Swift Cookbook

Over 50 hands-on recipes to help you create apps, solve
problems, and build your portfolio of projects in Swift

Cecil Costa

BIRMINGHAM - MUMBAI

Swift Cookbook

First published: April 2015

Production reference: 1220415

Published by Packt Publishing Ltd.
Livery Place
35 Livery Street
Birmingham B3 2PB, UK.

ISBN 978-1-78439-137-9

www.packtpub.com

Credits

Author

Cecil Costa

Reviewers

Edgar Lanting

Sergio Martínez-Losa Del Rincón

Vladimir Pouzanov

Commissioning Editor

Sarah Crofton

Acquisition Editor

Kevin Colaco

Content Development Editor

Rahul Nair

Technical Editors

Ruchi Desai

Edwin Moses

Shruti Rawool

Copy Editors

Pranjali Chury

Janbal Dharmaraj

Rashmi Sawant

Project Coordinator

Leena Purkait

Proofreaders

Simran Bhogal

Safis Editing

Indexer

Tejal Soni

Production Coordinator

Alwin Roy

Cover Work

Alwin Roy

About the Author

Cecil Costa, also know as Eduardo Campos in Latin countries, is a Euro-Brazilian freelance developer who has been learning about computers since getting his first 286 in 1990. From then on, he kept learning about programming languages, computer architecture, and computer science theory. Learning is his passion as well as teaching; this is the reason why he worked as a trainer, giving on-site courses for companies such as Ericsson, Roche, TVE (a Spanish television channel), and lots of other companies. Nowadays, he also teaches through online platforms, helping people from every part of the world.

In 2008, he founded his own company, Conglomo Limited (`www.conglomo.es`), which offers development and training programs both on site and online.

Over his professional career, he has created projects by himself and also worked for different companies, from small to big ones, such as IBM, Qualcomm, Spanish Lottery, and DIA%.

He develops a variety of computer languages (such as Swift, C++, Java, Objective-C, JavaScript, Python, and so on) in different environments (iOS, Android, Web, Mac OS X, Linux, Unity, and so on) because he thinks that a good developer needs to learn every kind of programming language to open his mind, and only then will he really know what development is.

Nowadays, Cecil is based in the UK, where he is progressing in his professional career, working with augmented reality on mobile platforms.

I would like to thank Hope Mtshemla for assisting me in writing this book and Larry Tesler for creating the copy and paste feature on computers.

About the Reviewers

Edgar Lanting is an experienced IT engineer who specializes in database technology and operating systems. In his free time, he loves to experiment with development and really likes Apple's new programming language, Swift. He currently works as an engineer at the Dutch file transfer company WeTransfer and lives near Amsterdam with his wife and two dogs.

Sergio Martínez-Losa Del Rincón lives in Spain. He is a software engineer and serial entrepreneur. He always liked to write technical documents and enjoys programming in several languages.

He is always learning new programming languages and facing new challenges. Currently, he is creating applications and games for iPhone, Macintosh, Android, Google Glass, and OUYA. You can see part of his work at `https://itunes.apple.com/artist/sergio-martinez-losa-del-rincon/id380348699`.

Vladimir Pouzanov is a systems engineer and embedded enthusiast. He has spent countless hours hacking different mobile hardware, porting Linux to various devices that were not supposed to run it, and toying around outside the iOS sandbox. He has also been a professional iOS consultant and has been developing applications based on iOS ever since the first Apple iPhones became available. Later on, he switched his professional interest to systems engineering and cloud computing, but he still keeps a close eye on the mobile and embedded world.

www.PacktPub.com

Support files, eBooks, discount offers, and more

For support files and downloads related to your book, please visit www.PacktPub.com.

Did you know that Packt offers eBook versions of every book published, with PDF and ePub files available? You can upgrade to the eBook version at www.PacktPub.com and as a print book customer, you are entitled to a discount on the eBook copy. Get in touch with us at service@packtpub.com for more details.

At www.PacktPub.com, you can also read a collection of free technical articles, sign up for a range of free newsletters and receive exclusive discounts and offers on Packt books and eBooks.

https://www2.packtpub.com/books/subscription/packtlib

Do you need instant solutions to your IT questions? PacktLib is Packt's online digital book library. Here, you can search, access, and read Packt's entire library of books.

Why subscribe?

- ► Fully searchable across every book published by Packt
- ► Copy and paste, print, and bookmark content
- ► On demand and accessible via a web browser

Free access for Packt account holders

If you have an account with Packt at www.PacktPub.com, you can use this to access PacktLib today and view 9 entirely free books. Simply use your login credentials for immediate access.

Table of Contents

Preface

It was unbelievable in September 2014, when there were lots of apps available for iPhone and iPad, that Apple suddenly announced that there would be a new programming language for developing for iOS and OS X. So, Swift appeared and as with other languages, it came with its own peculiarities and tricks. This book is intended to update Objective-C developers who want to migrate to Swift and also to help Swift developers get a stronger base with better knowledge about this programming language.

If you enjoy creating small apps, this book is perfect for you. This book will show you how to create Swift apps from scratch. So, take your Mac, open your Xcode, and let's cook Swift!

What this book covers

Chapter 1, Getting Started with Xcode and Swift, introduces you to some Xcode features that are Swift-specific. This might sound a bit advanced for the first chapter, but it is not difficult and it is also very important, mainly for those people who would like to develop professionally.

Chapter 2, Standard Library and Collections, shows you how to manipulate arrays, dictionaries, sets, strings, and other objects using the Swift way. This chapter is very important for people who have been working with Objective-C.

Chapter 3, Using Structs and Generics, shows you how Swift structs are not the same as Objective-C (or even C) structs, and that generics is a feature that allows you to create functions that are not tied to only one type. Both features have their own tricks.

Chapter 4, Design Patterns with Swift, explains how to implement design patterns using Swift, especially if you like object-oriented programming.

Chapter 5, Multitasking, shows you how to use different types of multitasking, a feature that is present in almost every app nowadays.

Chapter 6, Playground, teaches you how to use Playground, a new Xcode feature that allows you to test your code before adding it to your project.

Chapter 7, Swift Debugging with Xcode, explains how to debug Swift code using Xcode, LLDB, and Instruments. Here, you learn some tricks for finding and solving bugs in your app.

Chapter 8, Integrating with Objective-C, shows you how Swift and Objective-C can live together and gives you a step-by-step guide on how to migrate your Objective-C app to Swift.

Chapter 9, Dealing with Other Languages, shows you how to use C, C++, and the assembly language with Swift since you already know Swift is not alone in iOS and OS X development.

Chapter 10, Data Access, shows you different ways of storing data, which can be local or remote.

Chapter 11, Miscellaneous, expounds some topics that are very important in the Swift development world, from new frameworks such as the WatchKit to the widely used ones.

What you need for this book

Developing on Swift requires Xcode 6 or higher, which by itself needs to be installed on Yosemite (OS X 10.10), which can only be installed on a Mac computer. So, this is basically what you need.

A few recipes can only be tested on a physical device (iPhone, iPad, or iPod); therefore, they can only be installed if you are enrolled on the Apple Developer Program.

Who this book is for

If you are an experienced Objective-C programmer and are looking for quick solutions to many different coding tasks in Swift, then this book is for you. You are expected to have development experience, though not necessarily with Swift.

Sections

In this book, you will find several headings that appear frequently (Getting ready, How to do it, How it works, and There's more).

To give clear instructions on how to complete a recipe, we use these sections as follows:

Getting ready

This section tells you what to expect in the recipe, and describes how to set up any software or any preliminary settings required for the recipe.

How to do it...

This section contains the steps required to follow the recipe.

How it works...

This section usually consists of a detailed explanation of what happened in the previous section.

There's more...

This section consists of additional information about the recipe in order to make the reader more knowledgeable about the recipe.

Conventions

In this book, you will find a number of text styles that distinguish between different kinds of information. Here are some examples of these styles and an explanation of their meaning.

Code words in text, database table names, folder names, filenames, file extensions, pathnames, dummy URLs, user input, and Twitter handles are shown as follows: "The XCPlayground also helped us with the `XCPCaptureValue` function."

A block of code is set as follows:

```
protocol Queue {
    typealias ElementType
    func enqueue(element:ElementType)
    func dequeue() -> ElementType
    var size: Int{
        get
    }
}
```

When we wish to draw your attention to a particular part of a code block, the relevant lines or items are set in bold:

```
override func viewDidLoad() {
    super.viewDidLoad()
    // Perform custom UI setup here
    var geekNib = UINib(nibName: "Geekboard", bundle: nil)
    self.view = geekNib.instantiateWithOwner(self, options: nil)[0]
        as UIView
    self.label.text = currentBinaryText
    self.nextKeyboardButton = UIButton.buttonWithType(.System) as
        UIButton
```

Any command-line input or output is written as follows:

```
xcode-select -p
```

New terms and **important words** are shown in bold. Words that you see on the screen, for example, in menus or dialog boxes, appear in the text like this: "When the application appears, click on **calculate**, without adding any information into the text fields."

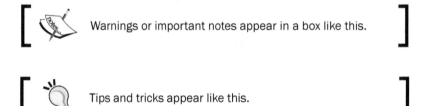

Warnings or important notes appear in a box like this.

Tips and tricks appear like this.

Reader feedback

Feedback from our readers is always welcome. Let us know what you think about this book— what you liked or disliked. Reader feedback is important for us as it helps us develop titles that you will really get the most out of.

To send us general feedback, simply e-mail feedback@packtpub.com, and mention the book's title in the subject of your message.

If there is a topic that you have expertise in and you are interested in either writing or contributing to a book, see our author guide at www.packtpub.com/authors.

Customer support

Now that you are the proud owner of a Packt book, we have a number of things to help you to get the most from your purchase.

Downloading the example code

You can download the example code files from your account at `http://www.packtpub.com` for all the Packt Publishing books you have purchased. If you purchased this book elsewhere, you can visit `http://www.packtpub.com/support` and register to have the files e-mailed directly to you.

Errata

Although we have taken every care to ensure the accuracy of our content, mistakes do happen. If you find a mistake in one of our books—maybe a mistake in the text or the code—we would be grateful if you could report this to us. By doing so, you can save other readers from frustration and help us improve subsequent versions of this book. If you find any errata, please report them by visiting `http://www.packtpub.com/submit-errata`, selecting your book, clicking on the **Errata Submission Form** link, and entering the details of your errata. Once your errata are verified, your submission will be accepted and the errata will be uploaded to our website or added to any list of existing errata under the Errata section of that title.

To view the previously submitted errata, go to `https://www.packtpub.com/books/content/support` and enter the name of the book in the search field. The required information will appear under the **Errata** section.

Piracy

Piracy of copyrighted material on the Internet is an ongoing problem across all media. At Packt, we take the protection of our copyright and licenses very seriously. If you come across any illegal copies of our works in any form on the Internet, please provide us with the location address or website name immediately so that we can pursue a remedy.

Please contact us at `copyright@packtpub.com` with a link to the suspected pirated material.

We appreciate your help in protecting our authors and our ability to bring you valuable content.

Questions

If you have a problem with any aspect of this book, you can contact us at `questions@packtpub.com`, and we will do our best to address the problem.

1
Getting Started with Xcode and Swift

In this chapter, we will cover the following topics:

- ▶ Installing Xcode from the App Store
- ▶ Downloading the Xcode image
- ▶ Starting a Swift project
- ▶ Using Swift project options
- ▶ Creating a conditional code
- ▶ Adding a developer account
- ▶ Compiling from the command line
- ▶ Using Swift as an interpreter
- ▶ Adding a control version system to an existing project

Introduction

In this chapter, we will learn the basics of creating a project with Swift. Even if you have already created your own project, it is worth reading the recipes of this chapter. You will learn how to interact with Xcode, how to test your code from the command line, and at the end, we will review the basics of this language.

Before downloading Xcode, you have to know that you can't use Swift with any version of Xcode; it must be 6.0 or higher. To install the version 6 of Xcode, you must have at least OS X Mavericks (OS X 10.9), so meet these requirements before installing it.

Installing Xcode from the App Store

The first way of installing Xcode is by downloading it from the App Store. The advantage of this method is that you will be warned about updates, and the system requirements will be checked before the download starts.

Getting ready

To download any program from the App Store, you must have an Apple ID; it's free and it won't take long to set up.

How to do it...

1. To download Xcode from the App Store, just open App Store from your dock or your applications folder.

2. The first time you open the App Store, it will ask you for your Apple ID details (email and password). After opening this application, just search for xcode in the textbox, which is located on the upper-right corner of this application.

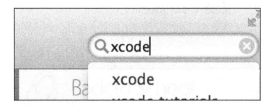

3. Make sure that you are installing Xcode from the right vendor (Apple); sometimes, we get results that lead us to think that they are what we want but they aren't.

4. Once you have found the Xcode app, just click on the **Install** button, and the next step is to go for coffee, or you can call a friend, because Xcode is 2.2 gigas, which means that it will take a while to download, so take a break now.

5. To check if Xcode has finished the installation, you just need to open the `Applications` folder or the Launchpad app, then have a look to see whether there is any progress bar under the Xcode icon.

How it works...

Like any other application that you will install from the App Store, you only need to open the App Store application, search for it, and install it.

There's more...

If you buy a new computer, you will see that Xcode will be offered to be installed into your new machine. This is because Apple keeps track of the applications you've already installed.

Downloading the Xcode image

The second way of installing Xcode is by downloading an image from the Apple Developer Center; this step is not free, it's only available to members of the Apple Developer Program (which costs approximately $99 a year) or for people who work in companies that are members of this program.

Getting ready

For this recipe, you will need to have 2.2 gigabytes of free space besides the space stored by the installed Xcode, but I will assume that you won't have this problem.

The advantage of downloading a DMG file is that you can save it onto a DVD as a backup (you never know when this version of Xcode will be removed from the App Store). Also, if you work in a team, it is very important to have every member working with the same Xcode version. Also, if you want to install any beta version of Xcode, it will only be available through the Apple Developer Center.

How to do it...

To download the Xcode image, follow these steps:

1. The first step is to open your web browser; go to `http://developer.apple.com`, log in where it says **Member Center**. If you are a member of more than one team, it will ask you which account you want to use. Choose the most appropriate one.

2. After this, you will see a table with some options, choose **iOS Dev Center** or **Mac Dev Center**.

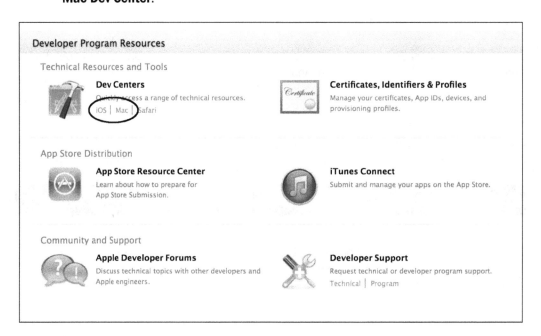

Developer Program Resources

Technical Resources and Tools

Dev Centers
Quickly access a range of technical resources.
iOS | Mac | Safari

Certificates, Identifiers & Profiles
Manage your certificates, App IDs, devices, and provisioning profiles.

App Store Distribution

App Store Resource Center
Learn about how to prepare for App Store Submission.

iTunes Connect
Submit and manage your apps on the App Store.

Community and Support

Apple Developer Forums
Discuss technical topics with other developers and Apple engineers.

Developer Support
Request technical or developer program support.
Technical | Program

You can download Xcode from iOS Dev Center, even if you are going to use it for OS X development or vice versa

3. After downloading the DMG file, double-click on it and drag the Xcode icon into your `Application` folder. Remember that you need the administrator's permission to copy files into the `Applications` folder.

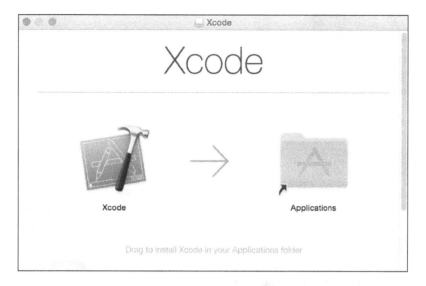

4. You can also install Xcode onto a different path like your home directory, but I wouldn't recommend this if it's not necessary.

 Don't search for download swift on your search engine as there is another programming language that is also called Swift, which has nothing to do with Apple devices.

How it works...

The DMG file ensures that you can always have a backup of this Xcode version, so if for any reason, you have problems with future versions of Xcode, you can install the previous version. It is also possible to have more than one Xcode version installed onto your computer.

There's more...

The Apple Developer Center is a good website to get Xcode resources. Here, you can find videos, guides, code samples, and addons.

Starting a Swift project

Usually, starting Swift is something that is very straightforward; however, it is good to know what is going on in every step.

Getting ready

Before you start a project, make sure that you know your project name and in which folder it will be saved. Changing this kind of parameter can create problems after the project has been created. Once you have Xcode installed, you can open it from your application folder, from the Launch pad, or even from your dock if you have added Xcode on it. As I'm a very lazy person, I prefer the latter; it's faster for me to have it on my dock.

How to do it...

The first time you open Xcode, it's possible that it will ask to install some additional packages, so do it. Some of these packages are important, depending on the type of application you are developing, and some of them are necessary to have access for some devices, mainly the newest ones.

1. Now, Xcode is asking you about the project you want to start or open. Check the option that says **Create a new Xcode project**.

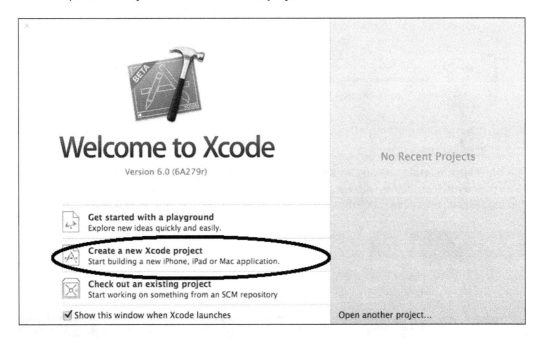

If, for any reason, this window is not shown to you, there is always the option to go to **File** (on the menu bar) | **New** | **Project**.

2. The next step is to choose the type of project that you want to develop. To do this example, I will use a **Single View Application** for iOS, but I'll make comments if there is anything different on OS X applications, or for another type of project.

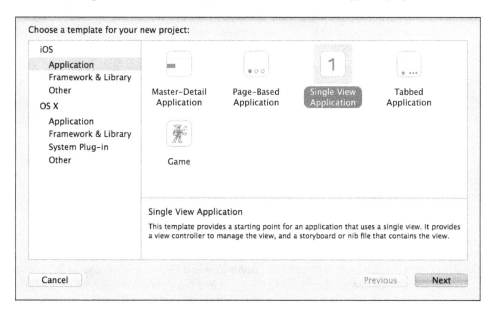

The next dialog will ask you for some project information, one example being the programming language that you want to use. In this example, we will use Swift.

3. Choose **Swift** as language and it will create the application with its delegate, with Swift code. Make sure that Core Data is unchecked to prevent having its code on the app delegate.

   You will also notice that Swift iOS applications now have no files called `main.m`, `main.mm`, or `main.swift`. OS X apps have a `main.swift` file, but it is smaller than the previous `main.m` file.

   As you should already know, the product name is your application name, the organization name is the proprietary of this software, and the organization identifier is the reversed Internet domain, for example, `uk.co.packtpub` instead of `packtpub.co.uk`.

4. Note that now there is no checkbox for creating unit tests because by default, it is created for you using XCTest. If you don't want it, just remove the group from your project. I wouldn't remove it, it usually doesn't hurt.

5. Now, it's time to choose a folder to store our project. Remember that during the development, you can add files, which will be stored in different locations. I don't recommend this kind of practice, but if you have to do so, try to have your project close to these files.

6. I also recommend you to check the option to use a Git repository, except if you have a subversion repository, of course. Even if you are the only developer, it's important to have a version control system. Remember that we are humans, and sometimes, we make mistakes and so have to go back.

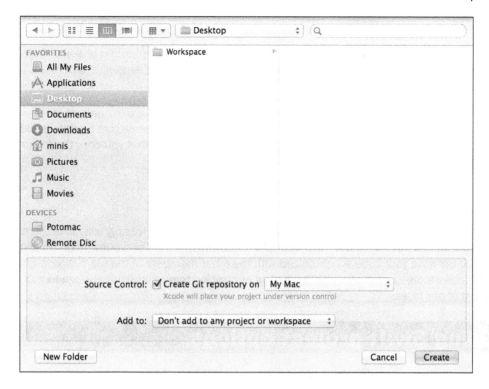

7. Once you have the project created, press the play button to see it working. If it's the first time you have installed Xcode, it will show you a dialog asking you to enable the developer mode. Click on the **Enable** button if you have the administrator password.

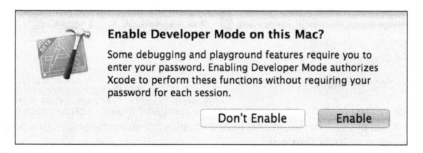

8. Ok, now you have your project up and running.

How it works...

Creating a project is not something difficult; you only need to pay attention at some steps. Make sure that you have selected Swift as the main programming language; otherwise, you will see a lot of stuff with Objective-C.

Pay attention to the folder where you will create your project. Xcode will create another folder with your project name, and inside of it, Xcode will create the project bundle, a folder with the source code. If you want to copy your project, make sure that you copy the folder that contains everything.

There's more...

If you want to work on a team that already started a project, you probably will clone the project using the **Check out an existing project** option. You will use a Git or a subversion repository, and you will have your code synchronized with the other members of the team. Xcode offers us the basic tools to work with a **VCS** (**version control system**); these are enough for 80 percent of our tasks.

Using Swift project options

Xcode projects comes with lots of options. Here, we will know some of them, mainly the Swift-specific ones.

Getting ready

To do this recipe, just create a new project, as shown in the previous recipe.

How to do it...

Follow these steps for changing some Swift options:

1. Once you've created a project, click on the navigator project icon or press *command + 1* if you prefer a keyboard shortcut, then click on your project icon (the first icon). Now, click on **Build Settings**.

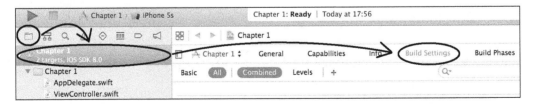

2. Look for **Embedded content contains swift code**; In this case, we will select **NO**, but of course, if you know that there is any extra content created with Swift, you should select **YES**.

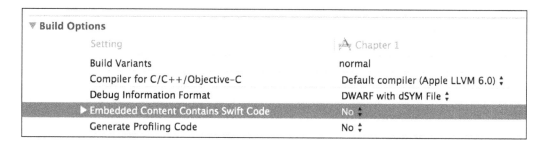

3. Go to the **General** tab and scroll down; you can see where you can add the embedded binaries.

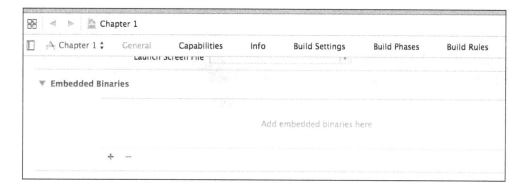

4. Now, look for **Optimization Level**. Here is where you tell the compiler how much time it should expend trying to make your code faster or compressing it. Usually, when we are developing (debug mode), we set for no optimization (-O0); however, when we are going to create the final product (release mode), we will usually set an optimization level such as-Os, which means fastest and smallest.

 Sometimes, with Objective-C, when you used to set a high level of optimization, the debugger used to loose some of the variable values. I haven't seen this phenomenon with Swift yet, but it's good to have it in mind.

5. Another important option is **Import paths**. This tells Swift where it should look for Swift modules. If you are linking your project with external libraries, you may need to specify where the module.map file is. If you have more than one path to search, you need to set them one per line. If you have different paths for debug and release, you can still use variables such as $(CONFIGURATION) or $(TARGET).

You can use absolute or relative paths, but I would give preference to the relative ones.

How it works...

Changing settings is something that you have to do mainly when your project starts growing. There are some options that you set differently for debug and release configurations.

There's more...

Xcode has a lot of configuration settings; showing all of them would be out of the scope of this book. I recommend that you at least look at some of them, mainly if you want to work with big projects. My main recommendation here is: do not change your settings without synchronizing with the other members of your team (mainly with the project manager). If you cause a conflict with the VCS, it could be hard work to fix it.

Creating conditional code

Usually when we are developing, we have some cases where we would like to have different pieces of code according to our needs. For example, let's imagine that we would like to compare the performance of some functions written by us with some equivalent functions that were created on a third-party library. In this case, we can create some macros for using only our functions or for using only the third-party functions, allowing us to have the same application working in two different ways.

In this recipe, we will show how to create a log according to a platform and we can also enable or disable it if the execution is being affected by the excess of logs.

Getting ready

Create a new project called Chapter 1 Conditional Code, as shown earlier, and let's code a little bit.

How to do it...

To create a conditional code, follow these steps:

1. After creating a new project, let's create a new file by navigating to **File | New | File...**. Now, choose **Swift File** and name it CustomLog.swift.

Don't save your files on a different folder from the project; this will give you problems in the future.

2. Now, add the following code:

```
func printLog(message: NSString){
    #if VERBOSE_LOG
        #if os(OSX)
            let OS="OS X"
        #else
            let OS="iOS"
        #endif

        #if arch(arm) || arch(arm64)
            let devicetype = "Mobile device"
        #elseif arch(x86_64) || arch(i386)
            let devicetype = "Computer"
        #else
            let devicetype = "Unkown"
        #endif

        NSLog("%@ on a %@ - %@", OS, devicetype, message)
    #endif
}
```

3. Now, go to the `viewDidLoad` method of your view controller, and add a call for this function, like this:

```
printLog("Hello World")
```

4. Try pressing play now; what do you see? The answer is—nothing! The reason is that the compiler knows nothing about the macro `VERBOSE_LOG`, which means that this macro is interpreted as *false* and the only thing that is created is an empty function.

5. Now, go back to your project build settings, search for `other swift flags`, and add `-DVERBOSE_LOG`, as shown in the following screenshot:

6. Click on play again and you will see the log message.

How it works...

Currently, the Swift compiler has two defined macros: `os()` and `arch()`. The first one can receive `OSX` or `iOS` as argument, and the second one can receive `x86_64`, `arm`, `arm64` and `i386`. Both macros will return a Boolean value. You can also create your own macro, defining it on your build settings.

The block that is evaluated as true will be compiled, and the other blocks will not be compiled; this way you can have code that calls OS-specific functions.

I would like to emphasize, mainly for those developers who are used to working with C projects, that the Apple documentation leaves a very clear message that Swift has no preprocessor; it only uses a trick on compilation time, so you can't use macros as we used to do on C or even on Objective-C. The only thing you can do is watch to see whether they are set or not.

There's more...

If you need, you can use the operators `&&`, `||`, and `!` as shown here: `#if arch(arm64) && os(iOS)`, but you can't use any kind of comparator operator such as `==`, `<`, and so on.

If you are interested in knowing more options that you can add to *other Swift flags*, check out the *Compiling from the command line* recipe in this chapter.

Adding a developer account

Usually, Apple tries to make the developer's life easier by improving Xcode and creating tools, but there is an exception when we talk about certificates. If you want to test your app on a physical device (iPhone, iPad, or iPod), you need a certificate. If you would like to upload it onto the App Store, you also need this certificate.

The idea of a certificate is to protect your code from malicious code or from being modified after being signed, but this idea has a price. To get a certificate, you will need to be enrolled on the Apple Developer Program.

Getting ready

I will assume that if you continue with this recipe, you are already enrolled on this program. Let's recycle the previous project; open it, and let's start.

How to do it...

Follow these steps to add an Apple developer account:

1. Once you've opened the project, click on the project navigator, then click on the combobox that shows our project, and select the target **Chapter 1** if it's not selected yet.

2. Now, have a look at the option called **Team**. In the case of programming a Mac application, this combobox is enabled only if you select the signing option to **Mac App Store** or **Developer ID**.

3. Usually, the **team** option starts with **None** selected. Click over this combobox and select **Add Account**.

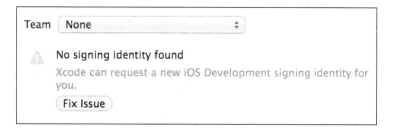

4. After selecting to add an account, Xcode will ask for your Apple Developer Program login data (e-mail and password). If you don't have it, you have the option to join the program.

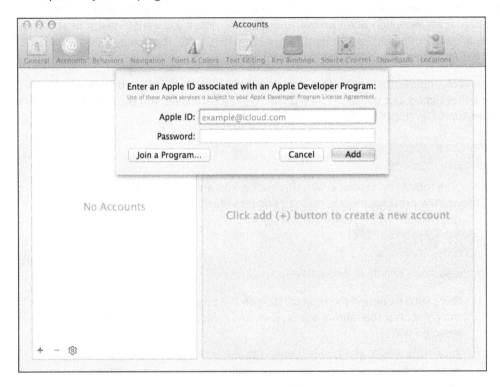

5. Once you've added this, you are supposed to use your account and run your app. If you have a device attached to your Mac, you can go to the **Window** option on the menu bar, and then you can select the **Devices** option.

   Your device should appear on the dialog, Xcode could take a while to read the device's symbols. In case of having this device attached for the first time, you will see that you will have to ask to change the status of this device to developer mode.

6. When you get the green light, it means that your device is ready to be used for development; now, go back to your project and change from the simulator to your device.

   If the device is enabled, but not listed by Xcode, it could mean that you have to decrease the iOS Deployment Target, which can be found on the project setting, under the **Info** tab.

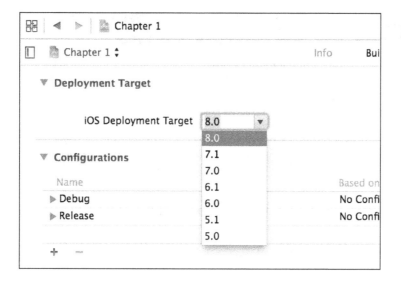

Lowering the iOS Deployment Target to the minimum value is an idea very common among programmers to cover the maximum sort of devices. Doing this will prevent your development from using new features. Check out the features that you need first, and then change your iOS Deployment Target.

How it works...

Signing a code is something done for security; the main restriction is that you must be up to date with the Apple Developer Program. Apple allows having up to 100 devices per account.

There's more...

Sometimes, the certificate gives us some headache; take care if it asks you to revoke your certificate; you may have to create a new one on the Apple Developer Center, and if you are working on a team, you may have to wait for the administrator's approval.

There are a few times that you need to change the code signing option on the build settings; it happens mainly when you get code from another organization ID.

Testing your code on a device is something that is very useful; it's where you can test the real user experience. Whenever you have some low-level code, such as assembly code or something written in C language that uses type sizes or byte orders, it's good to test your project on a device. Remember that Apple's devices have CPUs based on ARM and ARM64, which are different to the Intel CPU that is used on Mac computers.

Compiling from the command line

I know that nowadays a lot of users and even developers think that using the command line is something from the past. The reality is that even today a lot of tasks that can be done from the command line, mainly automations tasks such as continuous integration, must be done using the command line.

This recipe will show you that it's not difficult, and better than this, you will have a better understanding of the concept about what Xcode does behind the scenes.

 If you've never worked with a command line, I would suggest you read a book about it; *Linux Shell Scripting Cookbook, Packt Publishing*, is a good one in my opinion, even knowing that some commands are Linux specific.

Getting ready

Open a Finder window using the key combination *command* + *Shift* + *U* or open your Launchpad and click on the `others` folder. Here, you can see an icon called Terminal, open it and you should see a window similar to following one:

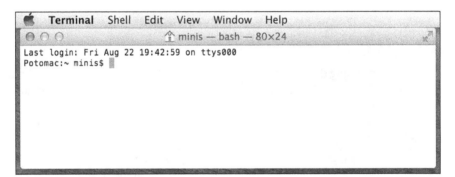

How to do it...

Here is how you can compile from the command line:

1. Just type `xcode-select -p`; this should give to you one path, for example, `/Applications/Xcode.app/Contents/Developer`, If you don't have more Xcode versions installed in your machine, you shouldn't worry about the path, it will probably be right. If for any reason you have more than one Xcode installed on your machine, you will need to change it by typing `xcode-select -s /Applications/XCODE VERSION.app/Contents/Developer`.

Remember that switching Xcode is a task that can only be done by an administrator, and it will affect every user.

2. Now, go to your project directory and type `xcodebuild -target "Chapter 1" -configuration Debug`. After this, you will see lots of commands on screen, but the most important message is the last one that should be ** **BUILD SUCCEEDED** **; which means that the project was built without errors.

How it works...

When you type a command, your system will look for this command using the paths specified by the `PATH` variable. You can check the directories included in your `PATH` variable by typing `echo $PATH` . By default, the directory `/usr/bin` is included.

This directory contains Xcode commands, such as `xcodebuild`. When you want to use commands from other Xcode version, you need to use `xcode-select` to overwrite these files to use the ones according to the version you want.

Once you have set it, you can compile your project. As your project is a set of lots of files such as source codes, images, and so on, it would be hard work if we had to do every single action (compiling, copying files, code signing, and so on) one by one. This is the reason it's easier to ask Xcode to do it by himself using the command `xcodebuild`.

The `xcodebuild` command has a lot of parameters, so you can specify the configuration to be Debug or Release, the target you want to compile, as many other options. Type `xcodebuild -help` to get a list of options.

 The `-help` argument is very common on Xcode commands. Try to use it when you have any doubt.

There's more...

Another good feature about the `xcodebuild` command is that it shows the commands that are being used with all its arguments. So, you can appreciate that when you compile an Objective-C project, Xcode uses the clang compiler, but when you have a Swift project, Xcode uses the `swiftc` command. Type `swiftc -help` with its full path to check its options and use them into the build options of *other Swift flags*.

Keep in mind that `xcodebuild` is going to look for a file called `project.pbxproj`, which is inside your `.xcodeproj` directory. This file contains information of every file, settings, and steps to create a project; in case of wrong syntax or wrong references, `xcodebuild` and the Xcode IDE won't compile the project at all. In addition to this fixing, this file could be a hard work. Because of these reasons, I wouldn't change this file manually, and also, I would try to avoid conflict with the Version Control System.

Using Swift as an interpreter

Like some other script languages, you can use Swift with its interpreter on the command line. Sometimes it's very useful, mainly when you want to test code but you don't want to create a new playground.

Getting ready

Open a terminal window as it was shown in the previous recipe.

How to do it...

Follow these steps for using Swift as a command line interpreter:

1. The first step is to find where the Swift command is; even if you have used the `xcode-select` command, it is possible that the Swift command is not accessible from your PATH variable. So, you can localize your Swift command using `find / Applications/Xcode.app -name swift  -a -type f`. In my case, I got `/Applications/Xcode.app/Contents/Developer/Toolchains/ XcodeDefault.xctoolchain/usr/bin/swift`. However, current versions of Xcode have the Swift command at `/usr/bin`. If it is necessary, add this directory to your PATH variable with the command `export PATH="$PATH:/Applications/ Xcode.app/Contents/Developer/Toolchains/XcodeDefault. xctoolchain/usr/bin/"`. At this moment, we can enter into the Swift interpreter just typing `swift`.

2. If you want to use Swift from the command line, sometimes, it's a good idea to have this PATH variable set permanently. To make this, we need to add the previous command into our `.profile` file, such as `echo 'export PATH="$PATH:/ Applications/Xcode.app/Contents/Developer/Toolchains/ XcodeDefault.xctoolchain/usr/bin/" ' >> $HOME/.profile && chmod +x $HOME/.profile`. From now on, if you restart your computer, it won't be necessary to look for the Swift path and set the PATH environment variable again.

3. Now, let's enter into our Swift command line and type the following code:

```
var dividend = [3,2,1,0]
var divisor = 6
```

4. You will see a message showing the content of these variables after typing each of them. Now, type the following loop code:

```
for i in dividend {
    println("\(divisor) / \(i) = \(divisor / i)")
}
```

5. Now, you can see that we will receive the following result:

```
6 / 3 = 2
6 / 2 = 3
6 / 1 = 6
Execution interrupted. Enter Swift code to recover and
    continue.
Enter LLDB commands to investigate (type :help for
    assistance.)
```

6. As you can see, the last option failed because we can't divide by 0 and that's a fast way we can test some code, using the command line. Most of the time, we will test using a playground, but sometimes using the command line is much faster.

How it works...

Calling the Swift command gives you the possibility to test your code or even use Swift as a scripting language. The highlight here is that you need to know where your Swift command is; the command line helps you to find it.

There's more...

Most of Swift's options and `swiftc` options are common; it means that if there is something that you would like to test before compiling, you can do it.

Adding a control version system to an existing project

It's very common starting a project without any version control, and with the passage of time, we change our idea and decide to add one.

Unfortunately, Xcode doesn't give this option to us and we have to do by hand. I hope this option will be added on Xcode soon.

Getting ready

To do this recipe, let's create an empty project called `Chapter1 Git`; however, this time before we save the project, uncheck the option **Create Git CGRepository on**.

How to do it...

Follow these steps for creating a local repository on an existing project:

1. Open a Finder window again and use the shortcut *command + Shift + U*, or open the utilities folder from your Launchpad. Now, open the terminal and go to your project folder.

2. Change your folder using the terminal by typing `cd` followed by a white space. Now, without closing your terminal, open the Finder window, then go to your project folder, drag the folder from the title bar to your terminal window, and then press the *Enter* key.

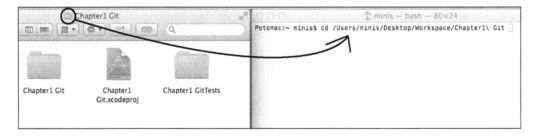

3. Now, just type the following commands:

```
git init
git add .
git commit -m "Initial commit"
```

4. Now, you can open your project and notice that Xcode already recognizes the VCS. If you want to be sure of it, modify a file, save it with *command* + *S* and check that you have the letter *M* on the right side of your file on the project navigator.

5. Once you are happy with your changes, you can deliver them by right-clicking on `AppDelegate.swift`, then go to the **Source Control** option and select `Commit AppDelegate.swift`.

6. Then, a dialog asking for a description will appear, write about your modification as comment, and click on **commit 1 file**.

How it works...

Unfortunately, if you forgot to add a Git repository to your project, Xcode doesn't provide any mechanism to add it to your project, so you have to add it by hand. Opening the command line allows you to use Git from the command line and Xcode detects that this feature has been added. Some versions of Xcode can only detect that the version control has been added when you open your project, so if you've done all steps and Xcode hasn't detected it, try closing and opening Xcode again.

 Xcode offers you some features to work with Git and SVN, but they are very limited. If you need more commands from your VCS, you can use them from the command line, or use an external tool for it.

There's more...

Even if you are not going to work as part of a team, I recommend that you use a version control system. When developing with Swift or other languages, you sometimes need to rollback or compare the current code with the previous versions of it, mainly when you have a new bug.

If you would like to know more on this topic, check out the book *Git Version Control Cookbook*, by Packt Publishing.

2

Standard Library and Collections

In this chapter, we will cover the following topics:

- ▸ Creating HTML manually
- ▸ Printing your object description
- ▸ Quizzing the user
- ▸ Searching for perfect numbers
- ▸ Sorting an array of products
- ▸ Finding the way out
- ▸ Working with sets
- ▸ Creating your own set
- ▸ Organizing a dinner room

Introduction

It's important to know the usage of collections and standard library, mainly for those people who come from Objective-C because there are some changes here.

In this chapter, we will create some apps to use these features. After these recipes, you should have good knowledge about the Swift programming language.

As mentioned in the previous chapter, most of our recipes will be created on iOS, but you can develop them on Mac OS X if you want.

Creating HTML manually

HTML started as a simple format for displaying web pages and links. Nowadays, this format has become very common and it is used everywhere. There are even frameworks such as PhoneGap that create applications with this file type.

In this recipe, we will create HTML using only strings; the main idea is to know about string manipulation. In this case, we will create the HTML code for a visiting card.

Getting ready

Open your Xcode and create a single view project called `Chapter2 HTML`.

How to do it...

Let's create HTML manually by following these steps:

1. Let's click on the storyboard and add the following layout:

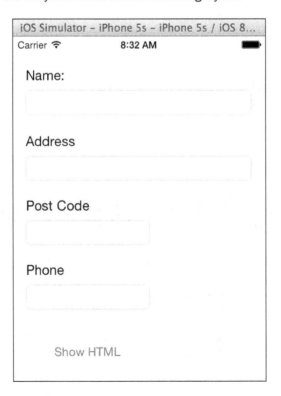

2. Then, connect the text fields with the following properties on the view controller:

```
@IBOutlet var nameTextField: UITextField!
@IBOutlet var addressTextField: UITextField!
@IBOutlet var postCodeTextField: UITextField!
@IBOutlet var phoneTextField: UITextField!
```

3. Link these properties with the corresponding text field on the view, and before creating an action button, we will create a card class with the following code:

```
class Card {
    private let TEMPLATE = "<div class=\"personalcard\">" +
                           "<p class=\"name\">#name#</p>" +
                           "<p class=\"address\">#address#</p>" +
                           "<p class=\
                             "postcode\">#postcode#</p>"+
                           "<p class=\"phone\">#phone#<
                             /p>" +
                           "</div>"
    var name:String?
    var address:String?
    var postCode:String?
    var phone:String?init(){}
}
```

As you can see, we are creating a class with the same information as our application. The main difference is that we have a constant called TEMPLATE, which has a model of our HTML.

4. Take note that this constant is private because it's something that we shouldn't see (for example, from the view controller). Also, notice that we have a plus sign at the end of each line that needs to continue on the next line. The reason is that we can't concatenate strings without using an operator as we used in Objective-C.

Swift doesn't need a semicolon at the instruction end. However, if you have a huge line, you have to tell the compiler that the line is going to continue, with a plus sign for example, or indicating on the next line that it is continuing from the previous one, for example, with a dot operator.

If you've been programming with Objective-C or C++, you may be asking why we've created an empty initializer. The reason is: it is not necessary; theoretically, because we only have constants and optional values. However, some Swift versions, for whatever reason, don't detect it and force you to create an empty initializer.

What are the attributes' initial values? The answer is *nil*. Have a look to see whether all of them are optional; otherwise, we will have to set their values to something.

Avoid using empty values such as empty strings to initialize an attribute; it is better to use optional attributes.

5. At this time, we have the basic structure. Now, we need to create the button event, so link the touch up event with the following action on the view controller:

```
@IBAction func showHTML(sender: AnyObject) {
        var card = Card()

        card.name = nameTextField.text
        card.address = addressTextField.text
        card.postCode = postCodeTextField.text
        card.phone = phoneTextField.text

        UIAlertView(title: "HTML", message: card.toHtml(),
        delegate: nil, cancelButtonTitle: "Dismiss").show()
    }
```

6. Now, we will have a look at whether this action is very clear. We will start creating a card object, then we will receive the information we need from our view, and at the end, display it.

Avoid spaghetti code, do not create an enormous action, and try to divide it into classes and methods. Have a look at the Model-View-Controller pattern on Wikipedia.

7. Everything is fine except for one detail: the card has no method called `toHtml`. No problem, let's implement it. Go back to our `Card` class and add the following method:

```
func toHtml() -> String{
    var html =
        TEMPLATE.stringByReplacingOccurrencesOfString("#name#",
        withString: self.name!)
    .stringByReplacingOccurrencesOfString("#address#",
        withString: self.address!)
    .stringByReplacingOccurrencesOfString("#postcode#",
        withString: self.postCode!)
    .stringByReplacingOccurrencesOfString("#phone#",
        withString: self.phone!)
    return html;
}
```

8. Now, it's time to test it, just press play on your Xcode IDE, fill the fields, and press the button, and you should see a message like the one shown here:

> **HTML**
>
> <div class="personalcard"><p
> class="name">Cecil Costa</p><p
> class="address">15 Graham Road</
> p><p class="postcode">CB4 1YE</
> p><p
> class="phone">0-777-6-555-444</
> p></div>
>
> Dismiss

How it works...

Strings have a lot of methods; some of them are used to modify the current string, while others only return values and still others create a new string based on the original one. In our case, we used `stringByReplacingOccurrencesOfString`, which generates a new string by replacing our marks (`#something#`) with the corresponding attribute.

We can chain the result of each replacement to do the next one preventing reassignment on each line.

> Nowadays, iPhones and iPads have 1 gigabyte or more of RAM, which should be enough for most of the traditional HTML templates. However, if you have a very big template with lots of replacements, you might need to look for a more optimized method for it. Replacing strings on big string variables allocates a lot of memory, and you might get a poor performance.

There's more...

If you look at this method documentation, you will see that there are two additional arguments, one called `options` and another one called `range`. They are used to specify a special comparator to search our string mark, and the other one uses only part of our string. As we didn't have the need to use it and they are optional, we've just omitted them; it wasn't necessary to fill them with nil values as we used to do in Objective-C.

If your project has objects that need to create HTML, XML, or JSON code, you can create a base object with a method specific to the corresponding casting to standardize it.

Printing your object description

The idea of this recipe is to see the Swift way to create a string using variable values. In Objective-C, we have a class method called `stringWithFormat`, but this method isn't used in Swift with the same frequency as it is used in Objective-C because now we have interpolation. In this example, we will create an app, which will show to the user three possible products. When the user chooses one of them, the app must show the information of this product and also its price if it's available.

How to do it...

1. Create a new single view project called `Chapter2 Product Value`. Now, let's click on the storyboard and add three buttons, as shown here:

2. Once you've done this, you can add a new swift file called `Product`. Now, we will create a class with a product name, its price, and the manufacturer name.

    In this case, the only information that can be omitted is the product price; the other attributes are not optional. This means that we will need an initializer with at least the product name and the manufacturer name.

3. As we would like to use our product with interpolation, we need to implement the `Printable` protocol, which forces us to implement a property called `description`. Once we have this information, we can implement our class with the following code:

```
class Product:Printable {
    var price:Double?
    var name: String
    var manufacturer: String

    init(name: String, manufacturer: String){
        self.name = name
        self.manufacturer = manufacturer
    }

    var description:String {
            return "\(self.name) (\(self.manufacturer))"
    }
}
```

4. Now, we can go to the view controller and create three products as attributes; following our examples, we will create a television, a gabion, and a locker. So, let's add the following attributes:

```
private let television = Product(name: "Television",
    manufacturer: "Telefunken")
private let gabion = Product(name: "Gabion",
    manufacturer: "Maccaferri")
private let locker = Product(name: "Locker",
    manufacturer: "Danalockers")
```

5. The next step is to create an auxiliary function, which is going to convert a double into a string with two digits of precision. I will create this function on the view controller file, but outside its class. If in a project, you are going to use this function in more than one file, I recommend you create another file for this function using the following code:

```
func doubleFormatter(value: Double) -> String{
    return String(format: "%.2f", value)
}
```

It is a good idea to have one or more files dedicated to auxiliary functions and class extensions. This will make your code maintenance easier.

6. The last thing we need to do is to create the button action. As you know, we have three buttons, and all of them will perform the same function; the only difference is the product that will be displayed. For this reason, we will create only one function and differentiate the product according to its sender.

Avoid repeating code, even if they are next to each other or if they are small code. This is because when the project starts having changes, it will generate new bugs.

7. Another detail that I would like to mention is that in this example, I will show the product price adding its VAT (20%). This is to make you aware of the power of Swift string interpolation.

```
@IBAction func showDescription(sender: UIButton) {
  var message:String
  var product: Product

  if sender.titleLabel?.text == "Television"{
    product = television
  }else if sender.titleLabel?.text == "Gabion" {
    product = gabion
  }else if sender.titleLabel?.text == "Locker"{
    product = locker
  }else{
    return
  }
  message = "You've chosen \(product)"

  if let price = product.price {
    message += " which costs \(doubleFormatter(price *
      1.20)))"
  }

  UIAlertView(title: "Product information", message:
    message,
    delegate: nil,
    cancelButtonTitle: "ok, thanks for letting me know")
    .show()
}
```

In this sample, we used the buttons titles to know the product chosen, but it's a bad practice. It was done this way only to create a small example focused on string interpolation. Imagine that you need to translate your program to other languages or if you have to add small information in this label; it will make you fix a lot of code.

8. Now, our app is complete; try to press play and then the app buttons. You should see an alert view like this one:

> ## Product information
> ### You've chosen Locker (DANALOCKERS) which costs 190.80)
>
> ## ok, thanks for letting me know

How it works...

One of the greatest features of Swift is string interpolation; it allows you to have expressions like the one we did while calculating the price with the VAT included. This also allows you to call functions like we did calling `doubleFormatter` to have our number shown with two digits. This also allows us to print an object.

If we wanted, we can even call object methods or property for example. We can show the manufacturer name in uppercase changing our description to `\(self.name) (\(self.manufacturer.uppercaseString))`.

Remember that if you want to print your own object, it must follow the `Printable` protocol and implement the property called `description`. Some languages such as Java have the equivalent method (`toString` in case of Java) on a base class and you only need to override it. However, Swift has no base if you don't specify it and this is the reason you can't only overwrite the `description` property without specifying the usage of the `Printable` protocol.

To use string interpolation, just create a string, and when you need an external value just wrap it between `\(` (backslash and open parenthesis) and `)` (closed parenthesis), for example, `\(variable)`.

If the expression is getting too complex in a way that is difficult to use it, just create a new variable with its value inside the string. This is also a good practice in terms of software maintenance. Objective-C doesn't have this feature; you have to create a new string using a class method named `stringWithFormat`. We used the Swift equivalent one, which is now an initializer.

I also would like to point out that we created a constant inside our `if` statement. In this case, we are not verifying whether the price is true or if it is greater than zero, we are just checking if it does not have a nil value. In case of a product that costs 0, for example, it would also evaluate to true.

Last but not least, notice that our variable `message` is not optional, but it wasn't initialized where declared. The reason for this is that the compiler will check it before reading it and setting it, and there will be no possibility of having it uninitialized.

The initial value for this variable depends on the product value, which can't be nil; this is the reason we were forced to add an `else` statement and `exit` from our function. Otherwise, the compiler would find a possible way to have the product set to nil and it would fail due to our interpolation.

There's more...

Another good solution for our `doubleFormatter` function is to create an extension. To do this, just change our formatter code to the following one:

```
extension Double {
    func precision(numDigits: Int) -> String {
        return NSString(format: "%.\(numDigits)f", self)
    }
}
```

This means that now we've added a new method to double types, and we can call it whenever we want. Of course, we also have to change the interpolation that uses our double value. Now, we can use the class extension replacing the corresponding line with this one:

```
message += " which costs \((price * 1.20).precision(2)))"Adding
    different characters
```

Quizzing the user

Sometimes, we need to add some icons on our application, but depending on the icon you want, it's not necessary to add an image; you can use Unicode characters. Let's create a quiz app using strings alone.

The idea for this app is to create an app where the user needs to answer a question in 12 seconds. After the last quiz, the app will show to the user his score, such as the number of well-answered and badly-answered questions.

Getting ready

Once we know the concept of this program, let's create a new project and name it `Chapter 2 Unicode`.

How to do it...

To create a quiz app, follow these steps:

1. First, let's create a new file called `Quiz` and add a class with a question to it, with three possible answers and the right answer, as follows:

```
class Quiz {
    var question:String
    // First possible answer
    var ①:String
    // second possible answer
    var ②:String
    // third possible answer
    var ③:String
    // Right answer
    var 🦌:Int

    init(question:String, ①:String, ②:String, ③:String,
        🦌:Int){
        self.question = question
        self.① = ①
        self.② = ②
        self.③ = ③
        self.🦌 = 🦌
    }
}
```

> To add Unicode characters to your code, you can copy from a
> website or go to **Edit | Special characters**.

2. Now that we've got this happy class, we need to create another one to store our quizzes and manage the user answers.

```
class QuizManager {
    private var quizzes:[Quiz] = []
    private var currentQuestion = 0
    // Total right answers
    private var ♠ = 0
    // Total wrong answers
    private var ♥ = 0

    func addQuiz(quiz:Quiz) {
        self.quizzes.append(quiz)
    }

    func getCurrentQuestion() -> Quiz? {
        if currentQuestion < quizzes.count {
            return self.quizzes[currentQuestion]
        }
        return nil
    }

    // Answer to the current question.
    // Returns true if it was the right answer
    func answer(questionNumber:Int) -> Bool{
        var rightAnswer:Bool
        if getCurrentQuestion()!.♠ == questionNumber {
            rightAnswer = true
            ♠++
        }else {
            rightAnswer = false
            ♥++
        }
        return rightAnswer
    }

    func get♠() -> Int {
```

```
        return 👍
    }

    func get👎() -> Int {
        return 👎
    }
}
```

3. The next step is to add one label for the question, three buttons for the possible answers, and one label to show the timer. Don't forget to hide the navigation bar if you don't want to show it. Your screen should similar to this:

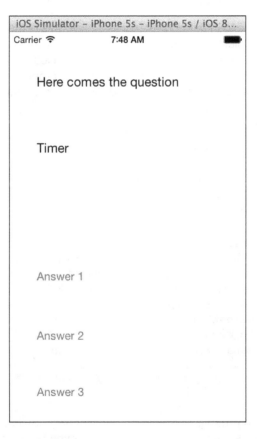

4. Now, it's time to create the corresponding properties on our view controller and link them. Besides these components, we will also need a timer, and another variable to know how much time has passed. Call these properties as shown here:

```
@IBOutlet var questionLabel: UILabel!
@IBOutlet var timerLabel: UILabel!
@IBOutlet var answer①Button: UIButton!
@IBOutlet var answer②Button: UIButton!
@IBOutlet var answer③Button: UIButton!
var quizTimer: NSTimer?
var elapsedTime:Int
var quizManager:QuizManager
```

5. Okay, now it's time to initialize these components. This is the reason we will create an initializer. In Objective-C, we used to set up the `viewDidLoad` method as this method is called after the controller's view has been loaded in memory, but now on Swift, every object must have each non-optional property initialized. This is the reason we will overwrite the `init` method. Don't worry about the meaning of each line; it will be explained soon.

```
required init(coder: NSCoder) {
    self.elapsedTime = 0
    quizManager = QuizManager()
    super.init(coder: coder)
    setupQuizManager()

}
private func setupQuizManager(){
    quizManager.addQuiz(Quiz(question: "What's the
        capital of Australia?", ①: "Sidney", ②:
        "Melbourne", ③: "Canberra", ✀: 3))
    quizManager.addQuiz(Quiz(question: "What is the
        smallest planet in the solar system?", ①:
        "The moon", ②: "Mercury", ③: "The sun", ✀: 2))
    quizManager.addQuiz(Quiz(question:
        "In which year was Harley Davison founded?",
        ①: "1903", ②: "2013", ③: "80BC", ✀: 1))
}
```

The first question you might have is: why did we use `required` instead of `override`? This is because the initializer was defined as required on the base class (`UIViewController`); in this case, we must re-implement this method.

6. The next step is to set `elapsedTime`. We will not use it now, but as it is not optional, we must set it here. Note that both, `elapsedTime` and `quizManager`, are initialized before the super class. After initializing the super class, we can add the questions to the quiz manager; which is the reason we have a call to `setupQuizManager`.

7. Okay, now we can show the first question on screen. To do this, we need the famous `viewDidLoad` function. We can't do it on the initializer because the labels and the buttons haven't been instantiated. You can also see the `prepareNextQuestion` method, which verifies whether there are more questions. If so, this shows the next question; if not, then it shows your score.

```swift
override func viewDidLoad() {
    super.viewDidLoad()
    prepareNextQuestion()
}
private func prepareNextQuestion(){
    if quizTimer != nil {
        quizTimer!.invalidate()
    }
    if let quiz = quizManager.getCurrentQuestion() {
        elapsedTime = 0
        questionLabel.text = quiz.question
        answer①Button.setTitle(quiz.①, forState:
          .Normal)
        answer②Button.setTitle(quiz.②, forState:
          .Normal)
        answer③Button.setTitle(quiz.③, forState:
          .Normal)
        quizTimer =
          NSTimer.scheduledTimerWithTimeInterval(1,
          target: self, selector: Selector("tick"),
          userInfo: nil, repeats: true)
        quizTimer!.fire()
    }else {
        // No more question
        UIAlertView(title: "Score", message: "Total
          \u{1F44D} \(quizManager.get👍())\nTotal
          \u{1F44E} \(quizManager.get👎())" , delegate:
          nil, cancelButtonTitle: "OK").show()
    }
}
```

8. There is something that is still missing, it's the timer callback. Remember that we would like to show the user the time he has left to answer the question, and after this, we have to skip to the next question. As you can see in the preceding method, we call a method named `tick`; this means that each second we have to increase the value of `elapsedTime`, and when the timer is over, we will consider that the question was answered wrongly.

```swift
func tick(){
    if elapsedTime < 12 {
        let baseCharCode = 0x1F550
        timerLabel.text =
            String(Character(UnicodeScalar(baseCharCode
            + elapsedTime)))
        elapsedTime++
    }else{
        quizManager.answer(0)
        prepareNextQuestion()
    }
}
```

9. If you press play now, you can see the app working except for one small detail. The user can't answer! Notice that there is no button action, so we need to add it, and remember that once the user has pressed the button it will go to the next question.

```swift
@IBAction func answer(sender: UIButton) {
    var userAnswer:Int
    switch(sender){
    case answer①Button:
        userAnswer = 1
    case answer②Button:
        userAnswer=2
    case answer③Button:
        userAnswer=3
    default:
        userAnswer = 0
    }
    quizManager.answer(userAnswer)
    prepareNextQuestion()
}
```

Cool, now we have our app working!

How it works...

In this recipe, we learned some ways of using Unicode happy characters. Now, you can create you own WhatsApp-like program. We saw that we can have variable names with Unicode characters; if you want, you can name your variables in Japanese! You can also create strings with Unicode values using `String(Character(UnicodeScalar(UNICODE_VALUE)))`, or you can also use it with interpolations such as `"Total \u{1F44D}"`.

> Take care while using Unicode characters; you may be complicating the other team members' lives. Remember that not everybody speaks Japanese or Chinese, and sometimes symbols are similar to others.

We also learned that it's possible to write an integer in hexadecimal; it's only necessary to add the prefix `0x`.

There's more...

If you want to see more Unicode symbols, there are some pages that can help us. I recommend `http://unicode-table.com` and `http://www.alanwood.net/demos/wingdings.html`.

Searching for perfect numbers

Believe it or not, when computers were born as giant calculators, and until now, their main function was to do powerful calculation. Let's add a little bit of math to our Swift project to create an app that will look for the first perfect number and show it to the user.

The main question you probably have now is: what's a perfect number? A perfect number is a positive integer that is equal to the sum of its divisors. For example, 6 is a perfect number because if you sum its divisors (1 + 2 + 3), its result is 6.

In this recipe, we will learn how to use the range operators.

Getting ready

Let's start by creating a new Swift project called `Chapter2 Perfect Number`.

How to do it...

Follow these steps to search for perfect numbers:

1. Click on the storyboard and create a layout similar to the one shown here:

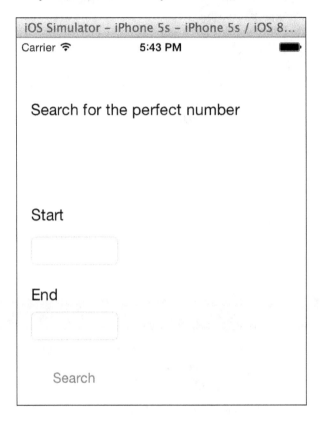

2. Now, let's link the text fields with the following properties:

```
@IBOutlet var startText: UITextField!
@IBOutlet var endText: UITextField!
```

3. Good, before we create the button action, we will create a function called `isPerfect`, which will check whether the number passed as argument is a perfect number or not. After this, we will create the button action.

```
func isPerfect(number:Int) -> Bool {
    var sum = 0
    for i in 1 ..< number{
        if number % i == 0 {
            sum += i
```

```
            }
        }
        return sum == number
    }


    @IBAction func search(sender: UIButton) {
        var rangeStart:Int = startText.text.toInt()!
        var rangeEnd:Int = endText.text.toInt()!
        for i in rangeStart ... rangeEnd {
            if isPerfect(i){
                UIAlertView(title: "Found", message: "\(i)
                    is a perfect number", delegate: nil,
                    cancelButtonTitle: "ok").show()
                return
            }
        }
        UIAlertView(title: "Found", message: "No perfect
            number found between \(rangeStart) and
            \(rangeEnd)", delegate: nil, cancelButtonTitle:
            "ok").show()
    }
```

How it works...

As you could see, we used a `for` loop twice. The first time we used the closed range operator, (...), which was used to include the last number (`rangeEnd`), because we want to check whether the last number the user entered.

The second time we used the half-open operator (..<) to exclude the last number because we don't want to include the last number into the sum.

The first version of Swift, the half-open operator, was only two dots (..). After some beta versions, it was renamed to ..<. For this reason, you can find some code on the Internet that is not going to work anymore.

There's more...

You can also use these operators on `switch` statements; they are very handy sometimes, mainly when you don't want to write the typical C `for` loop.

Sorting an array of products

In this recipe, we will learn how to manage an array in Swift. Here, we will create an array of products (very typical), add products to it, remove unavailable products, and sort the array by price.

Getting ready

Create a new Swift single view project called `Chapter 2 SortingProduct`.

How to do it...

Let's create and sort an array of products by following these steps:

1. Before we start with the view part, let's create the model part of our application. In our case, we will create the `Product` class. So, create a new file called `Product.swift` and type the following code:

```
class Product: Printable {
    var name:String
    var price:Double
    var available:Bool

    init(name:String, price:Double, available:Bool){
        self.name = name
        self.price = price
        self.available = available
    }

    var description: String {
        return "\(self.name): \(self.price)£ available:
          \(self.available)"
    }
}
```

2. As you can see, the idea of this class is to create objects with their name, price, and availability. We also inherited it from `Printable` to make use of its `description` property.

3. Now, you can click on the storyboard and add two labels, one for the full catalog, which means that it will show every product in its original order, no matter how much it costs or whether it's available or not.

4. The other label will show the same products but filtered for availability and sorted by price. So, now link your labels with the following properties and also create a product array as a property:

```
var products:[Product] = [] // this is our catalog
@IBOutlet var catalogLabel: UILabel!
@IBOutlet var availableLabel: UILabel!
```

5. You can create additional labels if you want to know their meaning. I created one with the title `Catalog` and another one with the title `Available Products`. It is also important to set a new number of lines on `catalogLabel` and `availableLabel`; otherwise, it will display only the first product.

6. The next step is to create the initialize; here, we only need to add some products to our array. As it's just a sample, the products will be hardcoded, but in real apps, we should retrieve them from a database or from the Internet.

```
required init(coder aDecoder: NSCoder) {
    super.init(coder: aDecoder)
    products.append(Product(name: "Shirt", price: 19,
        available: true))
    products.append(Product(name: "Socks", price: 1.99,
        available: true))
    products.append(Product(name: "Trousers", price: 22.50,
        available: false))
    products.append(Product(name: "T-Shirt", price: 10,
        available: true))
    products.append(Product(name: "Shoes", price: 32.20,
        available: false))
    products.append(Product(name: "Women shoes", price: 54,
        available: true))
    products.append(Product(name: "Men underwear", price:
        9.99, available: true))
    products.append(Product(name: "Bra", price: 12.5,
        available: true))
    products.append(Product(name: "Panty", price: 4.45,
        available: true))
    products.append(Product(name: "Tennis shoes", price:
        27, available: false))
}
```

7. After this, we can display our catalog when the view as loaded so that we can start using our catalog label.

```
override func viewDidLoad() {
    super.viewDidLoad()
    catalogLabel.text = "\n".join(products.map({
      (T:Product) -> String in
        return T.description
    }))
}
```

8. Okay, now it is time to add a button and create its action.

```
@IBAction func showAvailableProducts(sender: UIButton) {
    var availableProducts = products.filter {
      (product:Product) -> Bool in
        return product.available
    }
    availableProducts.sort { (product1:Product,
      product2:Product) -> Bool in
            return product1.price < product2.price
    }

    availableLabel.text =
      "\n".join(availableProducts.map({
      (product:Product) -> String in
        return product.description
    }))
}
```

The application is done; once you click on the button you will see a result similar to the one shown here:

iOS Simulator – iPhone 5s – iPhone 5s / iOS 8...

Carrier 🗢　　　　　4:18 PM　　　　　■

Catalog

Shirt: 19.0£ available: true
Socks: 1.99£ available: true
Trousers: 22.5£ available: false
T-Shirt: 10.0£ available: true
Shoes: 32.2£ available: false
Women shoes: 54.0£ available: true
Men underwear: 9.99£ available: true
Bra: 12.5£ available: true
Panty: 4.45£ available: true
Tennis shoes: 27.0£ available: false

Show available products

Available products

Socks: 1.99£ available: true
Panty: 4.45£ available: true
Men underwear: 9.99£ available: true
T-Shirt: 10.0£ available: true
Bra: 12.5£ available: true
Shirt: 19.0£ available: true
Women shoes: 54.0£ available: true

How it works...

Arrays in Swift are very similar to mutable arrays in Objective-C; they can add objects, remove them, and so on, but there are some differences. In the Swift programming language, you have to specify the object type that the array contains, like we did when we wrote the type between brackets.

You can create an array of any kind of object as we used to do in Objective-C declaring a variable as [AnyObject]. However, this should be avoided if it's not necessary. There is also the possibility to use NSArray instead of Array; in this case, we will have the same methods that we have for Objective-C.

You can also see something new on the `viewDidLoad` method; we called a closure named `map`, and this is because we want to create a big string with every product from our catalog delimited by a new line character (`\n`). To do this, we had to convert our `Product` array to a `String` array. The `map` function helps us with this because we can pass as argument one function that converts each element into the desired new type.

Another new function is the `filter` function; this function receives as argument another function, which returns a Boolean value. If the returned value is true, it means that the current element is valid and shouldn't be filtered; if the returned value is false, of course the new array will not contain this element.

Last but not least, we have the `sort` function. This function doesn't create a new array; it modifies the current one. Consider that in this case we have an array of our own class, something that the compiler doesn't know how to order it. In this case, we have to tell this function when two objects are ordered and when they are not.

 Take care when using functions that modifies an array; once it's done you can't roll back.

There's more...

There are two ways of declaring an array, one of them is the way we did using brackets, and the other form of declaring an array is using `Array<Product>`. There is no difference; they create the same kind of object. In both cases, you can't inherit from this type.

 Arrays were declared such as `Type[]` on the first version of Swift, then it was replaced by `[Type]`.

There are more array functions that can help us to manipulate the array such as `reduce`, `reverse`, or `removeRange`. If you've worked with NoSQL databases, you might be habituated to this kind of function. You can also create an array extension to manipulate arrays on your own way.

Finding the way out

In this recipe, you will learn about tuples. This new type didn't exist in Objective-C and it's very useful in Swift, mainly when it's necessary to return more than one value. For example, there are a lot of functions that need to return a value and an error code. In other languages, we usually return the value and the error value is returned as an argument.

You will also learn how to use a two-dimensional array, array, which in Objective-C was more complicated. In this case, we will use an array of enumeration.

So, this time, we will create an application that will find the way out of a maze. Of course, we will not waste our time designing a maze; we will present the result into a text view.

Getting ready

Create a new Swift single view project called `Chapter 2 Maze`.

How to do it...

1. First, let's create the model part of this maze. The maze for us is an array with four different possibilities: walls that we can't pass through, aisle where we can walk through, way out that is our goal, and *used*, which means that we've already used this path so we shouldn't use it again; this will prevent walking around in circles. So, the first thing we will do is to create a file called `Maze` and add the following code:

```
enum BlockType{
    case AISLE,
        WALL,
        USED,
        WAYOUT
}
```

2. Before we start implementing our `maze` class, we know that we will need a type to store one coordinate of the maze, and another one to know whether the path was found, and in case, it was found, we should have the path that was found:

```
typealias Position = (x: Int, y:Int)
typealias Way = (found: Bool, way: [Position])
```

3. Good, now it's time to create our class, in this case, we will need a two-dimensional array that represents the maze, another array that will contain the path to the way out, and two properties to know the width and the height of the maze:

```
class Maze{

    private var maze:[[BlockType]] = []
    private lazy var stack:[Position] = []
    private var width: Int
    private var height: Int
```

4. The first method that we will create is the initializer; in this case, it will be necessary to create a maze specifying its size. When we create the two-dimensional array, we will fill it with `AISLE`; to create walls, we will use another method that we will create afterwards.

```
init(width: Int, height: Int){
    self.width = width
    self.height = height
    for _ in 1...height{
        var row:[BlockType] = []
        for _ in 1...width{
            row.append(.AISLE)
        }
        maze.append(row)
    }
}
```

5. Now, we need methods to create the walls and the way out. In a more completed case, we should check whether the position is valid or not, but in this case, we will not bother ourselves with every detail. So, here are the methods:

```
func addWall(position: Position) {
    maze[position.y][position.x] = .WALL
}

func setWayout(position: Position){
    maze[position.y][position.x] = .WAYOUT
}
```

6. The next operation is to create the main method that will try to figure out one way to exit from the maze. In this case, the programmer shouldn't give the start point so that this method will have no argument, but we need to walk through the maze. However, the idea is to create a recursive function that will receive a new position and look for the next position, which is why this second function is private.

```
func findWayOut() -> Way{
    self.initStack()
    return self.next((0,0))
}

private func next(position: Position) -> Way {

    stack.append(position)
    if self.maze[position.y][position.x] == .WAYOUT {
        return (true, self.stack)
```

```
}

maze[position.y][position.x] = .USED

// UP
if position.y > 0 &&   (
  maze[position.y-1][position.x] == .AISLE ||
  maze[position.y-1][position.x] == .WAYOUT)
{
    let result = next((position.x, position.y-1))
    if result.found {
        maze[position.y][position.x] = .AISLE
        return result
    }
}

// LEFT
if position.x > 0 && (maze[position.y][
  position.x-1] == .AISLE ||
  maze[position.y][position.x-1] == .WAYOUT)
{
    let result = next((position.x-1, position.y))
    if result.found {
        maze[position.y][position.x] = .AISLE
        return result
    }
}

// DOWN
if position.y+1 < self.height &&
  (maze[position.y+1][position.x] == .AISLE ||
         maze[position.y+1][position.x] ==
           .WAYOUT)
{
    let result = next((position.x, position.y+1))
    if result.found {
        maze[position.y][position.x] = .AISLE
        return result
    }
}

// RIGHT
if position.x+1 < self.width &&
  (maze[position.y][position.x+1] == .AISLE ||
```

```
            maze[position.y][position.x+1]  ==  .WAYOUT)
        {
            let result = next((position.x+1, position.y))
            if result.found {
                maze[position.y][position.x] = .AISLE
                return result
            }
        }

        maze[position.y][position.x] = .AISLE
        stack.removeLast()

        return (false, [])
    }

    private func initStack(){
        stack = []
    }
}
```

If you are a good observer, you may notice by this code that Swift has lazy evaluation. This is a good thing because we didn't have to create a nested `if` function when we had to check whether the position was inside the array bound.

7. Now, it's time to complete our sample. Go to the storyboard and add a text view and a button to it. Link the text view with your code, calling it `textView`. Then, create an action for your button adding the following code:

```
@IBAction func findWayOut(sender: UIButton) {
    var resultString = ""
    var maze = Maze(width: 8, height: 5)
    maze.setWayout((7,4))
    maze.addWall((1,0))
    maze.addWall((1,1))
    maze.addWall((1,2))
    maze.addWall((1,4))
    maze.addWall((3,0))
    maze.addWall((3,1))
    maze.addWall((3,3))
    maze.addWall((4,3))
    maze.addWall((5,1))
    maze.addWall((5,3))
    maze.addWall((6,1))
    maze.addWall((6,3))
```

```
maze.addWall((6,4))
maze.addWall((7,1))
let (found:Bool, way:[Position]) =
 maze.findWayOut()
if found {
    for position in way {
        resultString+=
          "(\(position.x),\(position.y)) \n"
    }
}else{
    resultString+="No path found"
}
textView.text = resultString
}
```

How it works...

A lot of code needs some explanation. Let's start from the beginning. We've created an enumeration with four possible values. It is better to use enumerations than an integer or a string because you prevent the usage of non-existing values.

After this, we've declared two type aliases; the idea of this instruction is to rename a type like we did with `Position` and `Way`. This doesn't create a new type but helps us in terms of software maintenance; for example, if you use an array of integers that has a possibility of being changed to an array of doubles, it's a better idea to use a `typealias` than replacing every declaration to `[Double]`. This feature is equivalent to `typedef` on the C programming language.

Now, let's talk about the attributes. The first attribute is not optional and this is inside double brackets, which means that it is a two-dimensional array. Usually, by human definition, we say that the first dimension of an array is the row and the second is the column.

When we talk about positions; for example, in a Cartesian plane, we refer to *x* as the columns and *y* as the rows, and this is the reason why you will see the *y* coordinate coming before the *x* one, such as `maze[position.y][position.x+1] == .AISLE`.

The stack is also a non-optional attribute because we don't need the nil value, but this means that we must initialize it with anything. As we initialize every time when `findWayOut` is called, the first time it will be initialized twice, one on the initializer and another inside the function itself. To prevent this double initialization, we will add the modifier `lazy`, which means that it should be initialized with the same value in the declaration only the first time that this variable is going to be read and if it wasn't initialized before.

It used to be @lazy instead of just lazy on the first version of Swift.

Let's talk about the initializer; to create a maze, it's necessary to receive the width and the height as arguments. As the arguments have the same name as the attributes, it's necessary to differentiate them. In this case, the attributes are called self.width and self.height, and the arguments are called width and height.

The next step is the wildcard expression, which means that the current value of the for loop is not used. In this case, instead of assigning it to a variable, we just use an underscore. Notice that the underscore is used in both loops and the inner loop doesn't affect the outer loop and vice versa.

There is another way to create an array in only one line; this should be even more efficient because it's different when you create an array with a capacity than adding each element one by one. Try replacing both the for loops with this single line:

```
maze = [[BlockType]](count: height, repeatedValue:
    [BlockType](count: width, repeatedValue: .AISLE))
```

The next two methods are very similar, but one of them has the prefix add and the other one has the prefix set. It's only for software maintenance; we can have lots of walls, but only one way out. In this code, we are not checking it but it should be in the future. In cases like this, instead of a setter we can use a property.

Another thing to add here is that when the attributes were assigned, it wasn't necessary to specify the enumeration type such as BlockType.WALL but only its value, for example, .WALL. The reason for this is that Swift knows the assigned type, and that it can be omitted.

Then, we have the method that will be called to find the way out. It only initializes the stack to ensure that it is an empty array and then it calls the next function. Note that this looks like we have a function with double parentheses, but it's not true, we are passing a tuple as argument.

Tuples are like array with a fixed size. To create it, use parenthesis instead of brackets. The interesting feature about tuples in Swift is that you can name the values as if it were a dictionary or an object. So, it's up to you to create a tuple as (0,0) or (x:0, y:0). In cases like the Way type, where the elements have different meaning, I would suggest that you name the values; otherwise, it would be very difficult to remember what the element on the first position represents, if there is a path for way out or not, and that the second one represents the path itself.

Also, have a look at the view controller when the `findWayOut` method returns its values. This looks like that they are assigned to a tuple, but it's not true, they are assigned to two variables; this feature we didn't have on C or Objective-C. This means that if you want to swap the values of two variables, you can just use a sentence, for example, `(var1, var2) = (var2, var1)`, without creating any auxiliary variable as we used to do on Objective-C.

In this recipe, we used an array as a stack to store the path that we've already walked through, and using the `removeLast` method we could return back a step, like if we had some kind of breadcrumb, and this is the secret to find the way out, we just need to follow a path, and if we get lost, we only need to collect the breadcrumbs and try another one.

After finding the goal, the user will see the path as shown in the following screenshot:

iOS Simulator – iPhone 5s – iPhone 5s / iOS 8...

Carrier 🔶   10:15 PM

Find path

(0,0)
(0,1)
(0,2)
(0,3)
(1,3)
(2,3)
(2,2)
(3,2)
(4,2)
(5,2)
(6,2)
(7,2)
(7,3)
(7,4)

There's more...

Tuples in Swift can be used in different ways; they are also very useful in some switch cases; however, don't try to substitute dictionaries or arrays with tuples, each type has its own function.

 The new Swift version 1.2 has a native type called Set that does what this recipe does.

Working with sets

Swift brought to us this new feature called tuples, but for some unexplained reason, the set type has disappeared, or at least, it's not implemented yet. We have two solutions: the first one is using the old NSSet, which will be demonstrated in this recipe, and another solution is to create a new set class, which will be shown in the next recipe.

For this recipe, the user will write on a text field the cities that he has already visited, and when he finishes, he will press a button and show the cities without repetition.

Getting ready

Let's create a Swift project called `Chapter2 NSSet`.

How to do it...

To demonstrate working with NSSet, follow these steps:

1. Click on the view controller and add a text field where the user will write a city name, a button that the user will press when he finishes writing the city name, and another button to display the introduced cities.

2. Now, go to the view controller and add the following attributes:

    ```
    var cities:NSMutableSet = NSMutableSet()
    @IBOutlet var textField: UITextField!
    @IBOutlet var label: UILabel!
    ```

3. As you can imagine, you have to link the text field and the label with these properties now. The next step is to create an action for the add button:

    ```
    @IBAction func addCity(sender: UIButton) {
        cities.addObject(textField.text.capitalizedString)
        textField.text=""
    }
    ```

    The `capitalizedString` property is for two reasons, the first one is to store our cities with a pattern; otherwise, we could have the same city repeated due to different letter cases. The other reason is to have a better presentation.

    The last instruction is to clean the text field. If we don't do this, the user will need to erase the last city every time he adds one.

4. To complete this recipe, we will need to create the display button:

```
@IBAction func displayCities(sender: UIButton) {
    var citiesString:[String] = []
    for i in cities {
        citiesString.append(i as String)
    }
    label.text = ", ".join(citiesString)
}
```

5. Test this app by adding some cities and repeating some of them to check that they won't be listed twice.

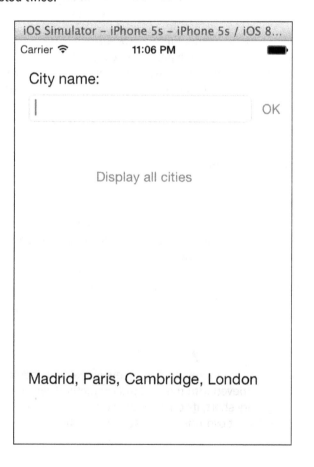

How it works...

As you could see we had to use the same Objective-C class: `NSMutableSet`. We have to use this in the same way we used to do with our old friend Objective-C. Remember that the Objective-C language used to work with a generic type called `id` or `instancetype`; there was no way to specify the type that our container had to store, as a result in Swift the stored type is `AnyObject`.

`AnyObject` is an empty protocol that doesn't inherit from anything, not even from `Printable`. This means that even if for us it's very clear that this set is storing only strings, the compiler can't do this assumption. And this is the reason we had to convert from our set to a Swift string array.

When the code needed to add the element into a new array, it was mandatory to convert this element into string, because in Swift, the types are checked in compilation time. Let's imagine that for whatever reason we had other object types than strings, in this case, we can improve our code by allowing it to check the type of element before casting. We can use the `for` loop as follows:

```
for i in cities {
    if i is String {
        citiesString.append(i as String)
    }
}
```

However, if you prefer to do this using a Swift way, you can use the operator `as?`. This operator tries to convert our element into the desired type, if it's not possible, it returns `nil`. With this in our mind, we can use the following code:

```
for i in cities {
    if let city = i as? String {
        citiesString.append(city)
    }
}
```

The last detail that I would like to emphasize about sets is that you should not forget that the equality in Objective-C was retrieved with the `isEquals:` method, which used to belong to `NSObject`. Making a long story short, if you want to use sets of your own classes, they must inherit from `NSObject` and must override the `isEquals` method.

There's more...

`NSSet` and `NSMutableSet` are not the only Objective-C containers in Swift, you can still use `NSArray`, `NSDictionary`, and `NSHashTable`. However, as you can see, they could make a lot of work. Try to use Swift types and avoid using a container for everything. If you need to use Objective-C types because you are migrating a project from Objective-C, it's okay, although you should have in mind that nobody knows how long Objective-C will be alive.

Creating your own set

As we can see with the previous recipe, sometimes, our old friend `NSSet` is not enough to solve our problems, so in this recipe, we will create our own set. The goal of this recipe is not only to show how you could create your own set, but also to overload operators.

For this recipe, we will create a simple shopping list program, where the user can write the product that he needs to buy and its quantity. If he tries to add it twice, the product will not appear twice, rather it will sum the quantity to the existing product.

There will be a switch button that when disabled means the user won't be able to add the product to the shopping list if it already exists, and of course, there will be a button to display our list.

Getting ready

As usual create a new project called `Chapter2 ShoppingList`, and then let's create a Swift file called `ShoppingList`. The idea here is to create our container and the type, which it will store, in this case, the `Product` class.

How to do it...

Product is something that is related with our container, we can even say that this is like a part of it. So, in this case, we can create a nested class to work with it. In this class, we will need only two attributes: its name and its quantity. Follow these steps to create your own sets:

1. In this case, we will create its description, and it will implement the `Comparable` protocol. We will use this protocol to know whether two objects represent the same product. Let's start coding:

```
class ShoppingList: Printable {
    class Product: Comparable, Printable {
        var name:String
        lazy var quantity:Int = 1

        init(_ name:String){
```

```
        self.name = name
    }

    var description: String {
        return "\(name): \(quantity)"
    }
}
```

2. Now, we need to create the shopping list attributes. We only need an array to store our products:

```
private var set:[Product] = []
```

3. As the shopping list is a set, we should implement the basic methods. One method is used to add a product and another one is used to know whether the shopping list already has a product. And of course, we will also add the `description` property:

```
func contains(product: Product)-> Bool{
    for currentProduct in set {
        if currentProduct == product {
            return true
        }
    }
    return false
}

func add(product:Product){
    for currentProduct in set {
        if currentProduct == product {
            currentProduct += product.quantity
            return
        }
    }
    set.append(product)
}

var description: String {
    return "\n".join(set.map({ (var product) ->
      String in
        return product.description
    }))
}
```

4. Note that we compared a product with another using the double equality operator (==). The main question is how does the compiler make the comparison. Actually, the compiler can't make this comparison without the programmer's help. First of all, as you can see, we used the `Comparable` protocol, in this program. This is not really necessary, but it's good to implement this protocol in case we also need to use a product with other containers.

5. Even if it's a comparable, we have to implement a function that will tell the runtime whether two products are equals or not. This function must be called == (yes, double equals), and it must be declared on the global scope, it means outside classes and functions. So, here we have the corresponding code:

```
func ==(leftProduct: ShoppingList.Product, rightProduct:
    ShoppingList.Product) -> Bool{
            return leftProduct.name.lowercaseString ==
              rightProduct.name.lowercaseString
        }
```

6. If we were implementing only the `Equatable` protocol, we wouldn't need to implement any other method; however, as we are implementing `Comparable`, we will also need to implement the operators <, <=, >, and >=.

```
func <=(leftProduct: ShoppingList.Product, rightProduct:
    ShoppingList.Product) -> Bool{
      return leftProduct.name <= rightProduct.name
}
func >=(leftProduct: ShoppingList.Product, rightProduct:
    ShoppingList.Product) -> Bool{
      return leftProduct.name >= rightProduct.name
}
func >(leftProduct: ShoppingList.Product, rightProduct:
    ShoppingList.Product) -> Bool{
      return leftProduct.name > rightProduct.name
}
func <(leftProduct: ShoppingList.Product, rightProduct:
    ShoppingList.Product) -> Bool{
      return leftProduct.name < rightProduct.name
}
```

7. As we are creating some operators, let's continue with them. Let's overload the += operator twice, once to add more units to a product and another to add a product into the shopping list:

```
func +=(shoppingList: ShoppingList, product:
    ShoppingList.Product) -> ShoppingList{
      shoppingList.add(product)
      return shoppingList
```

```
}

func += (product: ShoppingList.Product, quantity: Int) ->
    ShoppingList.Product{
      product.quantity += quantity
      return product
}
```

8. Note that it wasn't necessary to implement any protocol to overload this operator, and it wasn't necessary even for the previous operators, but it's a good idea to implement the `Comparable` protocol, to use with other functions or algorithms.

 Implement the `Comparable` or `Equatable` protocols when you can use it with other generic objects, for example, when you think the object could be ordered.

9. A good feature of Swift is that you don't need to overload only existing operators; you can also create new operators. In this case, we will create two new operators, `=>` that will tell us whether a product is in our shopping list and `!=>`, which is the opposite operator. I will explain in detail later. Use these operators in the following code:

```
infix operator => { associativity left precedence 140 }
infix operator !=> { associativity left precedence 140 }

func => (product:ShoppingList.Product,
    shoppingList:ShoppingList)->Bool {
      return shoppingList.contains(product)
}

func !=> (product:ShoppingList.Product,
    shoppingList:ShoppingList)->Bool {
      return !shoppingList.contains(product)
}
```

10. Now the model is done, let's create the view. Put two text fields: one for the product name and another one for the quantity, one switch to allow appending products or not; two buttons—one to add the product to the list and another one to display the list; and a text view. Let's connect them, except the buttons with the following attributes:

```
@IBOutlet var fieldQuantity: UITextField!
@IBOutlet var fieldProduct: UITextField!
@IBOutlet var appendSwitch: UISwitch!
@IBOutlet var textResult: UITextView!
```

11. Add an attribute that represents the application shopping list:

```
var shoppingList: ShoppingList = ShoppingList()
```

12. Now, we need to add the button actions. Let's start with the easiest thing, the display button that will show the description of the shopping list into the text view:

```
@IBAction func showList(sender: UIButton) {
    textResult.text = shoppingList.description
}
```

13. Now, we have to create the add button action. In this case, it will be necessary to check whether the user introduced a number on the quantity text field and also if it was possible to add the product to the shopping list:

```
@IBAction func addToList(sender: UIButton) {
    var product =
      ShoppingList.Product(fieldProduct.text)
    if  let quantity = fieldQuantity.text.toInt() {
        product.quantity = quantity
        if appendSwitch.on || product !=> shoppingList{
            shoppingList += product
        }else {
            UIAlertView(title: "Wrong product",
                message: "This product is already on your
                list", delegate: nil, cancelButtonTitle:
                "Ok, thanks for advising").show()
        }
    }else {
        UIAlertView(title: "Wrong value", message:
          "Ooops! I need a number on the quantity
          field", delegate: nil, cancelButtonTitle:
          "Ok, sorry").show()
        fieldQuantity.text = ""
    }
    clear()
}
```

The clear function is just an auxiliary method to empty the text fields every time we press the add button.

```
private func clear(){
    fieldQuantity.text = ""
    fieldProduct.text = ""
    fieldQuantity.becomeFirstResponder()
}
```

14. Now, you can click on play and add some products, repeat some products, and display, you should have a result like the one shown here:

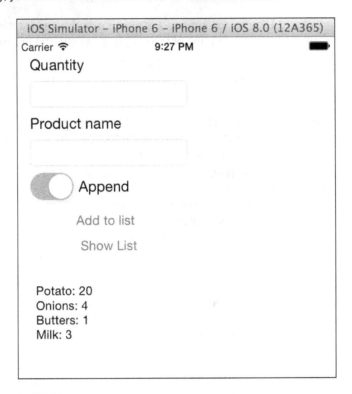

How it works...

Overloading operators is something very common in Swift; you can overload existing operators and you can create your own operator. If you want to create your own operator, the first thing you have to do is to report some properties of your operator. First, you have to choose if you type the usage:

▸ **Infix**: This means that the operator is used between two objects; for example, in our sample, we created the `!=>` operator to use it between a product and a set.

▸ **Prefix**: This means that the operator will operate only with the object that is on its right. For example, let's imagine that we would like to create the `!!!` operator, which could mean that we would like to empty the shopping list; in this case, we should use it as `!!!shoppingList`.

▸ **Postfix**: This operator will operate only with the object that is on its left, such as `shoppingList!!!`.

The next step is to write the word `operator` and the name you've chosen for it. After this, you have to add between braces the properties of this operator. Associativity values are left, right, and none. This is as follows

- ▶ **Left-associative**: This means that when there's more than one operator with the same precedence, the leftist one is going to be evaluated first
- ▶ **Right-associative**: This as you can imagine is the opposite of the left-associative
- ▶ **None-associative**: This means that it's not permitted to have more than one operator with the same precedence

Precedence is like a priority. Higher precedence is evaluated first.

There's more...

Swift allows changing the function of existing operators, for example, you can declare the following function:

```swift
func  + (i:Int, j:Int) -> Int {
    return 10
}
```

This will make every integer sum operator return `10`. This is something curious, but I wouldn't do that in sane conditions, and even worse is if you create recursive calls like this code:

```swift
func  + (i:Int, j:Int) -> Int {
    if i == 1 && j == 1 {
    return 10
    }else {
        return i + j
    }
}
```

Organizing a dinner room

In this recipe, we will learn how to use other features from the Swift programming language. We will copy the range of elements from an array, use dictionaries, subscripts, switches, and name a loop.

For this app, we will create a dinner for a company. In this case, it's not a wedding table where couples must be seated next to each other, we only need that people of the same group should be seated together on the same table, probably because they are from the same team or something like this.

We will create a class that represents a room. To add a new guest into this room, we will need to specify the name of someone who belongs to this group, which is already inside the room. If the person we want to add to this room is the first one, we will use the nil value as the name of the person who belongs to this group.

In the case of adding someone to a table, that is, full one group of this table must be reallocated to another table. Of course, we won't use the most optimized algorithm because that's not our main goal.

Getting ready

Create a new Swift single view project called `Chapter2 DinnerRoom`.

How to do it...

As usual we need to start with the model part of the Model-View-Controller. For this code, we will need a class for the room, another for a table that will store the seats with the person that is seated there, a group, which is the range of the table of people that belongs to the same team, and of course, we will also need a class to represent a person.

1. Let's start with the `person` class; in this case, we only need to store his name and the group where he belongs to. As there is a period where the person can be without any group, this attribute should be optional. So, create a new Swift file called `person.swift` and add the following code:

```
class Person: Equatable {
    var name: String
    var group:Group?
    init(_ name: String){
        self.name = name
    }
}
```

2. As you can see this class inherits from the `Equatable` protocol, it means that we must implement the `==` operator, as follows:

```
func ==(person1:Person, person2:Person)->Bool{
    return person1.name == person2.name
}
```

3. Good, now let's create the `group` class. Remember that a group doesn't have a name; it's just a range of a table of people who are sitting together. In this case, we need to store where the range starts, where it finishes, and its table. As you may imagine, let's create a file called `group.swift` and add the following code:

```swift
class Group {
    unowned var table:Table
    var rangeStart: Int
    var rangeEnd:Int
    var size:Int {
        return rangeEnd - rangeStart + 1
    }

    init (table:Table, entryPoint:Int){
        self.table = table
        rangeStart = entryPoint
        rangeEnd = entryPoint
    }

    func shift(){
        rangeStart++
        rangeEnd++
    }

    func increase(){
        rangeEnd++
    }
}
```

4. Note that the `size` property has no setters, only a getter and it's not related with a new attribute, that's what is called a computed property. Also, note that we had to add an `unowned` modifier to the `table` attribute; this is because if we had a UML class diagram, we can see that a room contains tables that contain people who belong to a group that knows its table. As you can see, we have a cycle, which by default would prevent the reference counter from reaching zero, and as a consequence, it would create a memory leak. Adding `unowned` will help us to avoid this problem.

5. The next class is the room. This class needs to store its tables, and also the guests that are already in the room. This second attribute is not mandatory, but it is faster for the computer looking into a dictionary than searching for it, and is also faster for the programmer because he will write less code. Add `room.swift` to your project and start adding the following code:

```
class Room:Printable {
    let STANDARD_TABLE_SIZE = 3
    var guests:[String: Person] = [String: Person]()
    var tables = [Table]()

    func add(table:Table){
        tables.append(table)
    }

    func add(person:Person){
        guests[person.name] = person
    }

    var description:String {
        return "\n".join(tables.map({ (table) -> String in
            "Table: \(table.description)"
        }))
    }
}
```

6. Now, look at the `guests` attribute, as we have two types between brackets and separated by a colon; this means that it's not an array, it's a dictionary. You can also write alternatively `Dictionary<String, Person>` instead of `[String: Person]`. One difference on dictionaries from Objective-C to Swift is that you must specify the key and the value types.

[When possible, try to use dictionaries instead of searching for elements, you will have a better performance.]

If you are a good observer, you can see that we repeated the add function. The difference is on the arguments type. This means that you can overload methods and functions in Swift.

7. Now, to check whether someone is already in this room, we will use the brackets operator, so we can type code such as `if room["Harry Potter"] == true {...};` to enable it in Swift, we have to write some kind of special function called subscript. In this case, we will write a read-only subscript:

```swift
subscript(name:String) ->Bool{
    get{
        if let guest = guests[name] {
            return true
        }
        return false
    }
    // No setter
}
```

8. Now, we only need to use the same idea to add someone in the room, remember that we have to specify someone's name from the same group or nil when it's the first person. Following this idea, we can add someone into the room with a code similar to `room["Harry Potter"] = Person("David Copperfield"):`

```swift
subscript(name:String?) ->Person{
    get{
        assertionFailure("Sorry, no subscript getter")
    }

    set(newValue){
        guests[newValue.name] = newValue
        // if the key is nil we will have to look for
        // the first table that is not null. If we
        // are not able to find it we have to create a
           new table
        if let personName = name {
            if let guest = guests[personName]{
                // now we need to find its table
                var guestGroup = guest.group!
                newValue.group = guestGroup
                // now we have to check the group table
                   is full
                if guestGroup.table.full {
                    // the table is full, if we have
                       only 1 group it is not possible
                       to add
                    // any one to this table, otherwise
                       the last group should move to
                       another table
```

```
                    if guestGroup.table.size ==
                       guestGroup.size {
                          // The group is bigger than the
                             supported size
                          assertionFailure("Group too
                             big")
                       }else{
                          // the last table group should
                             go to a new table

                          var lastGroup =
                             guestGroup.table.
                             getLastGroup()!
                          tables.append( guestGroup.
                             table.transferGroup(
                             lastGroup) )
                          // now the guestGroup table has
                             free space
                       }
                    }
                    guestGroup.table.add(newValue)
                    guestGroup.increase()
                }else
                {
                    assertionFailure("This guest should
                       exists")
                }

            }else {
                // this person belongs to a new group
                var table = freeTable()
                var index = table.add(newValue)
                var group = Group(table: table,
                   entryPoint: index)
                newValue.group = group
            }
        }
    }

    private func freeTable() -> Table {
        for table in tables {
            if !table.full {
                return table
            }
        }
```

```
    var newTable = Table(STANDARD_TABLE_SIZE)
    tables.append(newTable)
    return newTable
}
```

As you can see, we added an assertion into the getter method of the subscript, the reason is that subscripts can be read-only or read-write, but they can't be write-only. In this case, there is no sense of asking for a return value, so the only thing we can do is create an assertion to prevent problems.

 Don't use `assertionFailure` regularly; try to create code that can detect error and continue to work.

9. Create a new file called `table.swift`. Before we start coding the `Table` class, we need to know that a table will have an array of seats. We can have a free seat of an occupied one. If it's occupied, it's by someone, so we need to know who is occupying the seat. For cases such as this, Swift allows us to use enumerations.

```
enum TableSeat {
    case FREE,
    OCCUPIED(Person)
}
```

The only problem of enumeration is that we need to use switch cases a lot of times, so in this case where we want to know whether one seat is free or it is occupied by someone, it's a good idea to overload the operators `==` and `!=`.

```
func == (seat1:TableSeat, seat2:TableSeat) -> Bool {
    switch(seat1,seat2){
    case (.FREE,.FREE):
        return true
    case (.OCCUPIED(let person1),.OCCUPIED(let person2)):
        return person1 == person2
    default:
        return false
    }
}

func != (seat1:TableSeat, seat2:TableSeat) -> Bool {
    return !(seat1 == seat2)
}
```

10. Now, we can start typing the table class. Basically, we need to store an array of seats, but we can have some auxiliary computed properties and methods, as follows:

```
private var seats:[TableSeat]

init (_ size: Int){
    seats = [TableSeat](count: size, repeatedValue:
      TableSeat.FREE)
}

var full:Bool {
    return seats.last! !=  .FREE
}

var freeSeats:Int {
    var total = 0
        for i in seats.reverse() {
            if i == TableSeat.FREE {
                ++total
            }else{
                break
            }
        }
        return total
}

var nextFreeSeat:Int {
    return seats.count - self.freeSeats
}

var description:String {
    return ", ".join(seats.filter({ (seat) -> Bool in
        switch seat{
        case .FREE:
            return false
        case .OCCUPIED:
            return true
        }
    }).map({(seat) -> String in
        switch seat{
        case .FREE:
            assertionFailure("???")
        case .OCCUPIED(let person):
```

```
                return person.name
            }
        }))
    }

    private func shift(group:Group){
        seats[(group.rangeStart+1)...(group.rangeEnd+1)] =
          seats[group.rangeStart...group.rangeEnd]
        seats[group.rangeStart] = .FREE
        group.shift()
    }

    var size:Int {
        return seats.count
    }

    func getLastGroup() -> Group? {
        for seat in seats.reverse() {
            switch seat {
            case .OCCUPIED(let bySomeone):
                return bySomeone.group
            case .FREE:
                continue
            }
        }
        // no group
        return nil
    }

    func  transferGroup(group: Group)->Table{
        var newTable = Table(seats.count) //
          creating a new table with the same size
        newTable.seats[0...(group.size-1)] =
          seats[group.rangeStart...group.rangeEnd]
        seats[group.rangeStart...group.rangeEnd] =
          [TableSeat](count: group.size, repeatedValue:
          .FREE)[0...(group.size-1)]
        group.table = newTable
        return newTable
    }

func add(person:Person)->Int {
        var lastAllocatedSeat = self.nextFreeSeat-1
```

```
                    // return -1 if it wasn't possible
                    if self.full {
                        return -1
                    }
                    var index = lastAllocatedSeat + 1
                    if let group = person.group {
                        // who we have to shift the groups until we
                          find
                        // the new person's group and them we keep
                        // him (or her) on the array
                        searching:
                            while lastAllocatedSeat>=0 {
                                // in this case the seat should be
                                  always occupied
                                // but as the compiler doesn't know we
                                  have to retrieve
                                // its value
                                switch seats[lastAllocatedSeat] {
                                case .FREE:
                                    assertionFailure("shouldn't be any
                                      free seat here")
                                case .OCCUPIED(let groupPerson):
                                    if groupPerson.group !==
                                      person.group {
                                        // different groups, let's move
                                          the group to the right
                                        lastAllocatedSeat = groupPerson
                                          .group!.rangeStart-1
                                        shift(groupPerson.group!)

                                    }else{
                                        break searching
                                    }
                                }
                            }
                        index = lastAllocatedSeat + 1

                    }else{
                        // if the person group is null means that it's
                          a new group so
                        // can add him on the first available seat
                    }
                    self.seats[index] = .OCCUPIED(person)
```

```
        return index
    }
}
```

Before giving much explanation, we will test the previous code by adding `textView` to our view controller and some people into `room.swift`:

```
@IBOutlet var textView: UITextView!
var room:Room = Room()

override func viewDidLoad() {
    super.viewDidLoad()

    room[nil] = Person("Mr Peter File")
    room[nil] = Person("Ms Mary Simpson")
    room["Mr Peter File"] = Person("Mr Taro Mashimoto")
    room[nil] = Person("Mr Stuart Johnson")
    room["Ms Mary Simpson"] = Person("Mr Scott
        Chesterford")

    self.textView.text = room.description
}
```

How it works...

As you can see, we used some new features here. We were able to copy a range of seats using the . . . operator, which is an awesome feature that can save us from typing a lot of loops that do the same.

 Note that this slice operator (...) when working with a part of an array, the compiler can create a good optimization for a better performance.

Another good feature is the `switch` statement that can work with a combination of values, look at the == operator and you'll see that we don't need to create inner switched cases for each case. Talking about equalities operator, have a look at the `add` method that we used, `!==` instead of `!=`. The reason is that when we need to check whether two objects have the same instance, we have to use the operator `===` or `!==` to check whether they don't share the same instance.

We also used a label to name a loop (searching), the reason for that is by default the `break` statement will exit from the switch, not from our loop. We can control this situation with some Boolean variables, but we can avoid it breaking with `break searching`.

Another good trick was walking in the reverse way on our arrays. We did it using the method reverse. Of course, this we did it knowing that we have a small array; I can't imagine a table for one million people. Using reverse with big arrays is not a good idea because a new array will be created internally.

There's more...

You can still use the old NSDictionary class, but I will follow the same rule we saw with NSArray. Swift dictionaries are safer, and if you need dictionary, store completely different object types, it would be better to review your code; it could be very painful to maintain this code.

You just started learning about assertions, but further in this book, you will learn how to deal with assertion.

When you need to work with functions without specifying the input or output type, Swift gives you the feature of generics. We will learn more about this in the next chapter.

3

Using Structs and Generics

In this chapter, we will cover the following topics:

- ▸ Creating an exam app
- ▸ Checking the right answer
- ▸ Avoiding copying of structs
- ▸ Creating a generic array initializer
- ▸ Creating a priority list
- ▸ Creating a protocol for the priority queue

Introduction

We could say that structures are something similar to classes. They store values with attributes, and they have initializers and methods. But their usage is a bit different. The idea of **structs** in Swift came from Objective-C, which by itself was using the C struct.

We will also use generics, so we can create generic containers. The idea of generics is not new; other languages such as C++ and Java already had it. However, this feature didn't exist in Objective-C, so the programmer was responsible for casting the retrieved data and as a consequence of this, the code was unsafe.

Creating an exam app

In this recipe, we will create an exam app. For this exam, we will choose some random questions and the user will answer them. At the end, the app will show the user score and start again with a new exam.

Getting ready

First, open Xcode and create a project called `Chapter 3 Examination`, then create a file called `question.swift`. This is where we will define a question for an exam.

How to do it...

To create an exam app, follow these steps:

1. Open the storyboard and add a label and three buttons to the view controller. You will have something similar to the following screenshot:

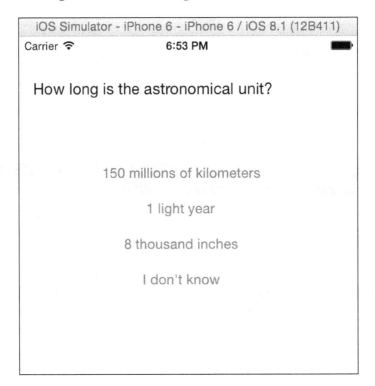

2. Copy the following code into the `question.swift` file:

```swift
struct Question {
    var question:String
    var answer1:String
    var answer2:String
    var answer3:String
    var rightAnswer:Int
    var userAnswer:Int?

    init(question:String, answer1:String, answer2:String,
      answer3:String, rightAnswer:Int){
      self.question = question
      self.answer1 = answer1
      self.answer2 = answer2
      self.answer3 = answer3
      self.rightAnswer = rightAnswer
    }
}
```

3. Ok, now we can create our array of questions. This will be like a template because it is not the exam yet; it will be a container of every question. So, go to the only view controller we have and add the following attribute:

```swift
private var examTemplate = [Question]()
```

4. The next step is to fill this array with questions; as you may imagine, we will not add a lot of questions for this recipe, but a real application can have many of them. In this case, we need to divide it into different methods by category, as follows:

```swift
private func addGeneralKnowledgeQuestions(){
  examTemplate += [
    Question(question: "In which year was Packt
      Pub founded?",
            answer1: "2001", answer2: "2004",
              answer3: "1978", rightAnswer: 2),
    Question(question: "What is the capital
      of Luxembourg?",
            answer1: "Luxembourg City", answer2:
              "Diekirch", answer3: "Viena",
              rightAnswer: 1)
        ]
}

private func addComputersQuestions(){
    examTemplate += [
```

```
            Question(question: "In which year did Bob Bemer,
                the creator of the 'escape key', die?",
                    answer1: "2004", answer2: "1980", answer3:
                        "He is still alive", rightAnswer: 1),
            Question(question: "How much RAM did Macintosh
                128Kb have?",
                    answer1: "1 Gb", answer2: "1 byte",
                        answer3: "128K", rightAnswer: 3)
        ]
    }

    private func addAstronomyQuestions(){
        examTemplate += [
            Question(question: "What is the name of the
                solar system star?",
                    answer1: "Antonio Banderas",
                        answer2: "Europe", answer3: "Sun",
                        rightAnswer: 3),
            Question(question: "How long is the
                astronomical unit?",
                    answer1: "150 millions of kilometers",
                        answer2: "1 light year", answer3: "8
                        thousand inches", rightAnswer: 1)
        ]
    }
```

5. Good! Now, we can initialize our exam, so let's create a method to do it. We will also need an attribute that will contain the current exam and another one that knows the current question.

```
    private lazy var exam:[Question] = []
    private lazy var currentQuestion = 0
    private func createExam(){
        func containsQuestion(question:String) -> Bool{
            for i in exam{
                if question == i.question{
                    return true
                }
            }
            return false
        }
        exam = []
        currentQuestion = 0
        while exam.count < 3 {
```

```
            var question = examTemplate[
              Int(arc4random_uniform(UInt32(
              examTemplate.count)   ))]
            if !containsQuestion(question.question) {
                exam.append(question)
            }
        }
    }
}
```

6. Okay, it's time to start! We only need to show the question with its possible answers like the method shown here:

```
@IBOutlet var labelQuestion: UILabel!
    @IBOutlet var buttonAnswer1: UIButton!
    @IBOutlet var buttonAnswer2: UIButton!
    @IBOutlet var buttonAnswer3: UIButton!
    @IBOutlet var buttonAnswerIdontKnow: UIButton!

    private func showCurrentQuestion(){
        if currentQuestion < exam.count {
            labelQuestion.text =
              exam[currentQuestion].question
            buttonAnswer1.setTitle(exam
              [currentQuestion].answer1, forState: .Normal)
            buttonAnswer2.setTitle(exam[currentQuestion]
              .answer2, forState: .Normal)
            buttonAnswer3.setTitle(exam[currentQuestion]
              .answer3, forState: .Normal)
            buttonAnswerIdontKnow.setTitle("I don't know",
              forState: .Normal)
        }else {
            var total = 0
            for i in exam {
                total += i.rightAnswer == i.userAnswer?
                  ? 1 : 0
            }
            UIAlertView(title: "Score", message: "Your
              score is \(total)", delegate: self,
              cancelButtonTitle: "Start again").show()
        }
    }

    func alertView(alertView: UIAlertView,
      clickedButtonAtIndex buttonIndex: Int){
        createExam()
```

```
            showCurrentQuestion()
    }
```

7. Now, we only need to add this action for the buttons:

```
    @IBAction func answer(sender: UIButton) {
        switch sender {
        case buttonAnswer1:
            exam[currentQuestion].userAnswer = 1
        case buttonAnswer2:
            exam[currentQuestion].userAnswer = 2
        case buttonAnswer3:
            exam[currentQuestion].userAnswer = 3
        default:
            println("I don't know")

        }
        currentQuestion++
        showCurrentQuestion()
    }
```

8. If you click on play now, you will realize that the app still doesn't work; we have to initialize it, so let's finish this application by filling the `viewDidLoad` method, as follows:

```
    override func viewDidLoad() {
        super.viewDidLoad()
        addGeneralKnowledgeQuestions()
        addComputersQuestions()
        addAstronomyQuestions()
        createExam()
        showCurrentQuestion()
    }
```

How it works...

The main difference between a class and a structure is that structures are copied every time they are assigned. What does this mean? This means that in this case if we've created this program with classes, the exam attribute and the exam template will point to the same objects (questions).

With this problem in mind, you can see that if we used classes when we start again, the new exam would come with the previous user's answers. And there is more; if you would like to store the exams with their answers, you would have to clone the objects; otherwise, everybody would have the same answers. Now, using structs, you don't have to worry about it; every time you create a new exam, you have new objects.

Another interesting part that I'd like to comment on is the `createExam` function. As you can see, we have another function inside of it. Swift allows you to have auxiliary functions. This is very useful, mainly when we want to divide our code into small tasks.

On the same function (`createExam`), you can see that we had a large call for creating a random number. The reason for this weird call is that Swift doesn't have a function for random numbers yet. Actually, Objective-C didn't have a random function either; we have to use the C function `arc4random_uniform`.

Such a function receives as argument a 32-bit unsigned integer, but Swift can't convert its integer to this type. So, we used `UInt32` to convert this number. As this function also returns an unsigned integer, it is necessary to cast its result to the Swift integer.

There's more...

There are more functions to retrieve random numbers, such as `rand`, `random`, and `arc4random`. Have a look at the manual page of the command line and check their differences.

Checking the right answer

This recipe will complete the previous one by checking the user's answer. If for any reason the answer receives a value out of range, this will be set to `nil`. Of course, in this application, it's not possible to answer with a wrong value, but remember that a good developer is always thinking about the possible software evolution.

Getting ready

Copy the previous recipe; if you like, you can rename the product name to `Chapter 2 Examination 2` by simply renaming the target name, as shown here:

How to do it...

Follow these steps in order to check the answers:

1. Go to the `question.swift` file. Now, replace the current class with the following one:

```swift
struct Question {
    var question:String
    var answer1:String
    var answer2:String
    var answer3:String
    var rightAnswer:Int
    var userAnswer:Int? {
        willSet(newAnswer) {
            if newAnswer? < 2 || newAnswer? > 3 {
                userAnswer = nil
                println("Wrong value, fixing it")
            }
        }
        didSet(oldValue) {
            valid = userAnswer? == rightAnswer
        }
    }
    var valid = false

    init(question:String, answer1:String,
      answer2:String, answer3:String, rightAnswer:Int) {
        self.question = question
        self.answer1 = answer1
        self.answer2 = answer2
        self.answer3 = answer3
        self.rightAnswer = rightAnswer
    }
}
```

2. Now, return to the view controller and replace the `showCurrentQuestion` method with the following code:

```swift
private func showCurrentQuestion() {
    if currentQuestion < exam.count {
        labelQuestion.text =
            exam[currentQuestion].question
        buttonAnswer1.setTitle(exam[
            currentQuestion].answer1, forState: .Normal)
```

```
buttonAnswer2.setTitle(exam[
    currentQuestion].answer2, forState: .Normal)
buttonAnswer3.setTitle(exam[
    currentQuestion].answer3, forState: .Normal)
buttonAnswerIdontKnow.setTitle(
    "I don't know", forState: .Normal)
}else {
    var total = 0
    for i in exam {
        total += i.valid ? 1 : 0
    }
    UIAlertView(title: "Score", message:
        "Your score is \(total)", delegate: self,
        cancelButtonTitle: "Start again").show()
}
}
}
```

3. This recipe can stop here; however, as we want to check this, an out of range value will be corrected to `nil`; we can replace the `answer` method with this one here:

```
@IBAction func answer(sender: UIButton) {
    switch sender {
    case buttonAnswer1:
        exam[currentQuestion].userAnswer = 1
    case buttonAnswer2:
        exam[currentQuestion].userAnswer = 2
    case buttonAnswer3:
        exam[currentQuestion].userAnswer = 3
    default:
        exam[currentQuestion].userAnswer = 0
    }
    currentQuestion++
    showCurrentQuestion()
}
```

How it works...

Swift has a good feature for properties called **property observer**. This feature is equivalent to triggers on relational databases. With `willSet`, you can correct the input and with `didSet`, you can trigger actions that are needed after the value has been changed.

We also changed the way we check a valid answer; this is done because the logic of a question should be inside its class or structure.

As you can see, this recipe is related to the *Quizzing the user* recipe in *Chapter 2, Standard Library and Collections*. If you want to create a more complete example, you can merge both apps into one.

Avoiding copying of structs

There are times when we are working with structs and we don't want to copy it. In this recipe, we will see this example and the solution for it by creating a small app where the user can see the coordinates of two supposed characters, and we can press a button to change their coordinates to a center point between them.

Getting ready

Create a new single view project called `Chapter3 Vector2D`. For this recipe, we will need only one new file, which we will call it `Position.swift`.

How to do it...

Let's create the app that prevents copying of structs:

1. Let's start with the Model part as usual. Click on the `Position.swift` file. Let's create a struct with the same name, as follows:

```swift
struct Position:Printable {
    private var x:Int,y:Int
    init(){
        (x,y) = (0,0)
    }
    mutating func moveUp(){
        self.y--
    }
    mutating func moveDown(){
        self.y++
    }
    mutating func moveRight(){
        self.x++
    }
    mutating func moveLeft(){
        self.x--
    }
```

```
mutating func meet(inout position:Position){
    var newx = (self.x + position.x) / 2
    var newy = (self.y + position.y) / 2
    self.x = newx
    self.y = newy
    position.x = newx
    position.y = newy
}
var description:String {
    return "\(self.x)x\(self.y)"
}
}
```

2. Now, go to the storyboard and add nine buttons and two labels to it, something similar to the following screenshot:

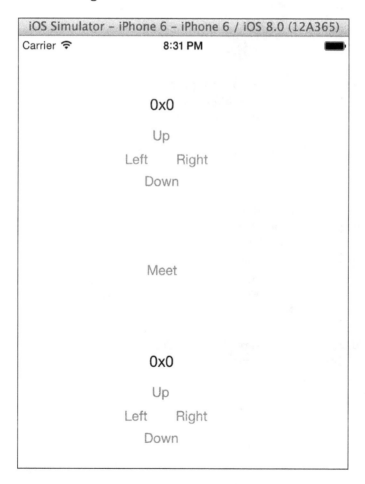

3. Now, let's link our labels with the following attributes:

```
@IBOutlet var labelC1: UILabel!
@IBOutlet var labelC2: UILabel!
```

4. After this, we will create two attributes that represent the coordinates of the characters. Of course, in a real game, these attributes will belong to objects of another type, probably of something like a character:

```
var character1 = Position()
var character2 = Position()
```

5. As you can see, these objects will start at the 0×0 position, but the labels won't know it if we don't initialize it with the `viewDidLoad` method. So, let's add the following code to the view controller:

```
override func viewDidLoad() {
    super.viewDidLoad()
    displayPositionC1()
    displayPositionC2()
}

private func displayPositionC1(){
    labelC1.text = character1.description
}

private func displayPositionC2(){
    labelC2.text = character2.description
}
```

6. Now, we can add the events that move the characters. As you can imagine, they are very straightforward because each action will proxy to the equivalent method on the struct. Here is the code for this:

```
@IBAction func upC1(sender: UIButton) {
    character1.moveUp()
    displayPositionC1()
}

@IBAction func downC1(sender: UIButton) {
    character1.moveDown()
    displayPositionC1()
}
@IBAction func leftC1(sender: UIButton) {
    character1.moveLeft()
    displayPositionC1()
```

```
    }

    @IBAction func rightC1(sender: UIButton) {
        character1.moveRight()
        displayPositionC1()
    }

    @IBAction func meet(sender: UIButton) {
        character1.meet(&character2)
        displayPositionC1()
        displayPositionC2()
    }
```

7. Now, the application is done. Click on play and move the characters with the buttons. The most important part is that no struct was copied or cloned.

How it works...

As you can see, we had to add a modifier on the methods of our structs. This is because struct methods, by default, are constants. If you need to change an attribute, you have to use the mutating modifier.

When receiving an argument that you don't want to copy, such as a struct, you have to use the `inout` parameter. This parameter will allow you to modify the corresponding argument. However, when using this feature, you have to call the function adding an ampersand (&) before the variable and you can't pass expressions as arguments.

Creating a generic array initializer

In this recipe, we will learn how to use generics. This feature is used a lot in languages such as C++, Java, and C# because this way, we don't need to overload a function for each possible type that could be used in our function.

In this case, we will create a function that receives the input items and returns an array with these elements but completely shuffled.

Getting ready

Create a new Swift single view project called `Chapter3 Array initializer`.

How to do it...

To create a generic array initializer, follow these steps:

1. Add a new file called `ArrayInit` and add this code in it:

```
func arrayInit<T>(values:T...)->[T]{
    var newArray = values
    for var i=0;i < newArray.count * 2 ; ++i {
            let pos1 =
                Int(arc4random_uniform(UInt32
                (newArray.count)))
        let pos2 =
          Int(arc4random_uniform(UInt32(newArray.count)))
        (newArray[pos1], newArray[pos2]) =
          (newArray[pos2], newArray[pos1])
    }
    return newArray
}
```

2. Now, we need to add two buttons and a text view to our storyboard to see this function working. So, let's link the text view with the following property:

```
@IBOutlet var textView: UITextView!
```

3. The next step is to create the events of each button, so add these actions into your view controller:

```
@IBAction func arrayInt(sender: AnyObject) {
    var arr = arrayInit(5, 10, 15, 20, 25, 30)
    textView.text = "\n".join(arr.map({ (element)
      -> String in
        return String(element)
    }))
}

@IBAction func arrayString(sender: AnyObject) {
    var arr = arrayInit("Hello", "I'm",
      "Edu","Merry", "Christmas")
    textView.text = "\n".join(arr)
}
```

4. Now, it's time to test our code. Run your application and press each button, and you should have results like these screenshots:

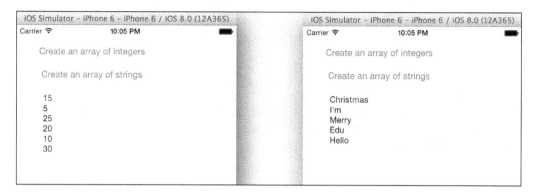

How it works...

One advantage of object-oriented programming is avoiding duplication of code. Some languages will force you to create a function for the array of strings and another one for the array of integers, and another new one for each new type that we need to use with this function.

Fortunately, Swift allows us to create a generic function. This means that we only need to implement the function once and the same code will be applied each time.

> Inside the function, the arguments are treated as a constant array, but calling the function with an array as argument has another meaning; the compiler will think that you have only one argument that is an array.

This function has something different: the ellipsis that is used after the input argument. This means that the function is not restricted to a number of arguments; this has a variable number of arguments. In our case, we can call it with six integers and with five strings. This feature is very useful, for example, when creating functions to calculate the average of some numbers.

There's more...

Overloading generic functions is allowed; it's used when there is a type that for any reason needs a different code. For example, now you can use this code to shuffle cards.

Creating a priority list

Let's imagine that we need to manage a queue of passengers on a flight. We know that the business class should embark first, then passengers of the first class, and finally, the economy class.

This is a typical case of a priority queue, but the nagging question is, can we create a priority queue only once? Or should we create a new priority queue in every new app? An Objective-C programmer who recently arrived at Swift probably will create this container storing objects of the type AnyObject. This solution can be acceptable; however, Swift has a better solution that is even safer: as you know, that is generics.

A priority queue needs to organize its elements using criteria. In this case, we can create our queue of any element but ensure that it is created for elements of a class which implements the Comparable protocol, that's what we call a type constraint.

Getting ready

Create a new Swift single view project called Chapter3 Flight.

How to do it...

Follow these steps to create a priority list:

1. Add a new Swift file called PriorityQueue.swift.
2. In this file, let's create a class with the same name. Here, we will need an array as an attribute to store our elements, and a few methods to work with this queue: enqueue for adding a new element; dequeue for removing the first element of the queue; size, which returns the number of elements on our queue; and toArray, which will return the elements of our queue to an array. So, add the following code into your file:

```swift
class PriorityQueue<T:Comparable> {

    private var elements = [T]()
    func enqueue(element:T) {
        elements.append(element)
        var index=elements.count-2
        while index>=0 && elements[index] <
          elements[index+1] {
            (elements[index],elements[index+1]) =
              (elements[index+1],elements[index])
```

```
            index--
        }
    }

    func dequeue() -> T {
        return elements.removeAtIndex(0)
    }

    var size: Int {
        return elements.count
    }

    func toArray() ->[T]{
        return elements
    }

}
```

3. Now, create a new file called `Passenger.swift`. Here, we will define a passenger with his data. Remember that we need to compare the priority of a passenger. For this reason, this class must implement the `Comparable` protocol:

```
class Passenger:Comparable, Printable {
    enum Class:Int {
        case ECONOMY=0, FIRST=1, BUSINESS=2

        var value:Int{
            return self.rawValue
        }
    }
    var classtype:Class
    var name:String
    var id:String

    init (name:String, id:String, classtype:Class =
      .ECONOMY){
        self.name = name
        self.id = id
        self.classtype = classtype
    }

    var description:String{
        var seattype:String
```

```
            switch self.classtype{
            case .ECONOMY:
                seattype = "economy"
            case .FIRST:
                seattype = "first"
            case .BUSINESS:
                seattype = "business"
            default:
                seattype = "unkown"
            }


        return "\(self.name), with id \(self.id) on
          \(seattype) class"
    }
}


// Operators
func <(lhs: Passenger, rhs: Passenger) -> Bool{
    return lhs.classtype.value < rhs.classtype.value
}

func ==(lhs: Passenger, rhs: Passenger) -> Bool{
    return lhs.classtype == rhs.classtype
}

func !=(lhs: Passenger, rhs: Passenger) -> Bool{
    return lhs.classtype != rhs.classtype
}

func <=(lhs: Passenger, rhs: Passenger) -> Bool{
    return lhs < rhs || lhs == rhs
}

func >=(lhs: Passenger, rhs: Passenger) -> Bool{
    return !(lhs < rhs)
}

func >(lhs: Passenger, rhs: Passenger) -> Bool{
    return lhs != rhs && !(lhs < rhs )
}
```

4. Now, open your storyboard and add two text fields (one for Passenger name and another one for his identification number, ID document), one table view to choose the seat type, two buttons to queue and dequeue, and a text field to display the current queue status. You should have a layout similar to the following one:

5. The next step is to open the view controller and add the protocol UITableViewDataSource:

```
class ViewController: UIViewController,
   UITableViewDataSource {
```

6. Ok, now link the corresponding components with the attribute, and besides this, create a passenger queue as an attribute:

```
@IBOutlet var passengerName: UITextField!
@IBOutlet var idDocument: UITextField!
@IBOutlet var seatType: UITableView!
@IBOutlet var textView: UITextView!

private var passengersQueue =
   PriorityQueue<Passenger>()
```

7. At this moment, we can start implementing the `tableview` code. As you know, we must implement at least the two mandatory methods of `UITableViewDataSource`. Let's start with the easiest one that returns the number of rows. Right now, there is no way to detect the number of elements of an enumeration, so we will hardcode this value:

```
func tableView(tableView: UITableView,
   numberOfRowsInSection section: Int) -> Int{
      return 3
}
```

8. The next step is to create the method that returns the seat type cells:

```
func tableView(tableView: UITableView,
   cellForRowAtIndexPath indexPath: NSIndexPath)
   -> UITableViewCell{
     var cell:UITableViewCell
     if let auxCell = tableView.
       dequeueReusableCellWithIdentifier("cell")
       as? UITableViewCell {
         cell = auxCell
     }else{
         cell = UITableViewCell()
     }
     switch indexPath.row {
     case 0:
         cell.textLabel!.text = "Economy class"
     case 1:
         cell.textLabel!.text = "First class"
     case 2:
         cell.textLabel!.text = "Business class"
     default:
         break;
     }

     return cell
}
```

9. If you click on play at this moment, you should at least see the table view with its values. Now, we need to create a method to display the current queue passengers:

```
private func displayQueue () {
     textView.text =
       "\n".join(self.passengersQueue.toArray().map{
     (var p)-> String in
     return p.description
     })
}
```

10. Now, we only need to create the actions for our buttons:

```
@IBAction func enqueue(sender: AnyObject) {
    if let indexPath =
      seatType.indexPathForSelectedRow(){
        var passenger = Passenger(name:
          passengerName.text, id: idDocument.text,
          classtype: Passenger.Class(rawValue:
          indexPath.row)!)
        passengersQueue.enqueue(passenger)
        self.displayQueue()
    }else {
        UIAlertView(title: "Error", message:
          "You must select the seat type", delegate:
          nil, cancelButtonTitle: "Dismiss").show()
    }
}


@IBAction func dequeue(sender: AnyObject) {
    passengersQueue.dequeue()
    displayQueue()
}
```

The app is done. Now, try to add different passengers and check how your queue grows.

How it works...

Generics save us from rewriting a lot of code, but as it needs to be safe, you can't use operators or methods that might not exist on the type that you are working with. To solve this problem, you can specify a constraint that will tell the compiler which methods are allowed to be used with this type. In our case, we specified that T is Comparable; so we can use the operators of Comparators on our code.

Some new knowledge that we can retrieve from this code is the nested enumeration. Swift has no namespace or package, but you can create nested enumerations, classes, and structs. This way we can avoid clashing names.

Another new feature is the typed enumeration; as you can see, we specified that each enumeration value is associated with an integer number. You can retrieve this value using `rawValue` or use `init(rawValue:)` to do the inverted process.

 The first version of Swift used to have a method called `toRaw()` instead of the property `rawValue`, and `fromRaw()` instead of using the initializer `init(rawValue:)`.

You can also implement your own function or computed property as we did in this enumeration; sometimes, it's better than using the raw value.

 Creating your function or computed property to convert enumerations is a good practice for software maintenance.

There's more...

There is more than one way to solve this problem; if you need performance, you might use a double linked list instead.

You can specify more than one constraint if you want by using the `where` clause. For example, if you would like to store elements that are also printable, you can change the class `header` to class `PriorityQueue<T:Comparable where T:Printable> {`.

Creating a protocol for the priority queue

In the previous recipe, we could create a generic code, which can be used in our future programs, but we have to remember that priority queues are only one kind of queue. It is good practice to define an interface for this abstract data type, and after this, have different implementations.

As you know, in Swift, we have protocols for cases such as this; however, we have a problem; protocols don't have generics. What is the solution? The answer is associated types.

Getting ready

Copy the project of the previous recipe and name it `Chapter 3 Flight Protocol`, and create a new file called `Queue.swift`.

How to do it...

To create a protocol for the priority queue, follow these steps:

1. Add the following code onto the `Queue.swift` file:

    ```swift
    protocol Queue {
        typealias ElementType
        func enqueue(element:ElementType)
        func dequeue() -> ElementType
        var size: Int{
    ```

```
        get
    }
}
```

2. Now, return to the priority queue and change its header to this one:

   ```
   class PriorityQueue<T:Comparable>:Queue
   ```

3. Click on play, and of course, the result is visually the same, but your code now is more recyclable. Try to remove one method such as `enqueue`, and you will see that the compiler will complain about the missing method of the protocol.

How it works...

Unfortunately, we can't create protocols with generics, but we can solve this problem with associated types. You only need to create `typealias` inside the protocol without specifying its real type, and then, we can declare the protocol's methods with this type. When you inherit from this protocol, your type can be anything, even a generic type `T`.

 Try to use protocols when you have a concept such as a queue, a list, or a stack. Then, you can have different implementations and use the best one for the occasion.

There's more...

Now that you learned how to make reusable code with generics, you will improve even more in the next chapter where we will use design patterns with Swift.

4

Design Patterns
with Swift

In this chapter, we will cover the following topics:

- ▶ Writing into a log file
- ▶ Creating a factory of musical notes
- ▶ Simulating a home automation
- ▶ Delivering some pizzas

Introduction

When object-oriented programming was introduced, the developers noticed that there were some objects or classes that were programmed following the same philosophy.

Xerox labs, for example, introduced the Model-View-Controller pattern in the 70s to develop programs using SmallTalk. A few other patterns were introduced by Xerox, but they were not called this.

When a book called *Design Patterns* was released in 1994, written by the Gang of Four, it brought solutions for common engineering problems. It demonstrated that the main problem with software development costs was maintenance; the usage of design patterns would cause a high cost in the first phase of software development but it would significantly reduce the maintenance costs.

Nowadays, design patterns are so important that it is very common to talk about them in job interviews. If you are experienced in Swift or Objective-C, you've already used some of these patterns without realizing.

In this chapter, we will cover a few design patterns; if possible, we will look at some common samples of these patterns in Swift.

> Before we start, I'd like to comment that design patterns are very questionable nowadays; for example, the singleton pattern that is shown in the *Writing into a log file* recipe of this chapter was criticized by some developers because it is very easy to implement and this is also the reason some programmers avoid this pattern. Others don't think that way, they think that you can use it, but only at the right moment, as the author explains in this URL: http://www.ibm.com/developerworks/library/co-single/. Anyway, arguing about this topic is out of the scope of this book, I will show you some patterns, and then you can decide whether to use them and when.
>
> Another detail I'd like to comment on is that some examples can look more complicated than those without patterns. Don't forget that design patterns are not based on simplicity, but in software maintenance.

Writing into a log file

This recipe is about a very simple and also a very common pattern design: the **Singleton** pattern. The idea of this pattern is to have an object with only one instance. You've already used this pattern in Swift or Objective-C, for example, when you used UIDevice or UIApplication.

For this recipe, we will create an object that will write out logs into a file. Note that it doesn't matter where we are in our application code, we should write only into one single file using one single object.

Getting ready

As we will write into a file, probably you would like to see its contents after running the application. Before we start, let's check whether we are able to see the destination folder.

If you use the simulator, open the Finder window and go to your home directory; you can use the shortcut *command + shift + H*. If you can't see a folder called Library, you have to press *command + J* to show the view options. Now, check the **Show Library Folder** option, as shown in the following screenshot:

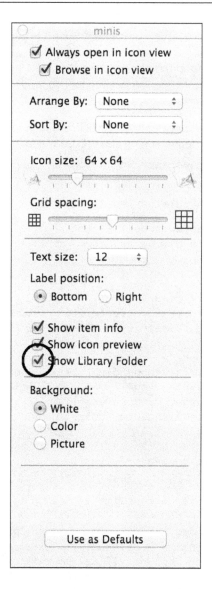

Of course, you won't have the application if you haven't ran it yet, so on your `viewDidLoad` method, paste the code `println(NSHomeDirectory())` to know your path, and then you can follow it.

 An easy way to open the document folder of the application is to print the home directory and copy it. Then, you can go to the Finder application, press *command + shift + G* and paste your path.

How to do it...

Let's create a small calculator and record the user actions. Remember that we don't need to instantiate the logger object every time we use the log; as it will be a singleton, you can call it from anywhere. So, let's get started.

1. Start a project called `Chapter 4 Log File` and create a file called `Log.swift`. Here is where we will define our log class. Copy the following code into the file:

```swift
private var myLogInstance:Log = Log()

class Log {
    private var handle:NSFileHandle

    class func getInstance() -> Log{
            return myLogInstance
    }

    private init(){
        var path:String =
          NSSearchPathForDirectoriesInDomains(
          .DocumentDirectory, .UserDomainMask, true)[0]
          as String
        let fullpath =
          path.stringByAppendingPathComponent(
          "application.log")
        NSFileManager.defaultManager(
          ).createFileAtPath(fullpath, contents: nil,
          attributes: nil)
        self.handle=NSFileHandle(
          forWritingAtPath:fullpath)!
    }

    private func getCurrentTime() -> String{
        let date = NSDate()
        let calendar = NSCalendar.currentCalendar()
        let components = calendar.components(
          .CalendarUnitHour | .CalendarUnitMinute |
          .CalendarUnitSecond, fromDate: date)
        let hour:Int = components.hour
        let minutes = components.minute
        let seconds = components.second
        return String(format: "%02d:%02d:%02d",hour,
          minutes, seconds)
    }

    func info(message:String){
      let finalMessage = "INFO:
        \(self.getCurrentTime()):\(message)\n"
```

```
        handle.writeData(finalMessage.dataUsingEncoding
          (NSUTF8StringEncoding, allowLossyConversion:
          false)!)
        handle.synchronizeFile()
    }

    func error(message:String){
        let finalMessage =
          "ERROR:\(self.getCurrentTime()):\(message)\n"
        handle.writeData(message.dataUsingEncoding(
        NSUTF8StringEncoding, allowLossyConversion:
        false)!)
    }

    deinit{
        handle.closeFile()
    }
}
```

2. Now, of course, we need to complete our application to check the usage of our code. Go to the storyboard and add two text fields, each of them will represent a number, a segmented control that will represent the current operator, a button to show the result, and a label where the result will be displayed. Your layout should be similar to the following one:

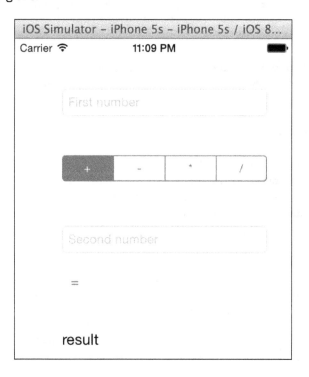

3. Now, let's code the view controller. First, let's add the attributes:

```
var chosenOperator:Character = "+"
        @IBOutlet var firstNumber: UITextField!
@IBOutlet var labelResult: UILabel!
@IBOutlet var secondNumber: UITextField!
```

4. Don't forget to link each graphic component with its attribute. Now, it's time to code our program methods; in this case, we will develop a method to save the chosen operator, and another to show the results:

```
@IBAction func operatorChanged(sender: UISegmentedControl)
  {
        switch sender.selectedSegmentIndex {
        case 0:
            chosenOperator = "+"
        case 1:
            chosenOperator = "-"
        case 2:
            chosenOperator = "*"
        case 3:
            chosenOperator = "/"
        default:
            Log.getInstance().error("Invalid value
              \(sender.selectedSegmentIndex)")
            return
        }
        Log.getInstance().info("User has chosen the
          following operator: \(chosenOperator)")
  }

    @IBAction func displayResult(sender: UIButton)
    {
        var number1:Double?
        var number2:Double?
        number1=(firstNumber.text as NSString).doubleValue
        number2=(secondNumber.text as NSString).doubleValue



        switch chosenOperator{
        case "+":
            labelResult.text = "\(number1! + number2!)"
            Log.getInstance().info("\(number1!) +
              \(number2!) = \(number1! + number2!)")
        case "-":
```

```
                labelResult.text = "\(number1! - number2!)"
                Log.getInstance().info("\(number1!) -
                  \(number2!) = \(number1! + number2!)")
            case "*":
                labelResult.text = "\(number1! * number2!)"
                Log.getInstance().info("\(number1!) *
                  \(number2!) = \(number1! + number2!)")
            case "/":
                if number2! == 0.0 {
                    Log.getInstance().error("Trying to divide
                      by zero")
                    UIAlertView(title: "Error", message: "Can't
                      divide by zero", delegate: nil,
                      cancelButtonTitle: "Ok").show()
                }else {
                    labelResult.text =
                      "\(number1!)/\(number2!)"
                    Log.getInstance().info("\(number1!) /
                      \(number2!) = \(number1! + number2!)")
                }
            default:
                break;
            }
        }
```

5. To finish our application, we should add a little bit of code on our application
    delegate. Filling these events will register when the user has opened the application,
    put the application on background, and returned to the application. Here is the code:

```
func application(application: UIApplication,
  didFinishLaunchingWithOptions launchOptions: [NSObject:
  AnyObject]?) -> Bool {
    println(NSHomeDirectory())
    Log.getInstance().info("Application has started")
    return true
}
func applicationDidEnterBackground(application:
  UIApplication) {
    Log.getInstance().info("Application has gone to
      background")
}
func applicationDidBecomeActive(application: UIApplication)
  {
    Log.getInstance().info("Application has become active")
}
```

6.   Now, click on play and test the program; then, press the **home** button and come back to the application. When you are done, go to the application documents folder, as demonstrated at the beginning, and open the file `application.log`. Note that every action was registered on the same file; it doesn't matter if it was an event produced by the app delegate or by the view controller.

How it works...

In this recipe, we will see the introduction of the access control. Swift has three access levels:

▸   **Public**: In this level, the object, attribute, or global variable can be used from anywhere, even from another module.

▸   **Internal**: In this level, the corresponding entity can be accessed from anywhere, except from another module.

▸   **Private**: In this level, the entity can be accessed only from the current file, even from the same module.

As you can see, the idea of a singleton is to make sure that there will be only one instance of a class. As the initializer of the class is private, it can't be called from anywhere, but only from a method or function that is in the current file.

So, we created a method called `getInstance` to access the only instance we have, and then we can access the object methods. Notice that we had to use classes, if we used structs, we would break the rule of one object only.

Sometimes, you will see the implementation of singleton accepting nil values, such as `private var myLogInstance:Log?`, and initializing it inside the `getInstance` method, such as `if myLogInstance == nil { myLogInstance = Log() } return myLogInstance`.

The reason is that some software architects think that you don't have to start your application instantiating every singleton object, except when you are going to use it. There are some singleton objects that are never called, and you shouldn't waste this memory. If you notice, this class also had a deinitializer. Technically speaking, this method won't be called if you are running your application on iOS because iOS apps usually don't finish. However, the application can still end in certain circumstances, and you might close the file handle in the right way.

Now, when talking about file usage, first of all, we have to know what the application document's folder path is, because this is the location we have chosen for writing the log file. There is a function called `NSSearchPathForDirectoriesInDomains` which returns the full path of a requested folder (actually, it returns an array of paths). After calling this function, we can create the file with the file manager, and open it using `NSFileHandle`.

Don't use paths by concatenating with the home directories in this manner: `NSHomeDirectory() + /Documents`. Apple can change its path in future versions like they did with the bundle on iOS 8.

If this class wasn't a singleton, you wouldn't open this file here; you would open and close it every time you had to write a message because you must avoid having two open handles for the same file. Opening and closing a handle is a slow operation; it can affect your application performance.

In the case of writing into the log file with a high frequency, you will have to avoid clashing the file writing or opening, but if you have a singleton, this problem is much easier to control.

To finish this recipe, I would like to comment that this simple log system is based on real log systems used on applications. Usually, log files try to register the log level, such as info, error, warning, or debug, and its time. With this information in mind, you can filter your log when it gets big, and figure out what is going on when the application has crashed.

There's more...

The solution we had for our singleton application was to keep the object instance on a global variable; the ideal solution for this pattern is keeping it on a class variable, also called a static attribute, but unfortunately, if you type the following code, the compiler will not accept it, as it is not implemented yet. So, we hope that soon we can have a code like this one:

```
class Log {
    class var instance:Log…
```

Another way to do this is by creating an internal struct with a static member, something similar to the following code:

```
class Log {
    private struct STATIC{
        static var myInstance = Log()
    }
```

And in this case, you can return the instance this way:

```
class func getInstance() -> Log{
    return Log.STATIC.myInstance
}
```

Creating a factory of musical notes

Composing music with computers is something very common nowadays. Creating software that allows a musician to create his own music looks easy but it is not, mainly because there are lots of possibilities for each note.

In this recipe, we will use the pattern **Abstract Factory**. This pattern will allow us to change the note type that we want to create, and it will also initialize the note type for us.

As you may know, there are a lot of note symbols; you can check this URL on Wikipedia if you want to know more about it: http://en.wikipedia.org/wiki/List_of_musical_symbols.

However, for this recipe, we will work with three types of notes: the drum quarter note, the piano quarter note, and the quarter rest note. Of course, this is only an example; in a real program, probably you will have to complete it with tied notes, and so on.

Getting ready

Create a project called Chapter 4 Musical Notes; now, download the pictures that correspond to this recipe from the Internet. In this case, we have these pictures: staff.png, quarter_rest.png, cnote.png, dnote, cdrum.png, and ddrum.png.

We will also need some MP3 sounds for this recipe. Download three sounds for the piano notes and another three for the drums; of course, we won't have any sound for the rest note.

Place the pictures that were downloaded into your images.xcassets folder. If you like, you can also add the same pictures with different resolutions for use in different resolution devices (iPad and iPhone).

Before you start, we will just need to add a framework called AVFoundation. This will enable our app to play sounds. To do this, just click on the project navigator, then click on build phases. After this, expand the **Link binary with Libraries** section, then click on the plus button. Select **AVFoundation** and press **Add**.

How to do it...

1. As usual, we will start with the models. First, let's create a note protocol, as we know that in future we can have more than one type of note and we should be prepared for it. So, create a new file called NoteProtocol.swift and put the following code:

    ```
    import Foundation
    import UIKit

    enum NoteStep {
    ```

```
        case NOTE_C,
        NOTE_D,
        NOTE_E
    }
    protocol NoteProtocol {
        var sound:String?{
            get set
        }
        var image:UIImage?{
            get set
        }
        var step: NoteStep {
            get set
        }
        var location:CGPoint {
            get set
        }
        func play()
    }
```

2. The next step is to create an implementation of this protocol. Create a file called `MusicalNote.swift` and add the following content in it:

```
import Foundation
import UIKit
import AVFoundation

class MusicalNote: NoteProtocol{
    lazy private var _player = AVAudioPlayer()
    private var _sound:String?
    var sound:String? {
        get { return _sound }
        set(newSound){ self._sound = newSound }
    }

    private var _image:UIImage?
    var image:UIImage?{
        get{ return _image}
        set(newImage){ self._image = newImage }
    }

    private var _step:NoteStep
    var step: NoteStep {
        get{ return _step }
        set(newStep){ self._step = newStep }
```

```
    }

    private var _location:CGPoint
    var location:CGPoint {
        get { return _location }
        set(newLocation){ self._location = newLocation }
    }

    func play(){
        if let mySound = _sound {
            var urlSound = NSURL(fileURLWithPath:
                NSBundle.mainBundle().pathForResource(
                mySound, ofType: "mp3")!)
            self._player = AVAudioPlayer(contentsOfURL:
                urlSound, error: nil)
            self._player.prepareToPlay()
            self._player.play()
        }
    }

    init(_ step:NoteStep = .NOTE_C){
        self._location = CGPointZero
        self._step = step
    }
}
```

3. Now that we have implemented our note class, see to it that this note is not piano-specific or drum-specific; we only need to build it in a different way according to the note type and step. So, now we need to define a factory of notes. With the same logic we had applied before, we now need to create a protocol of a note.

    The only method that we will define is `createNote`, and it needs to know the note step (C, D, or E) and its position on the staff. It's time to create a new file called `AbstractNoteFactory.swift` and type the following code:

    ```
    protocol AbstractNoteFactory {
        func createNote(noteStep:NoteStep, order:Int) ->
            NoteProtocol
    }
    ```

4. Once we have the definition of a note factory, we can start creating our own factories. Let's start with the simplest one: `SilenceFactory`; this factory will create only one kind of note, no matter its step. Type this code in a file called `SilenceFactory.swift`:

    ```
    import UIKit
    class SilenceFactory: AbstractNoteFactory {
    ```

```
func createNote(noteStep:NoteStep, order:Int) ->
  NoteProtocol{
    var note = MusicalNote(noteStep)
    note.image = UIImage(named: "quarter_rest.png")
    note.sound = nil
    note.step = noteStep
    var x = CGFloat(120) + CGFloat(40 * order)
    note.location = CGPointMake(x, 25)
    return note
  }
}
```

5. With this class, we will save some steps for when we need to create a new silent note. Following the same logic, let's create the piano factory and the drum factory. Use this code to create the piano factory:

```
class PianoNoteFactory: AbstractNoteFactory {
    func createNote(noteStep:NoteStep, order:Int) ->
      NoteProtocol{
        var note = MusicalNote(noteStep)
        note.step = noteStep
        var x:CGFloat = CGFloat(120.0) + CGFloat(40.0)  *
          CGFloat(order)

        switch noteStep {
        case .NOTE_C:
            note.image = UIImage(named: "cnote.png")
            note.location = CGPointMake( CGFloat(x), 57)
            note.sound = "piano_c"
        case .NOTE_D:
            note.image = UIImage(named: "dnote.png")
            note.location = CGPointMake( CGFloat(x), 44)
            note.sound = "piano_d"
        case .NOTE_E:
            note.image = UIImage(named: "dnote.png")
            note.location = CGPointMake( CGFloat(x), 36)
            note.sound = "piano_e"
        }
        return note
    }
}
```

And now, let's create the drum factory:

```swift
class DrumNoteFactory: AbstractNoteFactory {
    func createNote(noteStep:NoteStep, order:Int) ->
      NoteProtocol{
        var note = MusicalNote(noteStep)
        note.step = noteStep
        var x:CGFloat = CGFloat(120.0) + CGFloat(40.0)  *
          CGFloat(order)

        switch noteStep {
        case .NOTE_C:
            note.image = UIImage(named: "cdrum.png")
            note.location = CGPointMake( CGFloat(x), 57)
            note.sound = "bighit"
        case .NOTE_D:
            note.image = UIImage(named: "ddrum.png")
            note.location = CGPointMake( CGFloat(x), 46)
            note.sound = "cymbal"
        case .NOTE_E:
            note.image = UIImage(named: "ddrum.png")
            note.location = CGPointMake( CGFloat(x), 38)
            note.sound = "hithat"
        }
        return note
    }
}
```

6. Good, it's time to create our layout. For this recipe, we will need to add a staff (the Image View), which is where the notes will be displayed, a segmented control that will let us choose the note factory we want, and a play button that will appear after we create ten notes, and which will allow us to hear our music.

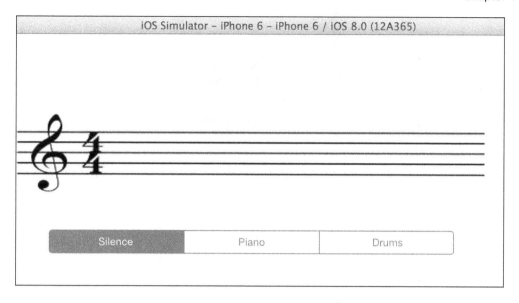

7. We won't allow the user to play the music before it is completely composed. For this reason, the play button must start as invisible. To do this, after adding the button to the view on the storyboard, click on it, go to the attribute inspector, and select the **hidden** option.

8. As you know, we now have to link the segmented control and the button with its attribute. Let's also add other attributes that are necessary for this app:

    ```
    @IBOutlet var segmentedControl: UISegmentedControl!
    @IBOutlet var playButton: UIButton!
    @IBOutlet var staff: UIImageView!
    var notes = [NoteProtocol]()
    var factory:AbstractNoteFactory = SilenceFactory()
    var timer:NSTimer?
    var pos = 0
    ```

> In this case, we had to specify the factory type as
> AbstractNoteFactory; if not, it will be declared as
> SilenceFactory, and it won't allow us to change the factory type.

9. Let's add the possibility to tap on the staff and add a note. To do this, we will add the following code on viewDidLoad:

    ```
    override func viewDidLoad() {
        super.viewDidLoad()
        let recognizer = UITapGestureRecognizer(target:
          self, action:Selector("handleTap:"))
    ```

```
        self.view.addGestureRecognizer(recognizer)
    }
```

10. As you can see, every time we tap on the screen, we have to check whether it is in a place where we can add a note. Let's implement this gesture action:

```
func handleTap(recognizer:UITapGestureRecognizer) {
    let point = recognizer.locationInView(staff)
    var noteStep:NoteStep = .NOTE_C
    switch point.y {
    case 105...125:
        noteStep = .NOTE_C
    case 95...105:
        noteStep = .NOTE_D
    case 80...95:
        noteStep = .NOTE_E
    default:
        return
    }
    var note = factory.createNote(noteStep, order:
      notes.count)
    notes.append(note)
    var imageView = UIImageView(frame: CGRect(origin:
      note.location, size: note.image!.size))
    imageView.image = note.image
    staff.addSubview(imageView)
    if notes.count == 10 {
        self.segmentedControl.hidden = true
        self.playButton.hidden = false
    }
}
```

11. As you can see, when we tap on the screen, we just ask for a new note; it doesn't matter which one is the current factory. Now, the segmented control will change the current factory when the user wants it.

```
@IBAction func changeFactory(sender:
  UISegmentedControl) {
    switch sender.selectedSegmentIndex {
    case 0:
        factory = SilenceFactory()
    case 1:
        factory = PianoNoteFactory()
    case 2:
        factory = DrumNoteFactory()
```

```
    default:
        break;
    }
}
```

12. To finish this app, we have to create an event for the play button. As we are not going to press the button for each note, we will initialize the timer and create a method to play each note after half a second:

```
@IBAction func playMusic(sender: UIButton) {
    playButton.enabled = false
    timer = NSTimer.scheduledTimerWithTimeInterval(0.5,
        target: self, selector: Selector("playNote"),
        userInfo: nil, repeats: true)
    timer?.fire()
}
func playNote(){
    notes[pos].play()
    pos++
    if pos >= notes.count {
        timer?.invalidate()
        pos = 0
        playButton.enabled = true
    }
}
```

13. Now, click on play and compose your music.

How it works

The abstract factory pattern saves us from performing a lot of steps after instantiating an object. As a programmer, we don't need to worry about the class that the object needs to use, only the base class; in this case, it created an object of the `NoteProtocol` type.

As every factory implements the same protocol, we don't need to check which the current factory is. We can also create new factories, and the code change wouldn't be painful.

There's more...

We will create another creational pattern that will allow us to create a home automation simulator.

Simulating a home automation

Technology is getting more and more popular every day; soon we will control even our door locks from our mobile phones. However, how does it work? Imagine when you walk into your living room, a sensor can detect that there is someone there and it will turn on the light. Also, if a barometer detects that it is going to rain, it can close the home windows. The examples mentioned here are good samples of objects that change their status and tell other objects about this change. For this case, we will use the pattern **Observer**, also known as the publisher-subscriber pattern.

In this recipe, we will create a sample of a home with only two windows, a door lock, and a clothes line. To make it simple, the application will read the sensor information from a file.

When we receive information from the radar, it may be that someone is approaching your home. In this case, the door lock must be locked and the windows should be closed, or when this person goes away, the windows can be opened again. Also, when the barometer detects that it is going to rain, the windows must be closed and the clothes line must collect the clothes. When the rain stops, these robots can do the opposite action.

Getting ready

Let's create a new project called `Chapter 4 Observer`. My first idea for this recipe was to create a list of actions into a file, but as with a few actions, it will be enough; we will create an array with actions instead.

How to do it...

1. First, let's create the simplest model, which in our case is the door lock. Basically, the only thing that we need to do here is to store its status, which can be opened or closed. So, create a file called `DoorLock.swift` and add the following code:

```swift
class DoorLock {
    enum Status {
        case OPENED, CLOSED
    }
    private var _status = Status.OPENED
    var status:Status {
        return _status
    }
    func open(){
        _status = .OPENED
    }
    func close(){
```

```
        _status = .CLOSED
    }
}
```

2. Once we've done the previous code, we can do something similar with the clothes line, so put the following code into a new file called `ClothesLine.swift`:

```swift
class ClothesLine {
    enum Status {
        case COLLECTED,
            LINED
    }
    private var _status = Status.LINED
    var status:Status {
        return _status
    }
    func collect(){
        _status = .COLLECTED
    }
    func line(){
        _status = .LINED
    }
}
```

3. Okay, now we need our last accessory, that is, the window. In this case, we have to store the count of times it was closed. Imagine that two people approach our house and one of them goes away, we have to keep the window closed because there is another person still near our house. So, create a file called `Window.swift` and add the following code:

```swift
class Window {
    enum Status {
        case OPENED, CLOSED(times:Int)
    }
    private var _status = Status.OPENED
    var status:Status {
        return _status
    }
    func open(){
        switch _status{
        case .CLOSED(var times):
            times = times - 1
            if times == 0{
                _status = .OPENED
            }else{
```

```
                        _status = .CLOSED(times:times)
                }
            default:
                _status = .OPENED
            }
        }
        func close(){
            switch _status{
            case .CLOSED(var times):
                times = times + 1
                _status = .CLOSED(times:times)
            default:
                _status = .CLOSED(times:1)
            }
        }
    }
}
```

4. Good, now it's time to create the radar. Remember that the radar needs to store some objects that will notify the status change, so we will create a nested class called `RadarObserver`. Start adding this class into a new file called `Radar.swift`, as follows:

```
class Radar{
    class RadarObserver{
        var onSomeoneAproaches: ()->Void
        var onSomeoneHasGoneAway: () -> Void

        init(){
            self.onSomeoneAproaches = { () -> Void in
            }
            self.onSomeoneHasGoneAway = {() -> Void in
            }
        }
    }
    var observers = [RadarObserver]()
        func addObserver(observer: RadarObserver){
            observers.append(observer)
        }
```

5. This feature can be added because we are creating a nested class; Swift doesn't allow us to create nested protocols. Now, create the methods that store or remove the observers. We will not remove any observer in this recipe but, as I told you earlier, always be prepared for the future.

6. The last part of this class is the methods that change the object status:

```
func detectedSomeone(){
    for observer in observers {
        observer.onSomeoneAproaches()
    }
}
func someoneHasGoneAway(){
    for observer in observers {
        observer.onSomeoneHasGoneAway()
    }
}
}
```

7. Once we've understood it, we can create the barometer following the philosophy, which we have used here:

```
class Barometer{
    class BarometerObserver{
        var onItsGoingToRain:() -> Void
        var onRainHasFinished:() -> Void

        init() {
            self.onItsGoingToRain = { () -> Void in
            }
            self.onRainHasFinished = { () -> Void in
            }
        }
    }
    private var observers = [BarometerObserver]()
    func addObserver(observer: BarometerObserver){
        observers.append(observer)
    }
    func removeObserver(observer:BarometerObserver){
        var index: Int?
        for (i,object) in enumerate(observers){
            if object === observer{
                index = i
                break
            }
        }
        if let indexFound = index{
            observers.removeAtIndex(indexFound)
        }
    }
    func detectedRain(){
```

```
        for observer in observers {
            observer.onItsGoingToRain()
        }
    }

    func detectedNoRain(){
        for observer in observers {
            observer.onRainHasFinished()
        }
    }
}
```

8. Okay, now we can create our display. For this recipe, we will add five labels, one for each accessory and one to show the last action. We also need a button to start simulating the reception of radar and barometer events. You can have a view similar to the following one:

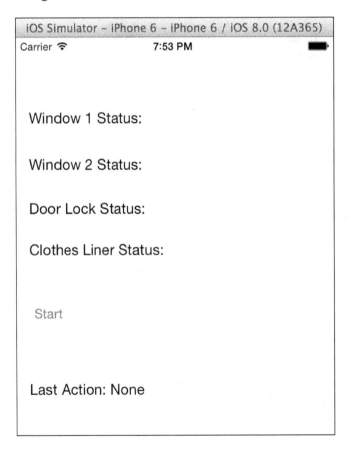

9. Now, let's link these components with the corresponding attributes:

```
@IBOutlet var labelWindow1: UILabel!
@IBOutlet var labelWindow2: UILabel!
@IBOutlet var labelDoorLock: UILabel!
@IBOutlet var labelClothesLine: UILabel!
@IBOutlet var labelLastAction: UILabel!
@IBOutlet var buttonStart: UIButton!
```

10. Now, let's go to the view controller and let's start completing the attributes. In this case, we need a radar, a barometer, two windows, a door lock, a clothes line, a list of actions that will be performed, and a timer to make the simulation easier for our eyes:

```
var radar = Radar()
var barometer = Barometer()
var window1 = Window()
var window2 = Window()
var doorLock = DoorLock()
var clothesLine = ClothesLine()
var actions=[String]()
var timer:NSTimer?
```

11. Now, let's create a private function that will update the labels. This function is an auxiliary function, so we don't need to repeat this code in every observer action:

```
private func updateLabels(){
    switch self.window1.status {
    case .CLOSED:
        self.labelWindow1.text = "Window 1 Status:
          CLOSED"
    default:
        self.labelWindow1.text = "Window 1 Status:
          OPENED"
    }

    switch self.window2.status {
    case .CLOSED:
        self.labelWindow2.text = "Window 2 Status:
          CLOSED"
    default:
        self.labelWindow2.text = "Window 2 Status:
          OPENED"
    }

    switch self.doorLock.status {
    case .CLOSED:
```

```
        self.labelDoorLock.text = "Door Lock Status:
           CLOSED"
    default:
        self.labelDoorLock.text = "Door Lock Status:
           OPENED"
    }

    switch self.clothesLine.status {
    case .COLLECTED:
        self.labelClothesLine.text = "Clothes Status:
           LINED"
    default:
        self.labelClothesLine.text = "Clothes Status:
           COLLECTED"
    }
}
```

12. Now, on our `viewDidLoad` method, we will add the observer's code. The following
    code only has the creation of the first two observers; you have to complete it following
    the same rule because it will be exhausting showing all of them:

```
override func viewDidLoad() {
    super.viewDidLoad()
    var radarObserver = Radar.RadarObserver()
    radarObserver.onSomeoneAproaches = { () -> Void in
        self.window1.close()
        self.updateLabels()
    }

    radarObserver.onSomeoneHasGoneAway = {
        () -> Void in
        self.window1.open()
        self.updateLabels()
    }
    radar.addObserver(radarObserver)

    radarObserver = Radar.RadarObserver()
    radarObserver.onSomeoneAproaches = { () -> Void in
        self.window2.close()
        self.updateLabels()
    }
    radarObserver.onSomeoneHasGoneAway = {
        () -> Void in
        self.window2.open()
```

```
                self.updateLabels()
            }
        radar.addObserver(radarObserver)
    }
    ...
```

13. Now, we can complete creating the simulator, the event of our button, which will initialize the actions and the timer, and a function that will be called by the timer and perform the corresponding action:

```
        func tick(){
            var action = actions.first
            actions.removeAtIndex(0)
            if actions.count == 0 {
                buttonStart.enabled = true
                timer?.invalidate()
            }

            if action == "someoneapproches"{
                radar.detectedSomeone()
            }else if action == "someoneleaves"{
                radar.someoneHasGoneAway()
            }else if action == "startrainning" {
                barometer.detectedRain()
            }else if action == "rainfinishes" {
                barometer.detectedNoRain()
            }

            labelLastAction.text = action
        }

    @IBAction func start(sender: AnyObject) {
        buttonStart.enabled = false
        actions = ["someoneapproches","someoneleaves",
          "someoneapproches","someoneapproches",
          "startrainning","someoneleaves","someoneleaves",
          "rainfinishes"]
        timer = NSTimer.scheduledTimerWithTimeInterval(1,
          target: self, selector: Selector("tick"),
          userInfo: nil, repeats: true)
        timer!.fire()
    }
```

It's done now! Click on play and watch it work.

How it works...

As you can see, the main goal of an observer is to execute an action, and to do this, we used closures. This Swift feature is equivalent to blocks on Objective-C and function variables in JavaScript. A closure knows where the object was created and can access its attributes even if it was stored in another object.

In our recipe, when the radar or the barometer detects something different, it will notify every observer who has subscribed for it. Each observer acts over the corresponding accessory (window, door lock, or that thing called a clothes line). Note that if we would like to write a traditional object method, it will be necessary to create new classes that inherit from the same observer and store in it the attribute that it is going to use. It wouldn't be a bad implementation, but using closures is much easier and more flexible.

If you are a Martin Fowler fan, you have probably noticed that some code here are very similar to the barometer observer and the radar observer. This is what Mr. Martin calls the smell of a code, meaning that the code doesn't need to be technically wrong but can smell bad.

That would be true in this case, except that this is just an example. Remember that in real life, probably the radar would have to notify the intruder's position, and the barometer would need to notify the precipitation, making the notifier's methods incompatible.

There's more...

We already learned about behavioral patterns and creational pattern. In the next recipe, we will use structural pattern, creating new object types based on a new feature.

Delivering some pizzas

Imagine that you have to create a new window type, which will have a border; the first idea is borrowed from a window class, and creating a new class called `BorderedWindow`. You can do the same thing with scroll bars; call it `ScrolledWindow`. Now, if we need to create a window with scroll and border, we have to create a new class called `ScrolledAndBorderedWindow`, but imagine that we now need to add a double and triple bordered window, we will have lots of combinations.

To prevent this kind of problem, there is a pattern called **decorator**; this pattern allows us to create new object types based on a new feature.

Getting ready

Create a new project called `Chapter 4 Pizzas` and add the pizza image into `Images.xcassets`. Now, heat up the oven and let's prepare some pizzas.

How to do it...

Let's execute these steps to deliver some pizzas:

1. First of all, let's create a base class that defines a pizza, so create a new file called `Pizza.swift` and create the following class:

```
class BasePizza {
    private var _price:Double
    var price:Double {
        get {
            return _price
        }
    }
    var name:String

    init(name:String, price:Double){
        self.name = name
        self._price = price
    }
}
```

2. As you can see, this class stores the price and the pizza or ingredient name. Now, we can define some pizzas with their prices:

```
class SimplePizza : BasePizza{
    init() {
        super.init(name: "SimplePizza", price: 4.50)
    }
}

class Peperoni: BasePizza{
    init() {
        super.init(name: "Peperoni", price: 7.50)
    }
}

class ChickenFiesta:BasePizza {
```

```
    init() {
        super.init(name: "ChickenFiesta", price: 7.50)
    }
}
```

3. Create a new file called `PizzaDecorators.swift`; here is where we will create the extra ingredients. First, we need to create a class that defines what a pizza decorator is:

```
class BasePizzaDecorator:BasePizza {
    var decoratedPizza:BasePizza?
    init(name:String, price:Double,
      decoratedPizza:BasePizza){
        self.decoratedPizza = decoratedPizza
        super.init(name: name, price: price)
    }

    override var price:Double {
        get {
            return super.price + decoratedPizza!.price
        }
    }
}
```

4. Now, let's add some extra ingredients. In this case, we will have Jalapeño, Cheese, Mushrooms, and Olives:

```
class Jalapeño:BasePizzaDecorator {
    init(decoratedPizza:BasePizza){
        super.init(name: "Jalapeño", price: 1.20,
          decoratedPizza: decoratedPizza)
    }
}

class Cheese:BasePizzaDecorator {
    init(decoratedPizza:BasePizza){
        super.init(name: "Cheese", price: 1.30,
          decoratedPizza: decoratedPizza)
    }
}

class Mushroom:BasePizzaDecorator {
    init(decoratedPizza:BasePizza){
        super.init(name: "Mushroom", price: 1.10,
          decoratedPizza: decoratedPizza)
    }
}
```

```
class Olive:BasePizzaDecorator {
    init(decoratedPizza:BasePizza){
        super.init(name: "Olive", price: 1.10,
            decoratedPizza: decoratedPizza)
    }
}
```

5. Good! Once you're done with that, we can create the view. We will add one label to display the total, four buttons for the extra ingredients, one text view to display the ingredients that we've already added to our pizza, and an Image View to make our application happier. At the end, we should have a layout similar to the one shown here:

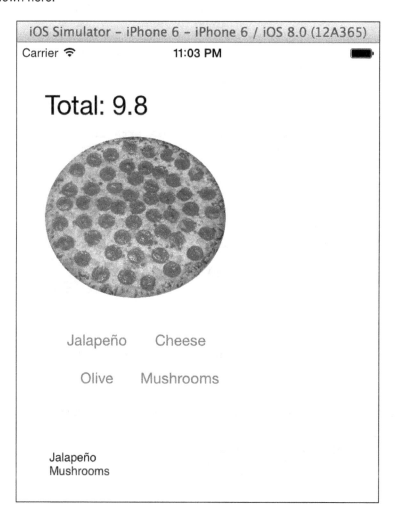

6. Now, we can create the view controller. Let's start with the attributes:

```
var myDeliciousPizza: BasePizza?
@IBOutlet var totalLabel: UILabel!
@IBOutlet var ingredientsList: UITextView!
```

7. Let's ask the user to select the pizza that he wants. In this case, we need to do it on `viewDidAppear` because we will do it with an action sheet, and this component doesn't work on the `viewDidLoad` method because the view is not ready to display action sheets yet:

```
override func viewDidAppear(animated: Bool) {
    var choosePizzaType = UIAlertController(title:
      "Pizza", message: "Choose your pizza",
      preferredStyle: .ActionSheet)
    choosePizzaType.addAction(UIAlertAction(title:
      "Simple", style: .Default, handler: { (action) in
        self.myDeliciousPizza = SimplePizza()
        self.refreshPrice()
    }))

    choosePizzaType.addAction(UIAlertAction(title:
      "Peperoni", style: .Default, handler:
      { (action) in
        self.myDeliciousPizza = Peperoni()
        self.refreshPrice()
    }))

    choosePizzaType.addAction(UIAlertAction(title:
      "Chicken Fiesta \u{1F389}", style: .Default,
      handler: { (action) in
        self.myDeliciousPizza = ChickenFiesta()
        self.refreshPrice()
    }))

    self.presentViewController(choosePizzaType,
      animated: true) {    }
}
```

8. We need to create a method called `refreshPrice`; it is as easy as this one:

```
func refreshPrice(){
    self.totalLabel.text = "Total:
      \(myDeliciousPizza!.price)"
}
```

9. To finish our application, you have to add the events that belong to the buttons; don't forget to link them:

```
@IBAction func addJalapeño(sender: UIButton) {
    myDeliciousPizza = Jalapeño(decoratedPizza:
      myDeliciousPizza!)
    self.ingredientsList.text =
      self.ingredientsList.text + "Jalapeño\n"
    self.refreshPrice()
}


@IBAction func addCheese(sender: UIButton) {
    myDeliciousPizza = Cheese(decoratedPizza:
      myDeliciousPizza!)
    self.ingredientsList.text = self.ingredientsList.text +
"Cheese\n"
    self.refreshPrice()
}


@IBAction func addOlives(sender: UIButton) {
    myDeliciousPizza = Olive(decoratedPizza:
      myDeliciousPizza!)
    self.ingredientsList.text =
      self.ingredientsList.text + "Olive\n"
    self.refreshPrice()
}


@IBAction func addMushrooms(sender: UIButton) {
    myDeliciousPizza = Mushroom(decoratedPizza:
      myDeliciousPizza!)
    self.ingredientsList.text =
      self.ingredientsList.text + "Mushrooms\n"
    self.refreshPrice()
}
```

Now the application is done, press play, choose a pizza, add some ingredients and enjoy your meal.

How it works...

The decorator pattern allows us to create a new object based on another one, which is very useful to prevent creating an uncontrolled numbers of classes based on combinations of features.

There's more...

There are more patterns. You can check them on Wikipedia (`http://en.wikipedia.org/wiki/Software_design_pattern`). Check which ones are the best for your project. There is also another feature, called anti-pattern, which explains common bad practices. In the next chapter, we will learn how to work with concurrent code with Swift, something that is very common nowadays, mainly if you like to develop games.

5
Multitasking

In this chapter, we will cover the following topics:

- ▸ Working of a device while you navigate
- ▸ Creating a SEO app
- ▸ Being aware of cyclones
- ▸ Links to our website

Introduction

Nowadays, multitasking is something very common; an application can do lots of things at the same time. If we have a multicore processor such as an iPhone 4S or newer, or an iPad 2 or newer, you can even improve the performance. Of course, you shouldn't use the multitasking feature for everything, because commuting from one task to another countlessly can harm the performance.

In this chapter, we will learn different types of multitasking and when you should use each of them. First, we will start with threads, then we will see NSOperations, and at last, we will look at ways to use GCD.

Working of a device while you navigate

Sometimes if you don't pay attention to multitasking, it might result in a frozen screen. As developers, knowing what is going on in the application, we can wait, but as users who don't know anything about the application operation, we can think that the app has hung and that it is necessary to restart.

In this recipe, we will create another thread to prevent this situation. Creating threads can also be some kind of mechanism for dividing tasks among different tracks, making debugging easier.

Let's pretend that we need to count the number of words in a document. We will have two buttons: one that will do this task without using a thread, and another that will do the same task using a thread.

Getting ready

Before you start, you must have a text file. You can use any text file you want, but to get a good result, you should have something big, like more than 30 KB. A suggestion is to download an RFC of any protocol.

So, let's create a new project called `Chapter 5 Thread`, add a file named `WordCounter.swift`, and start coding.

How to do it...

In this recipe, we will start by downloading a file from the Internet, and then we will work with it. Now, follow these steps:

1. Open your favorite web browser on your computer and download this text document `https://www.ietf.org/rfc/rfc2821.txt`

2. Drag the document into your project, preferably into your `Supporting Files` group.

3. Now, click on the `WordCounter.swift` file and create a class with the same name:

```
class WordCounter:NSObject {
    private var file:String
    lazy private var _words = [String:Int]()
    var words:[String:Int] {
        return _words
    }
```

4. Now, let's create an initializer; as you can see, the only attribute we need to initialize is the file attribute:

```
init(file:String){
    self.file = file
}
```

5. The next step is to type the `execute` method. Here, we will open our file and count the number of words. Of course, you can improve this method, but for now, this should be enough for us:

```
func execute(){
    _words = [String:Int]()

    // First step opening the file
    var manager = NSFileManager.defaultManager()
    var data = manager.contentsAtPath(
      NSBundle.mainBundle().pathForResource(file,
      ofType: "txt")!)!
    var content = NSString(data: data, encoding:
      NSUTF8StringEncoding) as! String

    // spliting the document into words
    var wordsArray =
      content.componentsSeparatedByString(" ")
    wordsArray = wordsArray.map({ (word) -> String in
        return word.stringByTrimmingCharactersInSet(
          NSCharacterSet.whitespaceCharacterSet())
    }) .map({ (word) -> String in
        return word.lowercaseString
    }) .filter({(word) -> Bool in
        var error:NSError?
        var regex = NSRegularExpression(pattern:
          "\\w+(-\\w+)*", options: .CaseInsensitive,
          error: &error)!
        let matches = regex.matchesInString(word,
          options: nil, range: NSMakeRange(0,
          count(word)))
        return matches.count > 0
    })

    // computing the results
    for word:String in wordsArray {
        if let tot = _words[word] {
            _words[word] = tot + 1
```

```
        }else{
            _words[word] = 1
        }
    }
  }
}
```

6. Now that we have the model part done, we can do the view and the controller part. Open your storyboard and add three buttons: one for counting the file words without using a thread, another one for using a thread, and another one to go to the website that is typed in the text field. As you can imagine, you have to add a text field and also a web view. You should have a layout similar to this one:

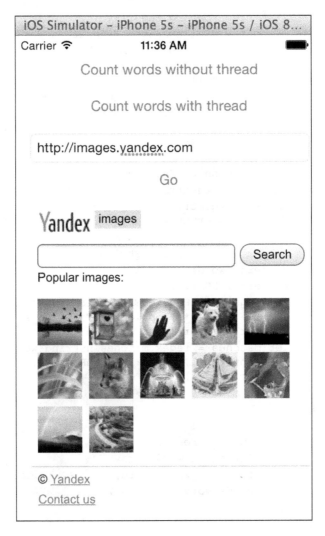

7. Now, let's link the text field and the web view to the corresponding attributes. We also need to create two attributes to know the time that we started counting the words and the time we finished doing it. So, let's complete our view controller with this code:

```
@IBOutlet var textField: UITextField!
@IBOutlet var webView: UIWebView!
lazy private var start = CFAbsoluteTimeGetCurrent()
lazy private var finish = CFAbsoluteTimeGetCurrent()
```

8. Once we have these attributes done, we can start with the easiest method. In this case, the method is the go button event, which loads the web page on the web view:

```
@IBAction func loadWeb(sender: UIButton) {
    var url = NSURL(string: textField.text)!
    var request = NSURLRequest(URL: url)
    webView.loadRequest(request)
}
```

9. Now, we have to create a method that will be called the word counter. This method should be common to both buttons, to the one that processes with a thread and the other that processes without a thread, so let's create a method now which is not bound by any button:

```
func countWords(file:String){
    var wordCounter = WordCounter(file: file)
    wordCounter.execute()
    finish = CFAbsoluteTimeGetCurrent()
    println("\(finish-start)")
    var result = ""
    for (total, word) in enumerate(wordCounter.words){
        result += "\(word) -> \(total)\n"
    }
    UIAlertView(title: "Result", message: result,
        delegate: nil, cancelButtonTitle: "Ok").show()
}
```

10. To finish the application, we have to create the click event for each button:

```
@IBAction func countWordsWithoutThreads(sender:
    UIButton) {
    start = CFAbsoluteTimeGetCurrent()
    countWords("rfc2821")
}

@IBAction func countWordsWithThreads(sender: UIButton)
    {
    start = CFAbsoluteTimeGetCurrent()
```

```
        var thread1 = NSThread(target: self, selector:
          Selector("countWords:"), object: "rfc2821")
        thread1.start()
    }
```

11. Now, it's time to test the application; pay attention to the different behaviors. First, press the button that processes the words without a thread, and after this, try to type anything on the text field. Until the word counter finishes, you won't be able to type anything. Once the operation is finished, press the button that works with a thread, and try to type a URL and navigate through it. Now, you will be able to navigate while the program is processing something else.

How it works...

Threads are like tracks of a program; even if you have lots of threads, you still share global variables or attributes like we did with the `start` attribute. People used to relate thread with earning on performance; that's not exactly true.

If you have an operation with IO, such as reading a file, or using a sensor such as Bluetooth, you can earn a good performance due to the fact that a processor can work while the IO doesn't send a reply.

Although you can earn on performance when using IO on our application, you probably can have a lower performance using threads. Why? This is because the program needs to waste time creating the thread and commuting between threads.

Why did we have a better usability when we created a thread on this app? The reason is that anything that you do with the user interface is done on the main thread. If you have a large operation on this thread, as we had while counting the words, it will prevent the program from rendering or answering an event until your operation is over.

Creating a new thread will make your application answer to the user interface while you are counting the words on another thread. In this case, we didn't earn or lose performance, but the user got a much better usability.

We can also see in this recipe the usage of regular expressions, which is a feature that made a computer language called Perl very famous, and other languages such as JavaScript also have this feature incorporated as part of the language. Unfortunately, that's not the case with Swift (or at least at this version). Regular expressions are very useful for finding patterns and also for creating some filters, such as validating e-mails, product codes, or URLs.

There's more...

Unfortunately, NSThread is not as complete as the functions of the posix threads, as we don't have, for example, the join method. If your thread function is a C function, you can still use functions such as pthread_create and pthread_join.

In the next recipe, we will learn about NSOperation, which is recommended by Apple.

Creating an SEO app

As you might know, nowadays, it's very common to analyze a website to get a better result on search engines. Counting the number of words on a website is a common way to know how search engines retrieve information from our website. As we already have a WordCounter class from the previous recipe, we will recycle it and create a new program, which is to count words on a website.

Getting ready

First of all, check some URLs from a website, the words of which you would like to count. It can be any website, but the idea is to have a few URLs to check with a lot of words.

To show that the task has finished, we will show an icon, so you can download it from the book resources or you can download your own icon.

Once you have your URL list and your icon ready, let's create a project called Chapter 5 SEO; add your icon and let's code.

How to do it...

Follow these steps to create an SEO app:

1. First, copy the WordCounter.swift file from the other previous recipe. To do this, just drag the file from a finder window to your project. Of course, it will be better if this file can be located on a common directory.

     When you have files that can be used on other projects, it's a good idea to store them into a common directory.

2. Now, click on this file; let's improve the code of this file. First, let's remove the file attribute because now we will read the file contents to the initializer. Secondly, we will create a new string attribute called content.

3. The next step is to modify the current initializer, just by transferring the code that opens and reads the file to the initializer. You also need to create a new initializer that will receive the contents instead of a filename. In summary, your `WordCounter` file may have a code like this one:

```
class WordCounter:NSObject {
    lazy private var _words = [String:Int]()
    var words:[String:Int] {
        return _words
    }
    lazy private var content:String = ""

    init(file:String){
        super.init()
        var manager = NSFileManager.defaultManager()
        var data = manager.contentsAtPath(NSBundle.
          mainBundle().pathForResource(file, ofType:
          "txt")!)!
        content = NSString(data: data, encoding:
          NSUTF8StringEncoding) as! String
    }

    init(content:String){
        super.init()
        self.content = content
    }

    func execute(){
        _words = [String:Int]()

        // splitting the document into words
        var wordsArray =
          content.componentsSeparatedByString(" ")
        wordsArray = wordsArray.map({ (word) -> String in
            return word.stringByTrimmingCharactersInSet(
              NSCharacterSet.whitespaceCharacterSet())
        }).map({ (word) -> String in
            return word.lowercaseString
        }).filter({(word) -> Bool in
            var error:NSError?
            var regex = NSRegularExpression(pattern:
              "\\w+(-\\w+)*", options: .CaseInsensitive,
              error: &error)
            let matches = regex?.matchesInString(word,
              options: nil, range: NSMakeRange(0,
              count(word)))
```

```
            return matches?.count > 0
    })

    // computing the results
    for word:String in wordsArray {
        if let tot = _words[word] {
            _words[word] = tot + 1
        }else{
            _words[word] = 1
        }
    }
}
}
```

4. It's time to create the application interface. In this case, we will need a text field to let the user enter a URL, a label to show a message, a button to indicate that the user has finished writing a URL, and a table view, which is something similar to the following screenshot:

5. Inherit the view controller from `UITableViewDataSource` and from `UITableViewDelegate`. Link the table view datasource and delegate it with the view controller. Don't worry if the compiler complains about some missing functions, we will implement them in a while.

6. Now, let's go to the view controller and create an auxiliary struct. This struct will help us to know whether the evaluation of the requested website is done and also the result. So, add the following code inside the view controller class:

```
struct UrlInfo {
    var url:String
    var finished:Bool = false
    lazy var words = [String:Int]()
    init(url:String){
        self.url = url
    }
}
```

7. The next step is to add some attributes. In this case, we will need a text field to enter the URL, a table view, an array of `UrlInfo`, and a queue for our operations:

```
@IBOutlet var urlTextField: UITextField!
@IBOutlet var urlsTables: UITableView!
var urls = [UrlInfo]()
var queue = NSOperationQueue()
```

8. Now, we can implement the button event, so link the button with a method called `analyze` and type its code, as follows:

```
@IBAction func analyze(sender: UIButton) {
    var url = urlTextField.
      text.stringByReplacingOccurrencesOfString(" "
      , withString: "", options: nil, range: nil)
    if url == "" {
        return
    }

    let position = self.urls.count
    self.urls.append(UrlInfo(url: url))
    self.urlsTables.reloadData()

    queue.addOperationWithBlock(){
        var data = NSData(contentsOfURL:
          NSURL(string: url)!)
        var textResponse = NSString(data: data!,
          encoding: NSASCIIStringEncoding) as! String
        println(textResponse)
```

```
var wordCounter = WordCounter(content:
    textResponse)
wordCounter.execute()
self.urls[position].words = wordCounter.words
self.urls[position].finished = true

NSOperationQueue.mainQueue(
    ).addOperationWithBlock({
        self.urlsTables.reloadData()
    })
    }
}
```

 While this code was written, my Xcode was updated and also the Swift API. So, it was necessary to fix some parts of it. Consider this kind of change when you are coding with Swift.

9. The next step is to implement the corresponding part of the table view. First, let's define the current number of cells in the table view:

```
func tableView(tableView: UITableView,
    numberOfRowsInSection section: Int) -> Int{
        return urls.count
}
```

10. Next, let's create a cell for the URL. In this case, when the URL has been computed, we will add an OK icon:

```
func tableView(tableView: UITableView,
    cellForRowAtIndexPath indexPath: NSIndexPath) ->
    UITableViewCell{
var cell =
    urlsTables.dequeueReusableCellWithIdentifier(
    "url") as? UITableViewCell
if cell == nil {
    cell = UITableViewCell(style: .Default,
        reuseIdentifier: "url")
    cell?.textLabel?.text = urls[indexPath.row].url
}

if self.urls[indexPath.row].finished {
    cell?.imageView?.image = UIImage(named:
        "ok.png")
}else {
```

```
                    cell?.imageView?.image = nil
            }
            return cell!
        }
```

11. And, of course, we need to show the result when the user selects a cell from the table view. This result will be shown only if the URL analysis has finished:

```
func tableView(tableView: UITableView,
    didHighlightRowAtIndexPath indexPath: NSIndexPath) {
    if urls[indexPath.row].finished {
        var result = ""
        for (total, word) in
            enumerate(urls[indexPath.row].words){
            result += "\(word) -> \(total)\n"
        }
        UIAlertView(title: "Result", message: result,
            delegate: nil, cancelButtonTitle:
            "Ok").show()
    }
}
```

Now, the application is done. Try to check a URL and see its results.

How it works...

NSOperation is something built on the top level of **Grand Central Dispatch** (**GCD**), which is the way Apple has for doing multitasks. The NSOperation class needs a queue that can be a new queue created by the programmer, or it can be an existing one.

As mentioned earlier, you have to consider that operations related to the user interface, such as refreshing the table view content, must be done on the main thread; speaking in NSOperation terms, it should be done on the main queue. You can also have a low priority queue for those tasks that don't need to finish as soon as possible.

One advantage about NSOperation over threads is that it is more optimized for multicore devices, meaning a better performance on Mac computers and new iPhones and iPads.

There's more...

Of course, you can use threads and NSOperation together, but you have to take care while using these. Avoid using NSOperation with a fork on the OS X, for example. In the next recipe, we will use GCD directly, which can give us more flexibility.

Being aware of cyclones

Sometimes it's good that our mobile phone or even our computer can tell us the weather predictions, mainly when some kind of disaster is going to come, such as a storm, an earthquake, or a cyclone. To do this, the application must continuously ask for the weather prediction from the Internet, but it shouldn't block the application's operation.

In this recipe, we will develop an application that will ask every 5 minutes for cyclone predictions; in the case of finding one cyclone, it will write down the URL where the user can retrieve information about the cyclone detected. If the application is running in the background, it will throw a notification.

Here, we will create a multitask using the Grand Central Dispatch, which is the way Apple recommends to use it.

Getting ready

Create an application called `Chapter 5 Cyclones` and add a file called `CycloneChecker.swift`. Also, check whether you have Internet connection on your computer or your device.

How to do it...

Follow these steps to create the `CycloneChecker` app:

1. First, we need to specify that this class (`CycloneChecker`) is a delegate of `NSXMLParserDelegate`, which forces us to inherit from `NSObject`, as follows:

   ```
   class CycloneChecker:NSObject, NSXMLParserDelegate{
   ```

2. Now, add its attribute. We will need a constant that will represent the frequency that the app will check on cyclones, another constant that contains the URLs where the application can check the cyclones predictions, an attribute that indicates the current website we are visiting, a queue to add our operation, an attribute to indicate whether the object is working or not, and a closure to run every time we find a cyclone. Here is the code for this:

   ```
   private let interval = 300
   private let urls =
     ["http://www.nhc.noaa.gov/nhc_at1.xml",
       "http://www.nhc.noaa.gov/nhc_at2.xml",
       "http://www.nhc.noaa.gov/nhc_at3.xml",
       "http://www.nhc.noaa.gov/nhc_at4.xml",
       "http://www.nhc.noaa.gov/nhc_at5.xml"]
   private var position = 0
   ```

```
private let queue = dispatch_queue_create(
    "cyclone.queue",DISPATCH_QUEUE_SERIAL)
private var started = false
var action: (String) -> (Void) = {(url) -> Void in
}
```

3. The first two methods that we will implement are the methods that make the object work or stop working:

```
func start(){
    started = true
    initQueue()
}
func stop(){
    started = false
}
```

4. As you can see, we need a method called `initQueue`, which will add the tasks to the object queue:

```
private func initQueue(){
    self.position = 0
    for i in 1...urls.count {
        dispatch_async(queue, { () -> Void in
            if self.started {
                println("checking \(self.position)")
                var xmlParser = NSXMLParser(
                    contentsOfURL: NSURL(string:
                    self.urls[self.position])!)
                xmlParser?.delegate = self
                xmlParser?.parse()
            }
        })
    }
    dispatch_async(queue, { () -> Void in
        if self.started {
            sleep(UInt32(self.interval))
            self.initQueue()
        }
    })
}
```

5. Once the object finds a cyclone, it needs to notify the user about it. So, here is the code to do this:

```
func parser(parser: NSXMLParser, didStartElement
    elementName: String, namespaceURI: String?,
    qualifiedName qName: String?, attributes
    attributeDict: [NSObject : AnyObject]){
    if elementName == "cyclone"{
        self.action(self.urls[self.position])
    }
}
```

6. To finish this class, we need to mark that the current XML has been parsed; next time, we will need to parse the next one:

```
func parserDidEndDocument(parser: NSXMLParser) {
    position += 1
}
```

7. The `CycloneChecker` part is done; the next step is to create the view, so click on the storyboard, add two buttons to it (one to start checking and another one to stop checking), a label to indicate the object status (running or stopped), and a text field to display the text that a cyclone is coming. This will look similar to the following screenshot:

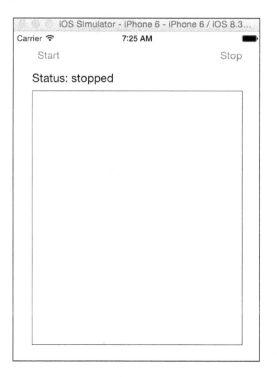

8. As you might imagine, now we will code the attributes, start linking the views we've added on the storyboard, and create an object, `CycloneChecker`, as follows:

```
var cycloneChecker = CycloneChecker()
@IBOutlet var buttonStart: UIButton!
@IBOutlet var buttonStop: UIButton!
@IBOutlet var textView: UITextView!
@IBOutlet var labelStatus: UILabel!
```

9. Let's initialize the application on the `viewDidLoad` method adding an action to `cycloneChecker`. In this case, we will add it to the text view and send a user notification if the application is running in the background:

```
override func viewDidLoad() {
    super.viewDidLoad()
    cycloneChecker.action = {(url) -> Void in
        if UIApplication.sharedApplication(
          ).applicationState == .Background    {
            var localNotification:UILocalNotification
              = UILocalNotification()
            localNotification.alertAction = "Cyclone
              found"
            localNotification.alertBody = "A cyclone
              was found. visit \(url) for more
              information"
            localNotification.fireDate =
              NSDate(timeIntervalSinceNow: 10)
            UIApplication.sharedApplication(
              ).scheduleLocalNotification(
              localNotification)
        }
        dispatch_async(dispatch_get_main_queue(), {
          () -> Void in
            self.textView.text =
              "\(self.textView.text)\nA cyclone was
              found. visit \(url) for more information"
        })
    }
    self.textView.text = ""
    self.textView.layer.borderWidth = 0.5
}
```

10. Now, we can finish the view controller adding the start and stop events, as follows:

```
@IBAction func start(sender: AnyObject) {
    cycloneChecker.start()
    labelStatus.text = "Status: started"
    buttonStart.enabled = false
    buttonStop.enabled = true
}


@IBAction func stop(sender: AnyObject) {
    cycloneChecker.stop()
    labelStatus.text = "Status: stopped"
    buttonStart.enabled = true
    buttonStop.enabled = false
}
```

11. To finish the application, you need to add on the app delegate—preferably on the `didFinishLauchingWithOptions` method—the following code to use notifications:

```
func application(application: UIApplication,
  didFinishLaunchingWithOptions launchOptions:
  [NSObject: AnyObject]?) -> Bool {
        if UIApplication.instancesRespondToSelector(
          Selector("registerUserNotificationSettings:"
          ))
        {

            application.
              registerUserNotificationSettings(
              UIUserNotificationSettings(forTypes:
              UIUserNotificationType.Sound |
              UIUserNotificationType.Alert |
                UIUserNotificationType.Badge,
                  categories: nil))
        }
        return true
}
```

12. Finally, you need to test the app, so click on the play button and check whether there is a cyclone near you. Hope not.

Don't forget to allow notifications if you are using iOS 8.

Your notification screen will look like this:

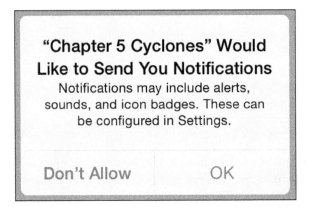

How it works...

Our app works using the Grand Central Dispatch, which will create a thread and a queue for running the assigned tasks. As it creates a separated thread, it doesn't block the user interface, and as it is not creating a thread for each task, the application doesn't lose performance due to thread commuting.

As you can see, when the queue was created, we had to specify that we would like a serial queue, meaning that a task doesn't start until the previous one finishes. We also used a function called `dispatch_async`, meaning that the caller will not wait to finish the task, so the code can continue running concurrently with the queue tasks.

Of course, when we find a cyclone, we need to write this information on the text view, which needs to be done on the main thread, so this is the reason that we had to create another task and add it to the main queue.

Another interesting part is that one task added to our queue had a call to the sleep function. As you know, the new queue is executed on a separated thread and the next task won't run until the current one finishes, so it's perfectly allowed to use this function.

If you haven't worked with notifications on the view controller, you have a sample of it. Don't forget that notifications work only with iOS 7 or higher and on iOS 8, the user must give permission to send notifications.

There's more

We still have two pending topics: the first one is to use concurrent queues and the other one is to prevent two tasks changing the same object at the same time. Both topics will be revealed in the next recipe.

Links on our website

In this chapter, we created an application that can help us position our website by checking its word frequency, but as you might know, SEO is not only about counting words, it's also about website links.

In this recipe, we will check the links on a website; in this case, as we are using the networks, we can do tasks in parallel.

Getting ready

Create a project called `Chapter 5 weblinks` and add a file called `LinkChecker.swift`. Please check whether you have an Internet connection on your simulator or device.

How to do it...

Once you have checked that your device or simulator has an Internet connection, follow these steps to create the Link Checker app:

1. Before we start creating the `LinkChecker` class, we will need to create an auxiliary class that will store the common information between objects of the type `LinkChecker`. This class will be called `UrlManager` and this needs to store the queue, a file handler to log the found URLs, an array with the URLs, and a constant to indicate the maximum number of links we want (some websites have a lot of links):

```
private class UrlManager {
    enum UrlAddStatus {
        case OK, FULL, REPEATED, WRONG_URL
    }

    private var _queue =
      dispatch_queue_create("concurrentqueue",
        DISPATCH_QUEUE_CONCURRENT)
    var queue:dispatch_queue_t{
        return _queue
    }
    private var fileHandle:NSFileHandle?
```

```
private lazy var _urls = [String]()
let LIMIT = 10
```

2. Now, let's create some auxiliary functions to help this object to know whether a URL should be stored or not. One of them will tell whether a URL is already stored in our list, the other one will tell whether the list is full, the third one will check whether the URL is valid or not, and the last one will log the URL on a file. Here is the code to do this:

```
func contains(url:String) -> Bool{
    objc_sync_enter(self._urls)
    for u in self._urls {
        if u == url {
            objc_sync_exit(self._urls)
            return true
        }
    }
    objc_sync_exit(self._urls)
    return false
}

var full:Bool {
    return self._urls.count >= self.LIMIT
}

private func validUrl(url:String) -> Bool{
    var error:NSError?
    var regex = NSRegularExpression(pattern:
      "^(https?:\\/\\/)?([\\da-z\\.-]+)\\.(
      [a-z\\.]{2,6})([\\/\\w \\.-]*)*\\/?$", options:
      .CaseInsensitive, error: &error)
    let matches = regex?.matchesInString(url, options:
      nil, range: NSMakeRange(0, count(url)))
    return matches?.count > 0
}

private func writeMessage(message:String){
    objc_sync_enter(self.fileHandle)
    self.fileHandle?.writeData(
      message.dataUsingEncoding(NSUTF8StringEncoding,
      allowLossyConversion: false)!)
    objc_sync_exit(self.fileHandle)
}
```

3. Now let's code the initializer; in this case, we only need to open the log file:

```
init(){
    var path:String =
      NSSearchPathForDirectoriesInDomains(
      .DocumentDirectory, .UserDomainMask, true)[0]
      as! String
    let fullpath =
      path.stringByAppendingPathComponent(
      "application.log")
    NSFileManager.defaultManager(
      ).createFileAtPath(fullpath, contents:
      nil, attributes: nil)
    self.fileHandle=NSFileHandle(
      forWritingAtPath:fullpath)!
}
```

4. To finish this class, we need to create the main method, which is `addUrl`. This function will return if it was possible to add the URL or not:

```
func addUrl(url:String) -> UrlAddStatus {
    if full {
        // WRITE FULL
        self.writeMessage("Couldn't store the url
          \(url). Buffer is full")
        return .FULL
    }
    if self.contains(url){
        self.writeMessage("Couldn't store the url
          \(url). Already on buffer")
        return .REPEATED
    }
    if !self.validUrl(url) {
        self.writeMessage("Couldn't store the url
          \(url). Invalid url")
        return .WRONG_URL
    }
    objc_sync_enter(self._urls)
    self._urls.append(url)
    objc_sync_exit(self._urls)
    self.writeMessage("Url \(url) successfully stored")
    return .OK
}
} // Class end
```

5. On the same file, we will create a class called `LinkChecker`; to do this, we will use `XMLParser` again.

 In this recipe, we are using `XMLParser` because it's built into the Swift standard libraries, but if you would like a better HTML parser, you can search on the Internet for a specific library, such as NDHpple (`https://github.com/ndavidsson/NDHpple/`).

6. Let's start with the attributes; for the implementation of this class, we will need an `NSXmlParser` delegate, an `UrlManager` object, and a closure to execute the function every time we find a URL:

```
class LinkChecker:NSObject, NSXMLParserDelegate {
    private var xmlParser:NSXMLParser
    private var urlManager:UrlManager
    var foundAction: (String) -> (Void) = {
        (url) -> Void in
    }
```

7. The next step is to create the initializers; in this case, we will develop two of them. The first one will be called from outside (the view controller) and the other one will be created by the same `LinkChecker`, receiving as argument the same `UrlManager` object, and this is the reason why it is a private initializer:

```
    init(url:String) {
        self.xmlParser = NSXMLParser(contentsOfURL:
          NSURL(string: url)!)!
        self.urlManager = UrlManager()
        super.init()
        self.xmlParser.delegate = self
        self.urlManager.addUrl(url)
    }

    private init(url:String, urlManager:UrlManager) {
        self.xmlParser = NSXMLParser(contentsOfURL:
          NSURL(string: url)!)!
        self.urlManager = urlManager
        super.init()
        self.xmlParser.delegate = self
    }
```

8. The next function is the `start` method, which will create the first task:

```
func start(){
    dispatch_async(urlManager.queue, { () -> Void in
        self.xmlParser.parse()
        return
    })
}
```

9. The last method of this `LinkChecker` class is the parser function of the
   `NSXMLParserDelegate` protocol. Here, we will check whether we've found a link,
   represented by the a HTML tag:

```
func parser(parser: NSXMLParser, didStartElement
    elementName: String, namespaceURI: String?,
    qualifiedName qName: String?, attributes
    attributeDict: [NSObject : AnyObject]){
        if elementName.lowercaseString == "a" {
            let href = "href"
            var newUrl = attributeDict["href"] as! String
            if let  range = newUrl.rangeOfString("#",
              options: .CaseInsensitiveSearch, range:
              nil, locale: nil){
                newUrl =
                  newUrl.substringToIndex(range.startIndex)
            }

            println("found link \(newUrl)")
            if self.urlManager.addUrl(attributeDict[href]
              as! String) == .OK {
                self.foundAction(attributeDict[href] as!
                  String)
                dispatch_async(urlManager.queue, { () ->
                  Void in
                    self.xmlParser.parse()
                    return
                })
            }
        }
    }
} // class end
```

10. Now, click on the storyboard. Let's create a screen with a text field to write a URL, a button to start analyzing it, and a table view to display the result, somewhat similar to this screenshot:

11. Now, inherit the `ViewController` from `UITableViewDataSource` besides `UIViewController`, and add the text field `tableview` and array of strings to store the URLs and a `LinkChecker` object as attributes:

```
class ViewController: UIViewController,
  UITableViewDataSource {
```

```
@IBOutlet var urlTextField: UITextField!
@IBOutlet var tableView: UITableView!
private var _urls = [String]()
private var linkChecker:LinkChecker?
```

12. Once it is done, we can add an event to our button to start analyzing the URL:

```
@IBAction func analyze(sender: UIButton) {
    linkChecker =
      LinkChecker(url:self.urlTextField.text)
    self.linkChecker?.foundAction = {
        (url) -> Void in
        self._urls.append(url)
        dispatch_async(dispatch_get_main_queue(),
            {() -> Void in
                self.tableView.reloadData()
        })
    }
    linkChecker?.start()
    self.urlTextField.resignFirstResponder()
}
```

13. To finish this class, let's implement the `tableview` methods, which will display the content of the `_urls` attribute:

```
func tableView(tableView: UITableView,
  numberOfRowsInSection section: Int) -> Int{
    return self._urls.count
}

func tableView(tableView: UITableView,
  cellForRowAtIndexPath indexPath: NSIndexPath) ->
  UITableViewCell{
    var cell = self.tableView.
      dequeueReusableCellWithIdentifier(
      _urls[indexPath.row]) as? UITableViewCell

    if cell == nil {
        cell = UITableViewCell(style: .Default,
          reuseIdentifier: _urls[indexPath.row])
        cell?.textLabel?.text = _urls[indexPath.row]
    }
    return cell!
}
```

14. Now, the application is done; text your web site and see how many links you get from it.

How it works...

Requesting something from the network is something that will take time; meanwhile the application can work with the next task. So, in this case, we need to create a concurrent queue instead of the serial queue.

With this in mind, we have to take care when working with some variables, mainly because the application can commute from one task to another when it hasn't finished working with a variable yet. To prevent tasks overlapping the same attribute or variable, we should control it using `objc_sync_enter` and `objc_sync_exit`.

 Unfortunately, Swift doesn't have any kind of mutex yet, so it needs to use the `@synchronize` method of Objective-C, and this is the reason for the prefixes of these functions.

There's more

As you can see, sometimes it's hard to work with concurrent tasks, and the developer needs to think in a lot of detail. Also, fixing an issue can be very difficult because sometimes, it's hard to reproduce it. In the next chapter, we will learn how to test our code without the need to run the whole application.

6
Playground

In this chapter, we will cover the following topics:

- ► Creating the first playground
- ► Watching some graphics
- ► Watching the temperature
- ► Stretching an image
- ► Beautifying your text
- ► Receiving JSONs
- ► Dangerous moves

Introduction

If you've ever programmed with an interpreted language such as Python, Perl, Ruby, or JavaScript, you probably noticed an advantage to these languages, over native languages such as C, Objective-C, or C++, which is the possibility of testing code without the need to add extra code to your project.

Sometimes, a developer needs to test a code before adding it to the project, mainly when you are learning the way Swift works. However, even if you are very experienced with Swift, there will be times when you will have new ideas, and you'll probably need to check whether this is a valid idea before coding it into your project.

For situations like these, Apple released the playground, a place where you can play with your code, test it, visualize it, and of course, decide on the usability of the code before adding it to your application.

It's quite impressive that Swift is a compiled language, but you can use playground to test your code as you go, similar to if you were on an interpreted language, viewing the results in real time.

Creating the first playground

In this recipe, you will get familiarized with the Xcode playground. Here, you will learn some basics of this Xcode feature, and after this, you will be able to test your own code using this new friend.

Getting ready...

Open your Xcode, but this time, instead of creating a new project, you have to choose **Get started with playground**, as shown here:

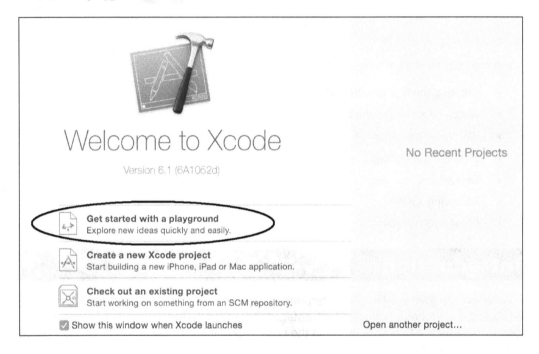

Once you have done it, you will see that the next dialog is a very simple one, which will ask only the project name and the platform (iOS or Mac OS). Call it Chapter 6 First Playground and select **iOS**, as shown here:

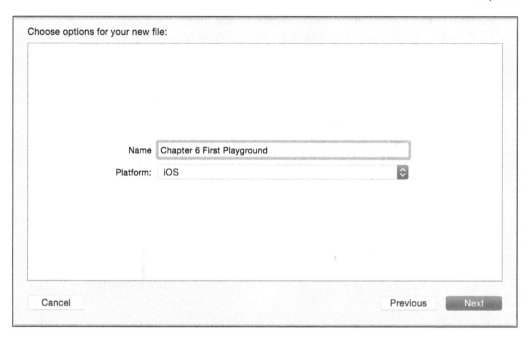

Then, you will see the famous dialog that asks you where to store your app. Choose a folder that you want for it. If you have doubts, choose the documents folder.

Before we start with our playground, open the Finder window corresponding to the folder where you saved your project, right-click (or control click) on your playground project, and click on **Show package contents**.

Now, you can see that there are three files: contents.xcplayground, results.playgrounddata, and section-1.swift. Right now, you can imagine what these files do, but I would like to emphasize that as your playground grows, the number of files also increases. Remember that the playground has its own bundle in which you can add pictures and other stuff.

How to do it...

Follow these steps to create the first playground:

1. Return to your Xcode and have a look at your playground. It started importing the UIKit and a string variable which says Hello, playground. You can also see, on the right hand, the result of this variable.

2. Let's start defining another variable called `name` before the `str` variable, and changing the `str` variable to have an interpolation, something like the following code:

```
var name = "Cecil Costa"
var str = "Hello, \(name)"
```

Now, you will see that on your right, you have both the variables processed.

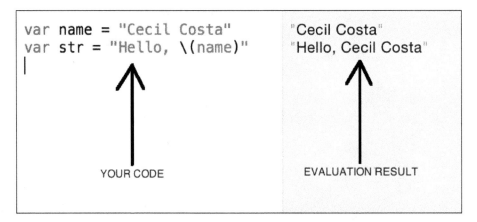

```
var name = "Cecil Costa"          "Cecil Costa"
var str = "Hello, \(name)"        "Hello, Cecil Costa"
```

YOUR CODE   EVALUATION RESULT

3. Once you've understood this, let's complete this code with an `if` statement. So, after the previous code, add an `if` statement like this one:

```
var myCity = "Cambridge"
var yourCity = "New York"

if myCity == yourCity {
    println("We live in the same city")
}else {
    println("We live in different cities")
}
```

4. After coding it, see to it that you have the result for one statement, but not for the other one. This is shown in the following screenshot:

```
var myCity = "Cambridge"                              "Cambridge"
var yourCity = "New York"                             "New York"

if myCity == yourCity {
    println("We live in the same city")———▶

}else {
    println("We live in different cities")———▶    "We live in different cities"
}
```

5. It's time to try a loop; let's calculate, for example, the famous Fibonacci function:

```
var fib_n = 1
var fib_n_1 = 1

for i in 3...10 {
    var sum = fib_n + fib_n_1
    fib_n_1 = fib_n
    fib_n = sum
}

fib_n
```

Now, you can appreciate the result in a different way. Instead of displaying the variable value, you can see the number of times that the instruction was executed. If you move your mouse pointer over the result of each instruction, you can see that two small icons will appear.

6. The first symbol, which is like an eye, is for viewing the variable result representation; the other one is for the timeline, which shows the values assigned to the variable on each loop iteration. We will talk about this later in the *Watching some graphics* and *Beautifying your text* recipes. The following screenshot gives a glimpse of these:

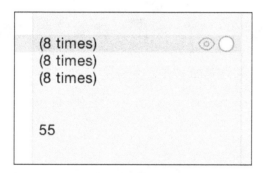

7. The reason why we wrote the `fib_n` variable alone at the end of our code is because this is the way you can visualize the final value of a variable. In this case, we can see that the result of our code is 55.

8. Now, we can compare this code with the equivalent one as a recursive function, then we can make a decision about which code will be used on our application:

```
func fib (n:Int) -> Int{
    if n == 1 || n == 2 {
        return 1
    }
```

```
        return fib(n-1) + fib(n-2)
    }

    fib(10)
```

9. After coding it, you can check two important pieces of information; the first one is the result, which is the same as the previous code. The second one is the number of times the function was called. As you can see, in this case, we had 54 times on the recursive function against the 8 of the interactive function.

How it works...

As you can see, every time you write a code, it is recompiled and executed; the advantage to this is that it gives you information about your code. You can use it to compare different code, and also check whether the idea you have in mind is the right one for your application.

There's more...

Now, you have a basic idea about how to use the playground. The next thing we will learn is how to visualize the information and its progress in a graphical way.

Watching some graphics

Knowing that a loop iterates eight times instead of 54 is fine. It gives you a good idea about the best algorithm to choose, but there are times when we need to visualize the variable's values during the loop iterations; for cases like this, Apple has created the timeline.

Getting ready

You can open your Xcode and click on **Get started with playground**, or if you already have your Xcode opened, you can go to **File | New | Playground**.

Name your project `Chapter 6 Timeline` and save it at your workspace folder.

How to do it...

In order to enable the app to watch some graphics, follow these steps:

1. First, let's type a code where we print some output. In this case, we will print a triangle with stars.

    ```
    for i in 1...5 {
        for j in 1...i {
    ```

```
        print("*")
    }
    println()
}
```

2. Once you've typed this code, you wouldn't appreciate the triangle yet. Go to the icon that looks like two overlapped circles and click on it. The icon is shown here:

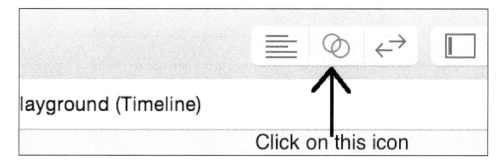

layground (Timeline)

Click on this icon

3. Behold, the Xcode split in two parts. The new part on the right is called the timeline. Now, you should see the console output, which should be similar to the following screenshot:

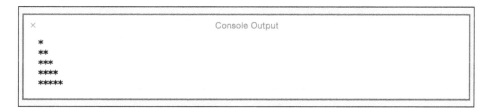

 If for any reason you close the console output, you can reopen it by just rerunning your code.

4. Now, let's see the values of a variable. In this case, we don't have many options, so we will check the value of the j variable. To do it, just type j after the `print` instruction, something like the following code:

```
    for j in 1...i {
        print("*")
        j // ← Yes, only the letter "j"
    }
```

5. Now, click on the round icon on the same level as the j variable.

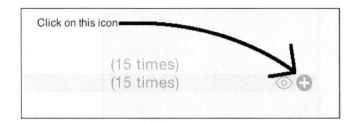

Click on this icon

(15 times)
(15 times)

6. Now, you can see the values of j according to the iteration on the following graphic.

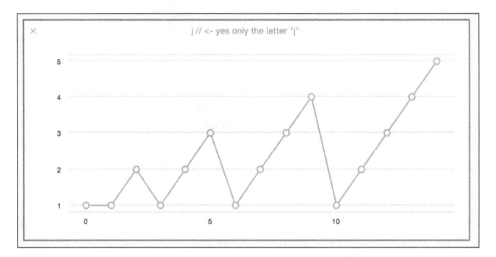

j // <- yes only the letter "j"

7. If you want to see the value of your variable more clearly, you can slide the red bar that is at the bottom of your Xcode screen.

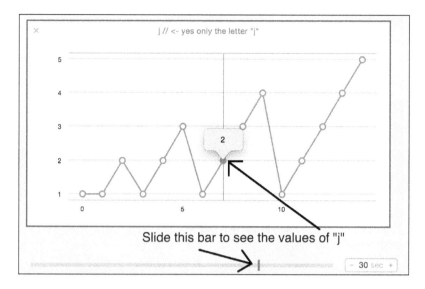

Slide this bar to see the values of "j"

8. If for any reason you have lots of graphs, you can close them to save space, but if you would like to keep some graphs, you can collapse them by double-clicking onto their titles, and of course, you can expand them by just double-clicking on them again.

×	j // <- yes only the letter "j"

As you can see, in this case, you've got only the title `j // ← yes only the letter j` instead of the whole graph.

How it works...

The timeline has three different editors, **the Standard Editor**, which gives us more space to code and watch our code routine; **the Assistant Editor**, which gives us more information about our code execution; and **the Version Editor**, which shows us the modifications that our playground has.

The Assistant Editor gives us more accuracy about the variables evolution and their values. Using a graph helps us to know how a variable is changing its value.

The console output is also important; note that if you try to visualize the print instruction only, you will see lots of stars, each of them on a different line. This kind of information is not useful for the developer.

There's more...

Playground isn't limited to displaying graphics only; you can also add some colors to it. In the next recipe, you will work with colors on your playground.

Watching the temperature

When Xerox engineers created the Window system based on Smalltalk, they brought a big concept to the computer world—the idea of analog representation on digital devices (computer).

This means that for us, human beings, it is easier to understand how long a process will take watching a progress bar instead of watching a percentage on screen. Here, we will watch some colors instead of numbers.

In this recipe, we will watch the color of a temperature instead of watching its value; this way, you can have a better idea about the chill.

Getting ready

Open your Xcode and create a new playground called `Chapter 6 Color`, remove the `str` string, but leave the UIKit import as it is.

How to do it...

Follow these steps to create a playground that will watch the temperature:

1. First of all, let's create an array with temperatures; in this case, the temperatures are measured in Celsius degrees:

   ```
   var temperatures = [15, 8, 3, -1, 2, 3, 3, 9, 14, 18,
      23, 27, 30, 34, 20, 30, 35, 39, 41]
   ```

2. The next step is iterating over the array. For each iteration, we will store the result into a variable called `color`:

   ```
   for temp in temperatures {
       var color:UIColor
       if temp <= 0 {
           color = UIColor(red: 0.0, green: 0.0, blue:
              1.0, alpha: 1.0)
       } else if temp >= 40 {
           color = UIColor(red: 1.0, green: 0.0,
              blue: 0.0, alpha: 1.0)
       }else {
   ```

```
    var proportional = CGFloat(temp) / CGFloat(40)
    color = UIColor(red: proportional, green: 0,
      blue: CGFloat(1) - proportional, alpha: 1.0)
  }
  color // Temperature representation
}
```

3. Now, you have to add the `color` variable from the last loop sentence to the timeline. You can see a result similar to the one shown here:

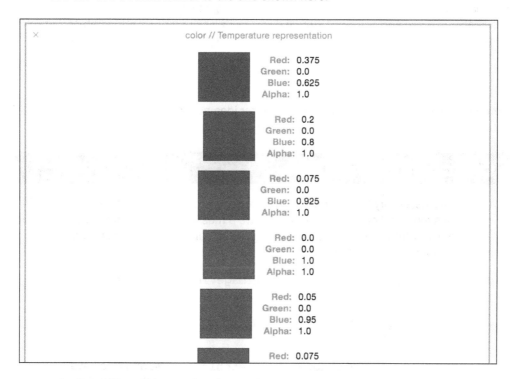

How it works...

Timeline is not only about displaying a number, it's also about giving us information where we can have a better idea about the code. Watching numbers, such as 13 degrees Celsius for example, sometimes is something that doesn't give us a good idea of what is going on, but watching a color can give us a better idea on whether it is cold or hot, mainly if you work with Fahrenheit values.

As you know, your computer screen works with three primary colors: red, green, and blue. `UIColor` also has a fourth factor, which is the alpha factor; zero means transparent and one means opaque.

In this recipe, we kept the **Alpha** value as 1 and the **Green** value as 0 in every case, but for cold days, we assumed that we need a high level of blue and a low level of red. For warm days, we had to create a color with a high level of red and low level of blue. This means that an intense blue color is saying that we had a very low temperature and an intense red color means a very hot temperature.

What about the intermediate temperature? In this case, we will have a purple color, which is the color created with 50% of red and 50% of blue.

Note that this kind of measure is more useful using playgrounds rather than using it on an app. Presumably, in a real app, you won't store a color, you will store the real temperature, but you can get an idea as to whether the values you have are of your liking or not before coding it.

There's more...

In this case, we used the colors for getting a better idea about our values, but what else can we use? In the next recipe, you will learn how to use images.

Stretching an image

Sometimes, it's necessary to have more than one sample of a picture in order to see which ratio is the desired one. Let's imagine that we have a message, but we don't want to show it to the user; we only want to show something that gives him an idea that there is something and the application will show the correct ratio later.

For cases like these, you can use `UIImage` and `ImageView`, and visualize it on the playground.

Getting ready

Create a new playground called `Chapter 6 Stretching Image` and also have an image ready for this recipe. I would recommend that you download the image file `secret_message.png` that is included with the resource files of this book.

How to do it...

To create a playground that stretches an image, follow these steps:

1. Close the Xcode and open a Finder window, go to the folder where you saved the playground, click on the project that you created, and right-click (or control-click) on it. On the menu, choose the option **Show Package Contents**, as we learned in the beginning of this chapter.

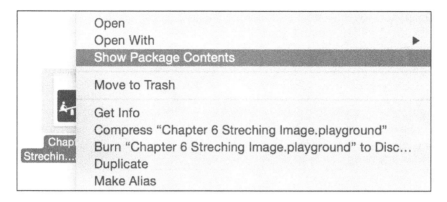

2. Now, create a folder called `Resources` and copy your image file in to it. After this, reopen your playground.

3. Remove the `str` variable because we will not use it. Let's create a new class where we have an `ImageView` object, its size, and the number of times that the `ImageView` object was stretched:

```
class ImageStretcher{
    var imageView:UIImageView
    var times = 0
    var currentFrame:CGRect
    init(){
        var image = UIImage(named: "secret_message")!
        imageView = UIImageView(image: image)
        currentFrame = imageView.frame
    }

    func stretch(){
        currentFrame.size.height *=  CGFloat(1.1)
        currentFrame.size.width *=  CGFloat(0.9)
        imageView.frame = currentFrame
        times++
    }
}
```

4. Once you've coded it, we need to create an object of this type, so add the following code to your playground:

```
var imageStretcher = ImageStretcher()
```

5. Good, now you have an object, but the image is still on; it's on its original size. If you call the `stretch` method, you will see the image stretched only once, so let's repeat this to get a better idea of how much we should stretch the picture:

```
for i in 1...15 {
    imageStretcher.stretch()
}
```

6. For visualizing the different results, you can click on the value history icon and then you can see lots of samples:

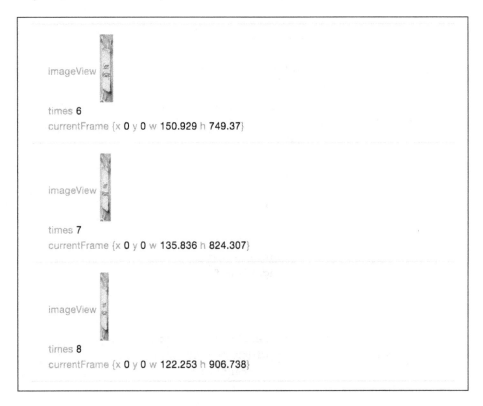

imageView

times **6**
currentFrame {x **0** y **0** w **150.929** h **749.37**}

imageView

times **7**
currentFrame {x **0** y **0** w **135.836** h **824.307**}

imageView

times **8**
currentFrame {x **0** y **0** w **122.253** h **906.738**}

7. To get a better idea of the `ImageView` object, you can click on the right side of the sample row, where there is an eye icon. Click on the number **10**, for example, and see what you've got:

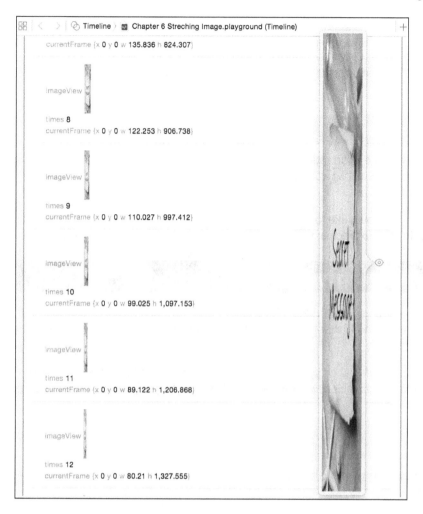

How it works...

Views are allowed to be used on the playground; you can previsualize, for example, how your `UIImageView`, `UILabel`, and `UITextField` will be drawn. In this case, we had to repeat it a few times, which means that only the ImageView wouldn't give us the complete information.

The best way we could do this was to create our own class and store the information we need, such as how many times we've stretched the ImageView, and the current size of the ImageView.

On the right-hand side of the result, as you can see, there is a small eye icon (quick look). It will show you how the view was displayed at that moment.

It's very common to work with a framework called **CoreImage** when you want to use a filter on an image (for example, hiding a secret message); unfortunately, this framework doesn't work with playground yet.

There's more...

If you need to store information with your playground, you'll probably want to print the constant XCPSharedDataDirectoryPath. This will show you where the playground stores its information.

Sometimes, we would like to hide a message, and sometimes, we would like to make it more readable. In the next recipe, we will learn how you can previsualize a text with different fonts.

Beautifying your text

Have you ever heard the phrase, "The quick brown fox jumps over the lazy dog?" Why is it so famous? The reason is that it is an English pangram, which means a phrase with every letter from the alphabet.

Pangrams are useful when you want to visualize properties of a font, such as size, color or bold. In this recipe, we will check different fonts using NSAttributedString and playground.

Getting ready

Create a new playground called Chapter 6 Text and remove the string that comes with it by default.

How to do it...

To add the beautifying text feature, follow these steps:

1. First, let's create our attributed string:

   ```
   var string = NSMutableAttributedString(string:
     "The quick brown fox jumps over the lazy dog")
   ```

2. After this, you will see a new icon with the letter appearing, which means that the playground has recognized it as an attributed string. Click on the quick look icon, and you will see the current string with its attributes.

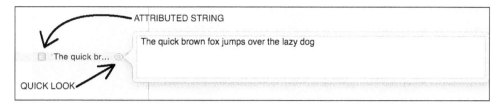

3. Now, let's choose some font sizes and colors for our text:

```
var fontSizes = [CGFloat(14.0), CGFloat(18.0),
   CGFloat(24.0)]
var colors = [UIColor.blackColor(), UIColor.blueColor(),
   UIColor.redColor()]
```

4. As we also would like to choose a few different fonts, we need to create another array; however, it can't be just a simple array of strings because we will call different methods. So, we will need to create an array of closures:

```
var fontSelectors = [
    {(size: CGFloat) -> Void in
        string.addAttribute(NSFontAttributeName , value:
          UIFont.systemFontOfSize(size), range:
          NSMakeRange(0, string.length))
    },
    {(size: CGFloat) -> Void in
        string.addAttribute(NSFontAttributeName , value:
          UIFont(name: "HelveticaNeue-Bold", size:
          size)!, range: NSMakeRange(0, string.length))
    },{(size: CGFloat) -> Void in
                string.addAttribute(NSFontAttributeName
                  , value: UIFont(name: "HelveticaNeue-
                  Italic", size: size)!, range:
                  NSMakeRange(0, string.length))
    }
]
```

5. Once we've done this, we'll have our playground ready to execute the main part. To do this, let's create three nested loops, each of them will iterate over one of our arrays:

```
for fontSize in fontSizes {
    for color in colors {
        for selector in fontSelectors {

                string.addAttribute(
                  NSForegroundColorAttributeName,
                  value: color, range: NSMakeRange(0,
                  string.length))
```

```
            selector(fontSize)

            string
        }
    }
}
```

6. If you prefer, instead of using `for` loops, you can use a more "swift way" of iterating over an array using the map closure:

```
fontSizes.map { (fontSize)-> Bool in
    colors.map { (color) -> Bool in
        fontSelectors.map { (selector) -> Bool in
            string.addAttribute(
              NSForegroundColorAttributeName, value:
              color, range: NSMakeRange(0, string.length))
            selector(fontSize)
            string
            return true
        }
        return true
    }
    return true
}
```

7. It doesn't matter which procedure you've chosen; click on the value history of the line that only contains the word `string`. Now, you can appreciate the samples of the attributed string.

×   string.addAttribute(NSForegroundColorAttribute...alue: color, range: NSMakeRange(0, string.length))

The quick brown fox jumps over the lazy dog

The quick brown fox jumps over the lazy dog

The quick brown fox jumps over the lazy dog

The quick brown fox jumps over the lazy dog

The quick brown fox jumps over the lazy dog

How it works...

Attributed strings are accepted by the playground, and this procedure is very useful when you have to choose a configuration for your app without running the full application.

If we were using Objective-C instead of Swift, we probably would have created an array of selectors rather than blocks. However, Swift doesn't follow this philosophy anymore, and the `performSelector` function now asks for a delay time to start.

Using blocks or closures is more flexible, and this also makes the code easier to maintain. One limitation you can see here is that you can't copy the array of functions from the quick look. In other words, you can do it, but the only text that you would copy is a function, which is not very useful.

There's more...

Here we had our own text, but what if we need some text from a remote server? In the following recipes, we will learn how to treat HTTP requests on playground.

Receiving JSONs

Asking for remote information is something very common today. What happens if your playground finished before you receive a server response? In this recipe, we will learn how to deal with this problem

Getting ready

Create a new playground called `Chapter 6 Requesting JSONs`, and just in this case, check your internet connection.

How to do it...

To receive JSONs on your playground, follow these steps:

1. First, we need to locate a URL, which can return more websites. In this case, we will use this URL: `https://api.github.com/users/mralexgray/repos`.

2. Create a constant with the URL mentioned earlier:

    ```
    let url = NSURL(string:
        "https://api.github.com/users/mralexgray/repos")!
    ```

3. Click on the quick look icon and check that you receive a JSON response.

You can use the quick look icon with NSURL for checking websites. If you are testing something, which is modifying a website, you can use quick look to check the new website look.

4. Now, let's create a request for our URL:

```
let request = NSURLRequest(URL: url)
```

5. The next step is to request the content of the URL:

```
NSURLConnection.sendAsynchronousRequest(request, queue:
  NSOperationQueue(), completionHandler:{ (response:
  NSURLResponse!, data: NSData!, error: NSError!)
  -> Void in
    if error != nil {
        error.description
    }else {
        data
    }
})
```

6. Check the playground result. Unfortunately, the playground finished before we got the response. Go to the beginning of your playground and add the following lines:

```
import XCPlayground

XCPSetExecutionShouldContinueIndefinitely(
  continueIndefinitely: true)
```

7. Now, we will be able to receive a response; however, you can see that the response won't be the one that we were waiting for. Fixing this issue will require us to implement a new class and set it as an NSURLConnection delegate. Place this code before sending your asynchronous request:

```
class HttpDelegate: NSObject, NSURLConnectionDelegate {

    func connection(connection: NSURLConnection,
      canAuthenticateAgainstProtectionSpace
      protectionSpace: NSURLProtectionSpace) -> Bool{
        return true
    }

    func connection(connection: NSURLConnection,
      didReceiveAuthenticationChallenge challenge:
      NSURLAuthenticationChallenge){
        challenge.sender.useCredential(
          NSURLCredential(trust:
          challenge.protectionSpace.serverTrust!),
          forAuthenticationChallenge: challenge)
```

```
        }
    }
    let delegate = HttpDelegate()
    var total = 0
    XCPCaptureValue("total",total)
    let connection = NSURLConnection(request: request,
      delegate: delegate, startImmediately: true)!
```

8. The total variable will be used later; for now the only thing you need to do is check whether we could receive the response as we expected. However, only one request might not be enough to create a benchmark; in this case, we need to go to the line where we are inspecting the `data` argument and add the following code:

```
        total++
        XCPCaptureValue("total",total)
        var err: NSError?
        var firstResponse =
          NSJSONSerialization.JSONObjectWithData(data,
          options: NSJSONReadingOptions.MutableContainers,
          error: &err)   as [[String:AnyObject]]?

        for response in firstResponse!{
            for (key, value) in response{
                if (key as NSString).containsString("_url")
                  && value is String{
                    let valueString = value as String
                    if !(valueString as
                      NSString).containsString("{"){
                        let _url = NSURL(string: value as
                          String)!
                        let _request = NSURLRequest(URL:
                          _url)
                        NSURLConnection.
                          sendAsynchronousRequest(_request,
                          queue: NSOperationQueue(),
                          completionHandler: { (_response,
                          _data, err) -> Void in
                            total = total + 1
                            total
                            XCPCaptureValue("total",total)
                        })
                    }
                }
            }
        }
```

9. Good, now as you can see, we have a more acceptable result. If you'd like to get a better result for your benchmarking, reduce the running time of your playground by changing the number of seconds located at the lower-right corner to 3 seconds:

10. Now, check how many times you received a response; that's your real statistics.

How it works...

Playground has its own framework, it's called **XCPlayground**. This was created to add some features to your playground according to your test needs. In this case, we started using the `XCPSetExecutionShouldContinueIndefinitely` function, which keeps the playground running, even if it has reached the last code line.

The XCPlayground also helped us with the `XCPCaptureValue` function. This function allows us to store a value from different parts of our code and create a single graph for it, as we did with the total variable.

We also had to fix an issue regarding the connection, which was being denied by the HTTPS protocol. In this case, we tried to create the connection, and we could see that it was being rejected. This is a good reason for using playground before coding into your app, so we can solve this issue much faster.

At the end, we changed the execution limit time of our playground. By default it starts with 30 seconds, but this might be too much for cases such as this. Reducing this allowed us to get a better idea about how many requests our app is able to handle in a second.

There's more...

As you can see, the playground has its own framework. This allowed us to control and get better results from the playground. To complete this, in the next recipe, we will learn how to create personalized quick looks.

Dangerous moves

Quick look is a good tool that helps us to visualize the current status of an object, but sometimes when we create our own class with its own logic, quick look won't be able to draw something that represents the object without your help.

In this recipe, we will learn how to create our own class representation. To do this, we will create a class that represents a checker board.

Getting ready

Create a new playground called `Chapter 6 Checkers` with the **iOS** option selected. If you select **MacOS**, remember that you should import Cocoa and replace some types with the equivalent one, such as `NSBezierPath` instead of `UIBezierPath`.

How to do it...

Let's create our checkerboard that makes dangerous moves:

1. Let's start creating a class that inherits from `NSObject`:

   ```
   class CheckersBoard:NSObject {
   ```

   Before we go any further, we need to define the status of each square, as you know it could have a black piece, a white piece, or it could be empty:

   ```
   enum BoardSpace {
       case FREE,
       WHITE,
       BLACK
   }
   ```

2. Now, let's define the board. In this case, it's a two-dimensional array attribute and the initial value of each square must be `.FREE`:

   ```
   var board = [[BoardSpace]](count:8 , repeatedValue:
     [BoardSpace](count: 8, repeatedValue: .FREE))
   ```

   As we never know whether the board has the right size, we will create a constant that represents the size of a square. You can change this value if you think that the board is too big or too small:

   ```
   let squareSize = 24
   ```

3. The next step is to create a method called `debugQuickLookObject`. This is not a random name, it must be called like this only:

```
func debugQuickLookObject() -> AnyObject? {
```

 Use the `debugQuickLookObject` method on your application; Swift and Objective-C debuggers also use this method to give you an idea of your object.

4. Start creating an image context with the size of the checkers board:

```
UIGraphicsBeginImageContext(CGSizeMake(
    CGFloat(squareSize * 8),
    CGFloat(squareSize * 8)))
```

Create two loops that will draw each square of the board:

```
for row in 0...7 {
    for col in 0...7 {
```

Inside these loops, we need to calculate where the current position is.

```
let offsetx = CGFloat(col * squareSize)
let offsety = CGFloat(row * squareSize)
```

5. After this, we need to know whether we will draw a black square or a white one. To do this, the `row` and `col` variables will help us:

```
if col % 2 == row % 2 {
    UIColor.grayColor().setFill()
}else {
    UIColor.blackColor().setFill()
}
```

6. Now, let's fill the square with the current color:

```
var bezier = UIBezierPath(rect:
CGRectMake(offsetx, offsety,
CGFloat(squareSize), CGFloat(squareSize)))
bezier.fill()
```

7. Once we have painted the square, we will draw a circle that represents a player piece:

```
switch board[row][col] {
        case .WHITE:
            UIColor.whiteColor().setFill()
        case .BLACK:
            UIColor.brownColor().setFill()
        default:
            continue
```

```
          }
    bezier = UIBezierPath(arcCenter:
        CGPointMake(offsetx + CGFloat(
        squareSize / 2 ) , offsety +
        CGFloat(squareSize / 2)), radius:
        CGFloat(squareSize / 3), startAngle:
        CGFloat(0.0), endAngle: CGFloat(360),
        clockwise: true)
    bezier.closePath()
    bezier.fill()
```

8. The loops are done; we can now finish them, return the image, and finish the board class:

```
            }
        }

        let image =
            UIGraphicsGetImageFromCurrentImageContext()
        UIGraphicsEndImageContext()
        return image
    }
}
```

9. As you might imagine, we need to test our class by instantiating it, adding some pieces on the board, and visualizing it:

```
var board = CheckersBoard()

board.board[2][5]  =  .WHITE
board.board[2][3]  =  .BLACK
board.board[4][3]  =  .WHITE
board.board[2][1]  =  .BLACK
board.board[0][5]  =  .WHITE
board.board[1][0]  =  .BLACK
board.board[7][6]  =  .WHITE
board.board[5][6]  =  .BLACK

board
```

10. Now, click on the quick look of the board (last line), and you should see a result like the one shown here:

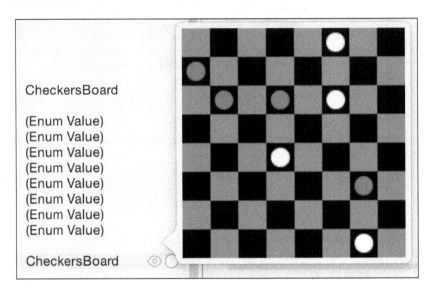

How it works...

To display a custom quick look, you have to create a class that inherits from NSObject and implements the debugQuickLookObject method. Although this method returns an object of type AnyObject, on its declaration, it should return anything that can be represented by the playground, such as colors, bezier paths, views, and so on.

In this recipe, we used a bezier path, which has a different coordinate system from the traditional views. Bezier paths have the initial point ($x = 0$ and $y = 0$) on the lower-left corner. This didn't affect us because we used only squares and circles, but bear this problem in mind because you can get wrong results.

UIColor has some methods that indicate what color should be used on the current context for filling a shape (setFill) and to draw its border (setStroke). These colors will be applied when you call the corresponding action to use them, such as bezier.fill().

There's more...

Sometimes, we need to indicate that we want to show a view on our playground. To do this, we have a function called XCPShowView, which is another way to visualize an object. In the next chapter, we will learn how to debug our app; it is very useful when we have too much code and we are not able to test it on the playground.

7
Swift Debugging with Xcode

In this chapter, we will cover the following topics:

- ► The Tax income simulator
- ► The best checker movement
- ► Debugging with LLDB
- ► Profiling an app

Introduction

Let's face it, nobody writes a full program without any issue. Even the best programmer will encounter some situations that hadn't been contemplated. Sometimes, it's easy to find the bug; sometimes, it is very hard, mainly, when we have a multithreaded app.

In this chapter, we will learn how to debug an app step by step; this will make it easier for you to find where the issue is.

The Tax income simulator

When we are developing an app, we know that some variables of a function shouldn't contain certain values, but are you sure of this? How can we develop and check that everything has its right value?

In this recipe, we will learn how to check that the values are right during the development stage. To simulate this, let's create an app where we are sure that there will be people trying to cheat the values; in this case, let's create an app to calculate tax income.

Getting ready

Create a project called `Chapter 7 Tax Income` and make sure that you are in debug mode. To do this, click on the project schema and select **Edit schema...**, as shown in the following screenshot:

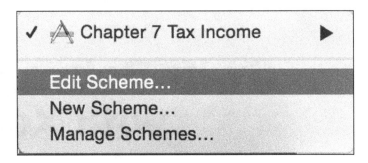

Click on the **Run** option located on the left-hand side, then make sure that the **Info** tab is selected, and finally, make sure that the build option is on the **Debug** mode. We will have some explanations later.

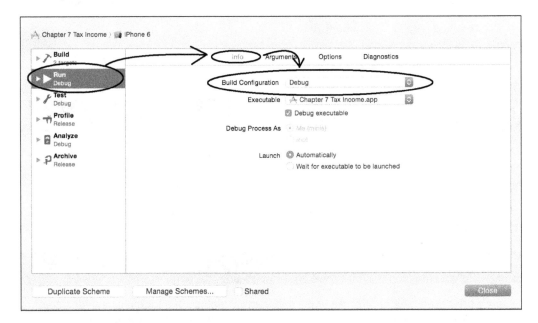

Once these steps have been checked, we need to open the project settings and create a macro called `DEBUG_MODE` only on the debug configuration.

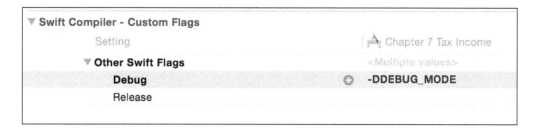

How to do it...

Let's create our very own tax income simulator by following these steps:

1. First, let's create a new file called `Assertions.swift`. Here, we will add some functions, all of them starting with `assert_`:

```swift
// element must be one of the elements in the set
func assert_in<T:Comparable>(element: @autoclosure () -> T,
    set: [T], message: @autoclosure () -> String){
    #if DEBUG_MODE
        if set.count == 0 {
        println("warning: comparing with an empty set")
        }
        assert(set.filter({(currentElement) -> Bool in
        return currentElement == element()
        }).count > 0, message)
    #endif
}

// element must be greater or equal to the other value
func assert_ge<T:Comparable>(value:T, otherValue:T,
    message:
    @autoclosure () -> String){
    #if DEBUG_MODE
        assert(value >= otherValue , message)
    #endif
}

// element can't be nil
func assert_not_nil<T>(element:@autoclosure () -> T?,
    message: @autoclosure () -> String){
    if element() == nil {
        #if DEBUG_MODE
```

```
            assertionFailure(message)
        #endif
    }
}
```

2. Now, we can create another file, which will contain a class that should be able to calculate the income tax. Create a new file called `IncomeTaxCalculator.swift` and start with the class header, as shown here:

```
class IncomeTaxCalculator:Printable {
```

3. The next step is to add its attributes; as you can imagine, we have to store a few values for it:

```
var title:String?
var name:String?
lazy var grossIncome:Double = 0.0
lazy var netIncome:Double = 0.0
lazy var children:Int = 0
lazy var education:Double = 0.0
```

As you can see, all of these are initialized or are optional; you don't need to create an initializer in this case, except if you are using one of the first versions of Swift. If so, use this:

```
init(){}
```

4. If you paid attention, this class must implement the `Printable` protocol. So, we need to add the description to this class:

```
var description: String {
    assert_not_nil(self.title, "Title cant be nil")
    assert_not_nil(self.name, "Name cant be nil")
    assert_in(self.title!, ["Mr", "Dr", "Miss", "Mrs"],
        "Wrong title")
    return "\(self.title!) \(self.name!) -
        \(self.calculate())"
}
```

5. To finish this class, we need a method that calculates the income tax based on the previous attributes. Of course, this is a fictional case; don't use this app to calculate your income tax.

```
func calculate() -> Double {
    assert_ge(self.grossIncome, 0.0, "Gross income
        can't be negative")
    assert_ge(self.netIncome, 0.0, "Net income can't be
        negative")
```

```
assert_ge(self.grossIncome, self.netIncome, "Net
   income cant be negative")

let totalAlreadyPaid = self.grossIncome -
   self.netIncome
var percentage:Double
if self.grossIncome <= 9000.0 {
    percentage = 0.0
} else if self.grossIncome <= 18000.0 {
    percentage = 0.15
} else {
    percentage = 0.40
}

let childrenBonus = Double(self.children) * 100.0

// 10 percent of education up to 1000 per child
var educationBonus:Double
var educationLimit = Double(self.children) * 1000.0
if 0.1 * self.education < educationLimit {
    educationBonus = 0.1 * self.education
}else {
    educationBonus = educationLimit
}

return self.grossIncome * percentage -
   childrenBonus - educationBonus - totalAlreadyPaid
   }
}
```

6. Once this is done, we have to create the graphical part of our app. So, go to the story board and create a layout with six text fields, one button, and six labels, something similar to the following screenshot:

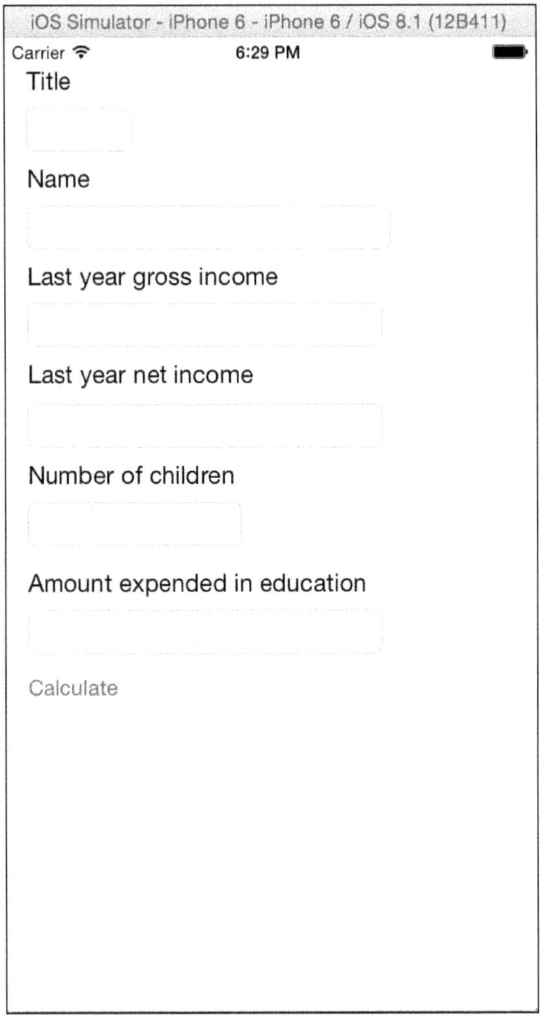

```
iOS Simulator - iPhone 6 - iPhone 6 / iOS 8.1 (12B411)
Carrier 🔋                    6:29 PM

  Title

  [          ]

  Name

  [                        ]

  Last year gross income

  [                        ]

  Last year net income

  [                        ]

  Number of children

  [                ]

  Amount expended in education

  [                        ]

  Calculate
```

7. As you might imagine, we need to create some attributes to link with the text fields:

```
@IBOutlet var titleTextField: UITextField!
@IBOutlet var nameTextField: UITextField!
@IBOutlet var lastYearIncomeTextField: UITextField!
@IBOutlet var numberOfChildrenTextField: UITextField!
@IBOutlet var LastYearNetIncome: UITextField!
@IBOutlet var educationTextField: UITextField!
```

8. To complete our graphical part, we need to add an event for the button:

```
@IBAction func calculateAction(sender: UIButton) {
    assert(countElements(self.nameTextField.text) >= 5,
      "Your name looks too short")
    var error:NSError?
    let regex = NSRegularExpression(pattern:
      "^[0-9]+[.[0-9]+]?$", options: .CaseInsensitive,
      error: &error)!
    if regex.matchesInString(
      self.lastYearIncomeTextField.text, options:
      nil, range: NSMakeRange(0, countElements(
      self.lastYearIncomeTextField.text))).count == 0{
        assertionFailure("Gross Income tax:
          wrong format")
    }
    let income = (self.lastYearIncomeTextField.text
      as NSString).doubleValue
    let incomeTaxCalculator:IncomeTaxCalculator
      = IncomeTaxCalculator()
    incomeTaxCalculator.title =
      self.titleTextField.text
    incomeTaxCalculator.name = self.nameTextField.text
    incomeTaxCalculator.grossIncome =
      (self.lastYearIncomeTextField.text as
      NSString).doubleValue
    incomeTaxCalculator.netIncome =
      (self.LastYearNetIncome.text as
      NSString).doubleValue
    incomeTaxCalculator.education =
      (self.educationTextField.text as
      NSString).doubleValue
    incomeTaxCalculator.children =
      self.numberOfChildrenTextField.text.toInt()!
    UIAlertView(title: "Income Tax", message:
      incomeTaxCalculator.description, delegate:nil,
      cancelButtonTitle:"Ok").show()
}
```

9. The last step is to test our application and watch the assertions work. Click on play. When the application appears, click on **calculate**, without adding any information into the text fields. You should see your application stop running and the Xcode should show you where.

```
"Your name looks too short")        Thread 1: EXC_BAD_INSTRUCTION (code=EXC_I386_INVOP, subcode=0x0)
```

The log console will open and show you what happened while printing the message that you have written, as shown here:

```
assertion failed: Your name looks too short: file /Users/minis/Desktop/
Workspace/Chapter 7 Tax Income/Chapter 7 Tax Income/ViewController.swift,
line 27
(lldb)

All Output ⌄
```

Let's complete this recipe by changing Debug configuration to Release; press play again and see that the first assert was ignored.

How it works...

Assertions are like functions that interrupt the application when they find an unexpected value. Of course, when a program is released, it needs to accept these values. This means that the developer shouldn't rely on the power of assertions forever; he must fix the value or at least interrupt the process.

Swift comes with only two assertions functions:

▶ `assert`: This is a function that has two arguments. The first one is a Boolean element, which, in the case of being false, will stop your program and show the next argument (the message) for the developer.

▶ `assertionFailure`: This function stops the program execution without checking any condition. This function is used when there is a way through which the app shouldn't go. Imagine that you have a `switch` statement, and theoretically, your program shouldn't go to the default case because it isn't considered. In such a case, you need to add an assertion.

Another nagging question is: what does **autoclosure** mean? The reason is this: `assert`, `assertionFailure`, and our other assertion functions actually don't receive a value as argument, the cause being laziness. This means that Swift won't evaluate the values before entering into the function.

Swift converts your argument into a function and the argument will be evaluated inside when the assert function calls it. Why? The reason is that assertions shouldn't work if you are compiling with Release configuration instead of Debug. Bear in mind that assertions stop your program, which is something good when you are developing, but for a user, this won't be a good sensation. This is the reason that we sometimes call the autoclosure function between `#ifdef NDEBUG` and `#endif`.

 Prior to the release of Xcode 6 beta 5, `@autoclosure` used to be written as `@auto_closure`. If you are going to look for something about this modifier on the Internet, try writing it both ways.

If assertions don't work on Release mode, why are they useful? The reason is that assertions are used to detect development errors; you should track the source of the error and modify it to ensure that the source won't give you a wrong value.

The reason we created a different file for our own assertion functions is that we may have this file shared between projects. Of course, you can use the `assert` function for everything, but I would recommend that you create assertion functions that can save work, like the one we have to check whether an element is inside of an array.

There's more...

In this recipe, we learned about using the Swift assertions, which is the equivalent to `NSAssert` in Objective-C. If you prefer using the other assertion features from the Objective-C foundation, such as `NSParameterAssert` and `NSAssertionHandler`, you are still able to use them in Swift.

Assertions are very useful for finding paths that are receiving wrong values; however, there are times when this needs to proceed step by step with the code. We will see how to do this with Xcode and Swift in the next recipe.

The best checker movement

If you have some experience with programming, you know that sometimes we need to proceed step by step with the code, mainly when we have those kinds of issues that nobody knows how it happened.

In this recipe, we will learn how to debug with Xcode and Swift. To do this, we will recycle our checkerboard. In this case, we will make the best movement using the white pieces. We will also leave the app ready for a second version; this app can also make use of kings.

We will not create the right algorithm in the beginning; the idea is to debug and find where the issue is, and then, we will correct the issues later.

Getting ready

Open your playground project from the previous chapter where you have the checkerboard. Leave it open because we will reuse this code. Once it's open, create a new project called `Chapter 7 checkerboard`. Let's start coding.

How to do it...

Follow these steps to visualize a checkerboard:

1. Create a new file called `CheckersBoard.swift`. Start coding by importing the UIKit if it is not imported yet:

   ```
   import UIKit
   ```

2. After this, you can paste the class code from the playground. Then, copy the last part from playground (variable instantiation and setup) and paste it on the `viewDidLoad` method on the view controller file:

   ```
   override func viewDidLoad() {
       super.viewDidLoad()
       var board = CheckersBoard()
       board.board[2][5] = .WHITE
       board.board[2][3] = .BLACK
       board.board[4][3] = .WHITE
       board.board[2][1] = .BLACK
       board.board[0][5] = .WHITE
       board.board[1][0] = .BLACK
       board.board[7][6] = .WHITE
       board.board[5][6] = .BLACK
   }
   ```

3. Now, let's create a breakpoint the third time we assign a piece, by clicking on the gray area on the left of the code, as shown here:

```
var board = CheckersBoard()
board.board[2][5] = .WHITE
board.board[2][3] = .BLACK
board.board[4][3] = .WHITE
board.board[2][1] = .BLACK
board.board[0][5] = .WHITE
```

4. Click on play, wait until the Xcode stops on your breakpoint, and move your mouse pointer over the board variable. This can be over any of them, such as the first one where the variable is being declared, or the other ones where to assign a piece.

   After a short interval, you will see a small dialog with two icons on the right. The first icon, which is an *i* with a circle around it, displays the content of the object with a text format similar to a JSON format.

```
(Chapter_7_Checkersboard.CheckersBoard) board =
0x00007fa5c8480520 {
  ObjectiveC.NSObject = {}
  board = 8 values {
    [0] = 8 values {
      [0] = FREE
      [1] = FREE
      [2] = FREE
      [3] = FREE
      [4] = FREE
      [5] = FREE
      [6] = FREE
      [7] = FREE
    }
    [1] = 8 values {
      [0] = FREE
      [1] = FREE
      [2] = FREE
      [3] = FREE
      [4] = FREE
      [5] = FREE
      [6] = FREE
      [7] = FREE
    }
    [2] = 8 values {
      [0] = FREE
      [1] = FREE
      [2] = FREE
      [3] = BLACK
      [4] = FREE
      [5] = WHITE
      [6] = FREE
      [7] = FREE
```

The other icon is very familiar to us because it's the same icon we've seen on the playground. This is the quick look icon, and we can also use it here. This way we will retrieve a more visual way of watching the checkerboard. The checkerboard should look similar to this:

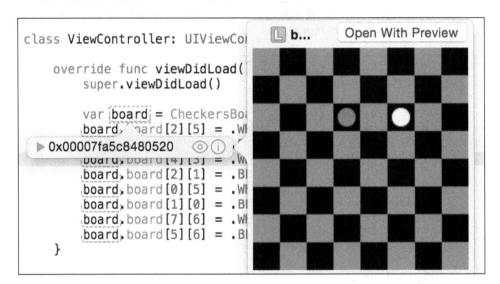

 Don't create the debugQuickLookObject method for every single class you have, but only for those classes that are hard to visualize and need to be debugged frequently.

5. Now that we know how to visualize our object, we need to differentiate traditional pieces from kings. Our next goal is to add a Boolean to the BoardSpace enumeration. Replace the previous enumeration with this one:

```
enum BoardSpace {
    case FREE,
    WHITE(Bool),
    BLACK(Bool)
}
```

6. Now, we need to display something different. In this case, we will add the letter *K* over the piece. Replace the switch statement inside the debugQuickLookObject method with the one shown here:

```
var isKing = false;

switch board[row][col] {
case .WHITE(let king):
```

```
            isKing = king
            UIColor.whiteColor().setFill()
        case .BLACK(let king):
            isKing = king
            UIColor.brownColor().setFill()
        default:
            continue
    }
```

7. Right, now after filling the pieces, we need to add code in the case of being a king in the current piece:

```
. . .
bezier.fill()
if isKing {
    ("K" as NSString).drawAtPoint(CGPointMake(offsetx +
        CGFloat( squareSize / 3 ) , offsety +
        CGFloat(squareSize / 5)), withAttributes: nil)
}
```

8. Now, we need to change the way we assigned the pieces with the one shown here:

```
        let board = CheckersBoard()
        board.board[2][5] = .WHITE(false)
        board.board[2][3] = .BLACK(false)
        board.board[4][3] = .WHITE(true)
        board.board[2][1] = .BLACK(false)
        board.board[0][5] = .WHITE(false)
        board.board[1][0] = .BLACK(false)
        board.board[7][6] = .WHITE(false)
        board.board[5][6] = .BLACK(false)
```

9. Let's repeat the operation by clicking on play and watching the board with quick look; now, you can click on the Step Over button (the *F6* key).

 New Apple keyboards have an assigned function for the *F6* key, so you will probably have to type this key together with the *fn* key.

10. Now, check the quick look and see that you have the letter *K* over one of our pieces, as shown here:

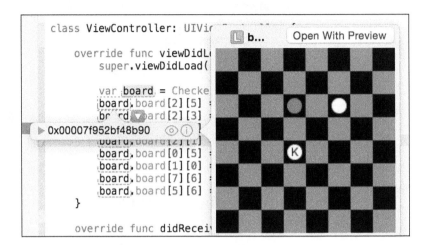

Ok, now that we know how to visualize the board, we will see whether we can win a game with only one turn. To do this, we will need to choose a piece and see every possibility we have. This means that we will need to clone our object frequently. Usually, we will create a struct for it, but in this case, we will create a method for cloning our object. We will give explanations later.

Let's start by executing these steps:

1. Just add this code inside your `CheckersBoard` class:

```swift
func clone() -> CheckersBoard {
    let board = CheckersBoard()
    for i in 0..<8 {
        for j in 0..<8 {
            switch self.board[i][j] {
            case .FREE:
                continue
            default:
                board.board[i][j] = self.board[i][j]
            }
        }
    }
    return board
}
```

2. The next step to worry about is how to capture the opponent's piece. To do this, we will need to test the directions that are possible. Let's create an enumeration inside our `CheckersBoard` class for helping us:

```
enum Direction {
    case NORTHWEST,
    NORTHEAST,
    SOUTHWEST,
    SOUTHEAST
}
```

3. Now, we need to create a method that will find for us the best movement, remember that we are using only the white pieces:

```
func bestMovementWhite() -> CheckersBoard?{
    var boardCandidate:CheckersBoard?
    for i in 0..<8 {
        for j in 1..<8 {
            var result: CheckersBoard?
            switch self.board[i][j]{

            case .WHITE(let king):
                if king {
                    result = bestMovementKingWhite(i,
                        y: j)
                }else {
                    result =
                        bestMovementSinglePieceWhite(i,
                        y: j)
                }
            default:
                continue
            }

            if let boardFound = result {
                if let currentBoard = boardCandidate {
                    if currentBoard.countBlack() >
                        boardFound.countBlack() {
                        boardCandidate = boardFound
                    }
                }else {
                    boardCandidate = boardFound
                }
            }
        }
    }
```

```
        }
      }
      return boardCandidate
  }
```

4. As you can see, we have two private methods: one for the best movement of a normal piece, and another for a king. Here, I will develop the single piece function; the other method, I'll leave it as homework for you; otherwise, it will be an extremely huge recipe. Now, add this code to the file:

```
private func bestMovementSinglePieceWhite(x:Int,
  y:Int) -> CheckersBoard {
    var clonedBoard = self.clone()
    if clonedBoard.capture(x, y: y, direction:
      .NORTHWEST) {
        return clonedBoard.
          bestMovementSinglePieceWhite(-1, y: -1)
    }

    if clonedBoard.capture(x, y: y,
      direction: .NORTHEAST) {
        return clonedBoard.
          bestMovementSinglePieceWhite(1, y: -1)
    }

    if clonedBoard.capture(x, y: y, direction:
      .SOUTHWEST) {
        return clonedBoard.
          bestMovementSinglePieceWhite(-1, y: 1)
    }

    if clonedBoard.capture(x, y: y, direction:
      .SOUTHEAST) {
        return clonedBoard.
          bestMovementSinglePieceWhite(1, y: 1)
    }
    return clonedBoard
}

private func bestMovementKingWhite(x:Int,
  y:Int) -> CheckersBoard? {
    // TODO Homework
    return nil
}
```

5. To complete this class, we need to add more methods: one that will count the number of black pieces and another that will capture the opponent's piece:

```
func countBlack() -> Int{
    var total = 0
    for row in self.board {
        for element in row {
            switch element {
            case .BLACK:
                total++
            default:
                continue
            }
        }
    }
    return total
}
private func capture(x: Int, y:Int,
  direction: Direction) -> Bool {
    var offset_x:Int
    var offset_y:Int
    switch(direction){
    case .NORTHWEST:
        offset_x = -1
        offset_y = -1
    case .NORTHEAST:
        offset_x = 1
        offset_y = -1
    case .SOUTHWEST:
        offset_x = -1
        offset_y = 1
    case .SOUTHEAST:
        offset_x = 1
        offset_y = 1
    }
    if x + 2*offset_x >= 0 && y + 2*offset_y >=
       0 && x + 2*offset_x < 8 &&  y + 2*offset_y < 8 {
        // we are inside the board range
        switch (board[x + 2*offset_x][y+2*offset_y],
          board[x + offset_x][y+offset_y]) {
            case (.FREE, .BLACK):
                board[x + offset_x][y+offset_y] = .FREE
                board[x + 2 * offset_x ][ y + 2 *
                  offset_y] = board[x][y]
```

```
                    board[x][y] = .FREE
              return true
              default:
              return false
         }
      }else {
          return false
      }
   }
```

Okay, now imagine that it's Monday; we had to type this entire code, and someone (probably your boss) tells you that there is a setup that doesn't find the best solution. Reviewing every single line of this code can be very boring and it can be hard to find where the problem is.

Let's debug starting with the setup that is not working, so replace the setup code with this one:

```
let board = CheckersBoard()
board.board[0][1] = .WHITE(false)
board.board[0][5] = .WHITE(false)
board.board[2][7] = .WHITE(false)
board.board[3][2] = .WHITE(false)
board.board[2][1] = .BLACK(false)
board.board[4][3] = .BLACK(false)
board.board[4][5] = .BLACK(false)
board.board[2][5] = .BLACK(false)
board.board[2][3] = .BLACK(false)
if let finalBoard = board.bestMovementWhite() {
    println(finalBoard.debugDescription)
}else {
    println("no solution")
}
```

The first thing you might have noticed is debugDescription. This is something similar to debugQuickLookObject, but instead of returning different kinds of objects, it only returns a text. We will complete this property later.

As you know, we have to debug the fourth white piece movement. To do this, go to the method called bestMovementWhite and add a breakpoint on the line where we call the bestMovementSinglePieceWhite method. Right-click on this breakpoint, and you will see a menu like this one:

| Edit Breakpoint... |
| Disable Breakpoint |
| Delete Breakpoint |
| Reveal in Breakpoint Navigator |

Choose **Edit breakpoint...**; as you know, we don't want to check what happened with the first three pieces. So if, for example, you want to ignore breakpoints three times before the app stops, choose **3**, as shown in the following screenshot:

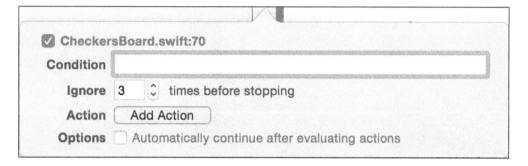

Sometimes, we know that we have to stop after a certain number of times; try to use this instead of clicking on play a lot of times. Add another breakpoint in this same method at the end (return boardCandidate) and edit it. Now, we will add a condition to make this work and change the action to sound. Unfortunately, most of the available sounds are too soft, I usually choose the glass one, but if you prefer, you can choose another one. To finish this breakpoint, select the **Automatically continue after evaluating actions** option, as shown here:

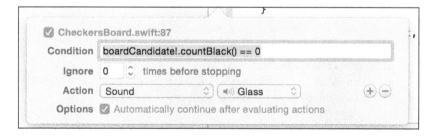

Now, click on play and wait until Xcode stops. Press the step into button (the one with an arrow pointing down) or press *F7*, and you will get into `bestMovementSinglePieceWhite`. Now, click on Step Over (or press *F6*) three times; check the board with quick look and have a look as we will return this board. After detecting the issue, we can replace our algorithm with this one:

```swift
private func bestMovementSinglePieceWhite(x:Int, y:Int) ->
    CheckersBoard {
    var clonedBoard = self.clone()
    var winner:CheckersBoard = self

    if clonedBoard.capture(x, y: y, direction: .NORTHWEST) {
        winner = clonedBoard.bestMovementSinglePieceWhite(
            x-2, y: y-2)
    }

    clonedBoard = self.clone()
    if clonedBoard.capture(x, y: y, direction: .NORTHEAST) {
        clonedBoard = clonedBoard.
            bestMovementSinglePieceWhite(x+2, y: y-2)
        if winner.countBlack() > clonedBoard.countBlack() {
            winner = clonedBoard
        }
    }

    clonedBoard = self.clone()
    if clonedBoard.capture(x, y: y, direction: .SOUTHWEST) {
        clonedBoard = clonedBoard.
            bestMovementSinglePieceWhite(x-2, y: y+2)
        if winner.countBlack() > clonedBoard.countBlack() {
            winner = clonedBoard
        }
    }

    clonedBoard = self.clone()
    if clonedBoard.capture(x, y: y, direction: .SOUTHEAST) {
        clonedBoard = clonedBoard.
            bestMovementSinglePieceWhite(x+2, y: y+2)
        if winner.countBlack() > clonedBoard.countBlack() {
            winner = clonedBoard
        }
    }
    return winner
}
```

Now, press play again, but instead of pressing Step Into, use Step Over. Check the board with the quick look inspector, and see that you now have the right solution. So, problem solved! However, don't celebrate too much, other issues are coming.

How it works...

Xcode allows us to debug step by step. Using the method that we used to debug on our playground, the project (`debugQuickLookObject`) can help us visualize the current object state. In this case, we can improve our method using the `drawAtPoint` method of `NSString`; right now, there is no equivalent method for Swift strings.

Another detail you can see is that we created our own method to clone the board instead of using a struct. The reason is that structs can't inherit values, and in this case, we need to do it due to our quick look method.

Breakpoints have some special features when using Xcode: you can ignore breakpoints a few times, which is very useful when you know that the issue happens after some repetitions. Imagine if you have to press a button continuously for 50 times, and then you have to repeat it again and again until you find a solution. You and your mouse will end the day exhausted.

As you can see, you can also add an action to the breakpoint, such as adding a debugger command and playing a sound, which is very useful for knowing that something has been done in the background. However, you don't want to stop logging a message that helps us to analyze the program trajectory.

There are some commands for debugging that a developer must know, such as Step Over, which executes the whole line of code and stops on the next one—Step Into, which goes inside the current function, Step Out (*F8*), which exits from the current function and stops at the same place where it was called, and continue (*control + command + Y*), which continues executing the program until the next breakpoint.

Unfortunately, there is no right or wrong procedure to find an issue, and sometimes, you have to use your sixth sense to solve it. The only way is to collect as much information as you can and go step by step.

There's more...

Actually, Xcode isn't debugging by itself; the reality is that it uses another debugger to do this task. In the next recipe, we will use the debugger from the command line.

Debugging with LLDB

Debugging with Xcode is fine, but sometimes we are limited, and we have to use the debugger with a lower level. To do this, we have to know that actually Xcode is not debugging anything, it uses another program called LLDB.

 Old versions of Xcode are used to debug with GDB instead of LLDB; don't try to use them with Swift because there is no support for Swift on GDB.

It's recommended that you know the LLDB commands if you want to debug big programs. These are also used in cases where you have to connect with another machine (a continuous integration, for example), where you have to do everything through an SSH shell.

Getting ready

Open the checkerboard program and check whether you have any breakpoint and remove all of them.

How to do it...

Debugging with LLDB will involve the following steps:

1. Click on play and when the program starts, click on the pause button; use the combination *control + command + U*. After this, you will see the LLDB console:

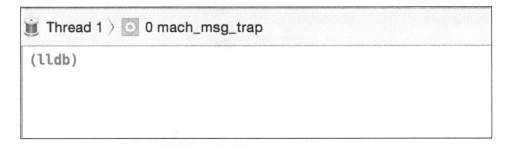

2. Now, click on the LLDB console and write `break s -r bestMovement*`; you'll see that the answer is `Breakpoint 1: 4 locations`. Then, let's list these breakpoints with `breakpoint list`. Here, you can see an ugly answer; but don't be scared, this is simpler than you think.

You can also write `thread info` to get some information about the current thread. See that this specifies the language of each frame; with this information, you can get a better idea as to what happened with your code in the case of crashing.

List your threads with `thread list`, switch to the thread 2 with `thread select 2`, and write `thread info` again.

3. Now, write a repl and see that the prompt changes to `1>`. In this case, we will write a new function to test our repl, so type the following code:

```
func num0(myArray:[Int]) -> Int {
    return myArray.reduce(0, {
        if $1 == 0 {
        return $0 + 1
    }else {
        return $0
    }})
}
```

4. Once this function is complete, let's test it:

```
num0([1,3,1,0,0,4,1])
```

As you can see, a repl can help you write functions in runtime, like we did with the playground.

How it works...

LLDB is the current Xcode debugger; you can set multiple breakpoints with regular expressions. Remember that what you do on LLDB isn't necessarily reflected on Xcode; the breakpoints we set are a good example.

Notice that three of our breakpoints have the filename and a line number such as `... at CheckersBoard.swift:158, ...`, which means your breakpoint is on the `CheckersBoard.swift` file at the line `158`.

We also used repl, which is a Swift command line. Here, you can create functions and test some code. Of course, you can also use playground, but sometimes, it is faster using the current debugger.

There's more...

Apple has some documentation about LLDB; it's worth having a look at it. Check this URL: `https://developer.apple.com/library/ios/documentation/IDEs/ Conceptual/gdb_to_lldb_transition_guide/document/Introduction.html`.

What about features that users complain of but are hard to debug, such as memory, performance, or energy? For these kinds of problems, you have to use another tool; we will learn about this in the next recipe.

Profiling an app

It's very common to hear about issues, but if an app doesn't have any important issue, it doesn't mean that it is working fine. Imagine that you have a program that has a memory leak, presumably you won't find any problem using it for 10 minutes. However, a user may find it after using it for a few days. Don't think that this sort of thing is impossible; remember that iOS apps don't terminate, so if you do have memory leaks, it will be kept until your app blows up.

Performance is another important, common topic. What if your app looks okay, but it gets slower with the passing of time? We, therefore, have to be aware of this problem. This kind of test is called **profiling** and Xcode comes with a very good tool for realizing this operation, which is called **Instruments**.

In this instance, we will profile our app to visualize the amount of energy wasted by our app and, of course, let's try to reduce it.

Getting ready

For this recipe you will need a physical device, and to install your app into the device you will need to be enrolled on the Apple Developer Program. If you have both the requirements, the next thing you have to do is create a new project called `Chapter 7 Energy`.

How to do it...

To profile an app, follow these steps:

1. Before we start coding, we will need to add a framework to the project. Click on the **Build Phases** tab of your project, go to the **Link Binaries with Libraries** section, and press the plus sign.

2. Once Xcode opens a dialog window asking for the framework to add, choose **CoreLocation** and **MapKit**.

3. Now, go to the storyboard and place a label and a MapKit view. You might have a layout similar to this one:

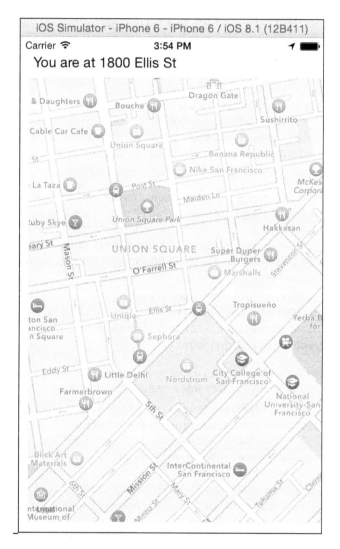

4. Link the MapKit view and call it just `map` and the `UILabel` class and call it just `label`:

```
@IBOutlet var label: UILabel!
@IBOutlet var map: MKMapView!
```

5. Continue with the view controller; let's click at the beginning of the file to add the core location and MapKit imports:

```
import CoreLocation
import MapKit
```

6. After this, you have to initialize the location manager object on the `viewDidLoad` method:

```
override func viewDidLoad() {
    super.viewDidLoad()
    locationManager.delegate = self
    locationManager.desiredAccuracy =
      kCLLocationAccuracyBest
    locationManager.requestWhenInUseAuthorization()
    locationManager.startUpdatingLocation()
}
```

7. At the moment, you may get an error because your view controller doesn't conform with `CLLocationManagerDelegate`, so let's go to the header of the view controller class and specify that it implements this protocol. Another error we have to deal with is the `locationManager` variable, because it is not declared. Therefore, we have to create it as an attribute. And as we are declaring attributes, we will add the geocoder, which will be used later:

```
class ViewController: UIViewController,
  CLLocationManagerDelegate {
    var locationManager = CLLocationManager()
    var geocoder = CLGeocoder()
```

8. Before we implement this method that receives the positioning, let's create another method to detect whether there was any authorization error:

```
func locationManager(manager: CLLocationManager!,
    didChangeAuthorizationStatus status:
      CLAuthorizationStatus) {
        var locationStatus:String
        switch status {
        case CLAuthorizationStatus.Restricted:
            locationStatus = "Access: Restricted"
            break
        case CLAuthorizationStatus.Denied:
            locationStatus = "Access: Denied"
            break
        case CLAuthorizationStatus.NotDetermined:
            locationStatus = "Access: NotDetermined"
            break
        default:
```

```
        locationStatus = "Access: Allowed"
    }
    NSLog(locationStatus)
}
```

9. And then, we can implement the method that will update our location:

```
func locationManager(manager:CLLocationManager,
    didUpdateLocations locations:[AnyObject]) {
    if locations[0] is CLLocation {
        let location:CLLocation = locations[0] as
            CLLocation
        self.map.setRegion(
            MKCoordinateRegionMakeWithDistance(
            location.coordinate, 800,800),
            animated: true)

        geocoder.reverseGeocodeLocation(location,
            completionHandler: { (addresses,
            error) -> Void in
                let placeMarket:CLPlacemark =
                    addresses[0] as CLPlacemark
            let curraddress:String = (placeMarket.
                addressDictionary["FormattedAddressLines"
                ] as [String]) [0] as String
                self.label.text = "You are at
                    \(curraddress)"
        })
    }
}
```

10. Before you test the app, there is still another step to follow. In your project navigator, click to expand the supporting files, and then click on `info.plist`. Add a row by right-clicking on the list and selecting **add row**.

11. On this new row, type `NSLocationWhenInUseUsageDescription` as a key and on value `Permission required`, like the one shown here:

Executable file		String	$(EXECUTABLE_NAME)
NSLocationWhenInUseUsageDescription		String	Permission required
Bundle identifier		String	com.packtpub.$(PRODUCT_NAME:rfc103

12. Now, select a device and install this app onto it, and test the application walking around your street (or walking around the planet earth if you want) and you will see that the label will change, and also the map will display your current position.

13. Now, go back to your computer and plug the device in again. Instead of clicking on play, you have to hold the play button until you see more options and then you have to click on the **Profile** option.

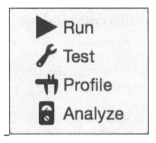

The next thing that will happen is that instruments will be opened; probably, a dialog will pop up asking for an administrator account. This is due to the fact that instruments need to use some special permission to access some low-level information.

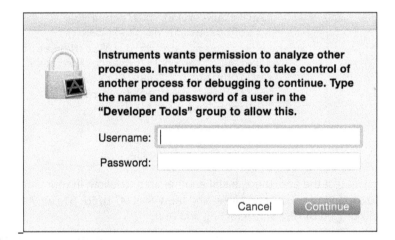

14. On the next dialog, you will see different kinds of instruments, some of them are OS X specific, some are iOS specific, and others are for both. If you choose the wrong platform instrument, the record button will be disabled. For this recipe, click on **Energy Diagnostics**.

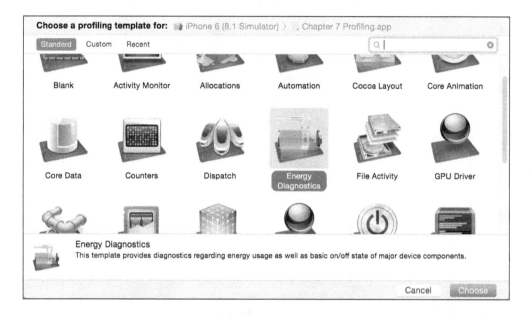

15. Once the **Energy Diagnostics** window is open, you can click on the record button, which is on the upper-left corner and try to move around—yes, you need to keep the device connected to your computer, so you have to move around with both elements together—and do some actions with your device, such as pressing the home button and turning off the screen. Now, you may have a screen that displays an output similar to this one:

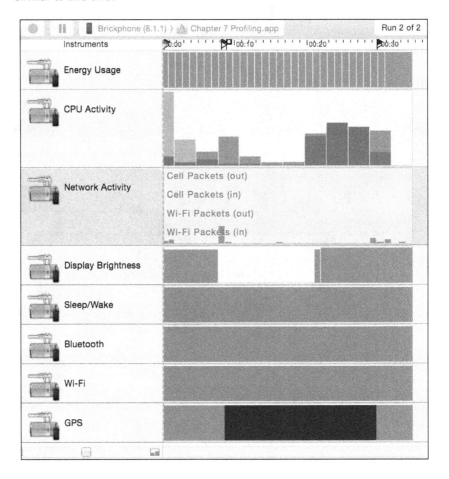

Now, you can analyze who is spending more energy on you app. To get a better idea of this, go to your code and replace the constant `kCLLocationAccuracyBest` with `kCLLocationAccuracyThreeKilometers` and check whether you have saved some energy.

How it works...

Instruments are a tool used for profiling your application. They give you information about your app which can't be retrieved by code, or at least can't be retrieved easily. You can check whether your app has memory leaks, whether it is loosing performance, and as you can see, whether it is wasting lots of energy or not.

In this recipe we used the GPS because it is a sensor that requires some energy. Also, you can check on the table at the bottom of your instrument to see that Internet requests were completed, which is something that if you do very frequently will also empty your battery fast.

Something you might be asking is: why did we have to change `info.plist`? Since iOS 8, some sensors require user permission; the GPS is one of them, so you need to report what is the message that will be shown to the user.

There's more...

I recommend you to read the way instruments work, mainly those that you will use. Check the Apple documentation about instruments to get more details about this (`https://developer.apple.com/library/mac/documentation/DeveloperTools/Conceptual/InstrumentsUserGuide/Introduction/Introduction.html`).

If you have experience with Objective-C, you might be asking how you can recycle your code using Swift. In the next chapter, we will see some recipes for this.

8
Integrating with Objective-C

In this chapter, we will cover the following topics:

- ▶ Calling a cab
- ▶ Hiring a van
- ▶ Porting from one language to another
- ▶ Replacing the UI classes
- ▶ Upgrading the app delegate
- ▶ Creating a framework

Introduction

Swift is out, and we can see that this will replace Objective-C in iOS development sooner or later. However, how should you migrate your Objective-C app? Is it necessary to rewrite everything all over again?

Of course, you don't have to rewrite a whole application in Swift from scratch; you can gradually migrate it. Imagine a 4-year app developed by 10 developers, it would take a long time to get this rewritten.

Actually, you've already seen that some of the code we used in this book has some kind of "old Objective-C fashion". The reason is that not even Apple computers could migrate the whole Objective-C code into Swift.

This chapter will help you migrate from Objective-C to Swift step by step.

Calling a cab

Let's imagine that we work for a taxi company, which already has an app that allows clients to call a taxi from it. As you may imagine, the company can start giving additional services rather than only using traditional cars; for example, let's imagine that they now want to offer hiring a van for people that have a lot of luggage.

In this recipe, we are going to start with a pure Objective-C application. After this, we are going to modify it so that we are prepared to add the Swift code in the future.

Getting ready

Let's start creating a project called `Chapter 8 Cab`, but in this case, select **Objective-C** instead of Swift as the programming language, as shown in the following screenshot:

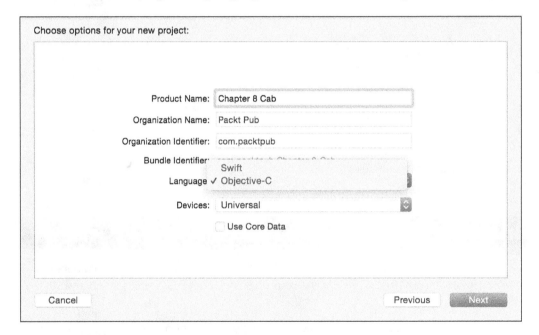

How to do it...

1. First, create a new file for your project, and select **Cocoa Touch Class**, which is located on the upper right-hand side of the iOS source:

2. Then, create a file called `Car`, which should be a subclass of `NSObject`, as shown here:

You will see that two files are created: `Car.h` and `Car.m`.

3. Click on the header file (Car.h) and add the following code:

```objc
#import <Foundation/Foundation.h>

@interface Car : NSObject{
    float fare;
}

@property (assign) float distance;
@property (assign) int pax;

-(id) init;
-(id) initWithFare:(float) fare;
-(float) getFare;

@end
```

4. Once the class interface is created, we have to implement this class, so click on the Car.m file and type the following code:

```objc
#import "Car.h"

@implementation Car
-(id) init{
    self = [super init];
    if(self){
        self->fare = 0.2;
        self.pax = 4;
        self.distance = 0;
    }
    return self;
}

-(id) initWithFare:(float) fare{
    self = [super init];
    if(self){
        self->fare = fare;
        self.pax = 4;
        self.distance = 0;
    }
    return self;
}

-(float) getFare{
```

```
        return self->fare;
}
@end
```

The model part is done, and now we need to create the view part.

5. Let's do something very straightforward. Just add a table view to the storyboard, and then link it to the view controller as an attribute, as a data source and as a delegate.

6. As you have to modify the header file (usually called `ViewController.h`), add an auxiliary attribute called `vehicles` of type `NSArray`:

```
@interface ViewController : UIViewController
   <UITableViewDataSource, UITableViewDelegate>{
      NSArray * vehicles;
      IBOutlet UITableView *tableView;
}
@end
```

7. Let's add some functionalities to this app. Go to the message file (usually called `ViewController.m`).

> Switching from the header file to its implementation or vice versa can be done using *command* + *control* + up arrow.

Now, let's start coding inside the ViewController.m file:

1. First let's import the `Car.h` file:

   ```
   #import "Car.h"
   ```

2. Then, add the data source content:

   ```
   - (NSInteger)tableView:(UITableView *)tableView
     numberOfRowsInSection:(NSInteger)section{
        return [vehicles count];
   }
   ```

   ```
   - (UITableViewCell *)tableView:(UITableView *)tableView
     cellForRowAtIndexPath:(NSIndexPath *)indexPath{
        UITableViewCell * cell;
        cell = [self->tableView
          dequeueReusableCellWithIdentifier:@"vehiclecell"];
        if(cell == nil) {
           cell = [[UITableViewCell alloc] initWithStyle
             :UITableViewCellStyleDefault
             reuseIdentifier:@"vehiclecell"];
   ```

```
        }
        Car * currentCar = [self->vehicles
          objectAtIndex:indexPath.row];
        cell.textLabel.text = [NSString stringWithFormat
          :@"Distance %.0f, pax: %d, fare: %.2f",
          currentCar.distance * 1000, currentCar.pax,
          [currentCar getFare] ];
        return cell;
    }
```

3. Now you have to initialize the `vehicles` attribute. Of course, here we are going to use just some hard code, otherwise we would have a very large amount of code:

```
- (void)viewDidLoad {
    [super viewDidLoad];
    Car * car1 = [[Car alloc] init];
    car1.distance = 1.2;
    Car * car2 = [[Car alloc] init];
    car2.distance = 0.5;
    Car * car3 = [[Car alloc] init];
    car3.distance = 5;
    Car * car4 = [[Car alloc] initWithFare:0.25];
    car4.distance = 4;
    vehicles = @[car1, car2, car3, car4];
    [self->tableView reloadData];
}
```

4. The last thing we need to do is create an event for the user, letting him choose a car for booking:

```
- (void)tableView:(UITableView *)tableView
  didSelectRowAtIndexPath:(NSIndexPath *)indexPath{
    Car * currentCar = [self->vehicles
      objectAtIndex:indexPath.row];
    // let's suppose that the current traffic allows
      us to drive at 50 km/h
    float time = currentCar.distance / 50.0 * 60.0;
    [[[UIAlertView alloc] initWithTitle:@"Car booked"
      message:[NSString stringWithFormat:@"The car will
      arrive in %.0f minutes", time] delegate:nil
      cancelButtonTitle:@"OK" otherButtonTitles: nil] show];
}
```

8. Now, test this app just to see whether it is working. The next step is to prepare this app to receive some Swift code. Before we add any swift file, we need to modernize this code. Fortunately, Xcode offers an option that does it automatically, so go to **Edit | Refactor | Convert to Modern Objective-C Syntax**, as shown here:

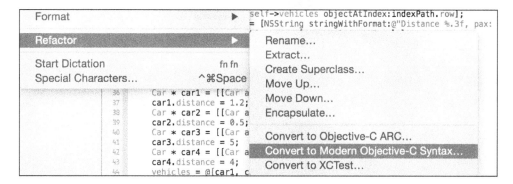

 Before you start modernizing your code, it's a good idea to commit your code in the version control system if you are using any.

9. When a dialog appears with some introduction text, click on **Next**, and then check every target that appears in the next dialog; usually they are checked, but just make sure of this. On the next screen, you will see some options to modernize your Objective-C code. You can leave all of them with their default values, but it is a better idea to make sure that every option is marked **Yes**, as shown here:

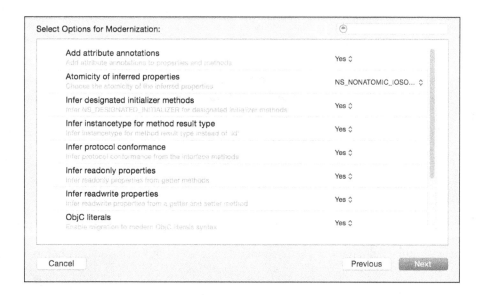

10. Now, you will see another dialog displaying the differences between the original code and the one that is going to be updated. Check the differences of each file by clicking on the filenames on the left-hand side. Your screen should look similar to this:

[Avoid modernizing your code without checking the differences between the old and new code; sometimes, you will find modifications that are not conceptually right.]

11. Click on **Next**, and you will see a new dialog asking whether you would like to enable automatic snapshots:

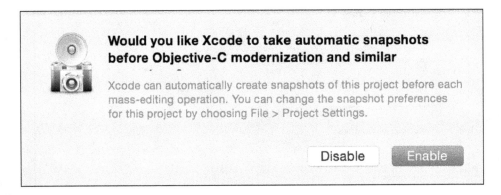

Now check whether your project has the changed code and that it still works as before.

How it works...

When you would like to migrate your Objective-C application to Swift, the first thing that you need to do is convert your code to Modern Objective-C Syntax. Thanks to this, your code will be ready to be compatible with Swift integration.

You can see that after modernizing your code, parts of your code are modified, for example, `id` is replaced with `instancetype`, initializers receive the modifier `NS_DESIGNATED_INITIALIZER`. Some functions are converted to properties, mainly those functions that start with `get` or `set`.

Usually, this kind of change is considered quite a massive change, which of course comes with the risk of needing to roll back to the previous state. This is the reason why Xcode recommends that you create a snapshot.

There's more...

In this recipe, we learned how to get an existing Objective-C app and used its code with Swift. Of course, sometimes you can do it automatically, and sometimes you have to change it manually. It is a good idea to check the modern Objective-C documentation. You can do so by visiting `https://developer.apple.com/library/ios/releasenotes/ObjectiveC/ModernizationObjC/AdoptingModernObjective-C/AdoptingModernObjective-C.html`.

Hiring a van

In this recipe, we are going to give more functionalities to the cab application. Here, we will assume that the application won't call only cars, but will also make van services available. In this case, the van needs to specify its capacity, and as we are modernizing the code, we will do it using Swift. Of course, there will always be some code to type in Objective-C, so bear that in mind.

Getting ready

In this recipe, we are going to continue with the previous app, so make a copy of the previous recipe and open the project copy. Renaming the app `Chapter 8 Car` to `Chapter 8 Vehicles` would be good way to differentiate them.

How to do it...

Let's add the functionality of hiring a van by following these steps:

1. First, click on the project navigator, then on the group, which contains the source code, and add a new Swift file called `Van.swift`. After we add the file, a new dialog appears asking whether you would like to create a bridge file. Click on **Yes**; otherwise, you have to create a header file yourself:

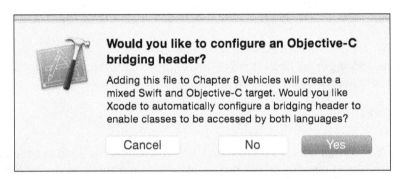

2. Once you have accepted it, go to build settings, type `bridging` in the search field, and check whether there is a file set in the **Objective-C Bridging Header** option:

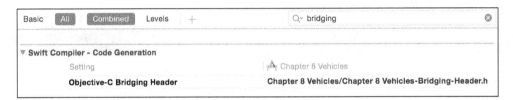

3. After this, check whether there is a new file in the project navigator called `Chapter 8 Vehicles-Bridge-Header.h`, and that its contents are basically empty (only a few comments). Then import the `Car.h` file:

```
#import "Car.h"
```

4. Now, click on `Car.h` and add the last modification. Let's create a property called `image`; this way, we can differentiate a car from a van. Use the following code:

```
@property (strong) UIImage * image;
```

5. You are going to receive an error because `Car.h` doesn't import UIKit, so go to the top of this file and add the following import instruction:

```
#import <UIKit/UIKit.h>
```

6. After this, you will have to click on `Car.m` to initialize this new property, so add the following code in both the initializers:

```
self.image = [UIImage imageNamed:@"car.png"];
```

7. Now, we can click on the Swift file and create a class that represents a van. In this case, we will add an attribute called `capacity`, which will represent the space measured in square meters, and as you may imagine, this class will be a subclass of a car:

```
class Van: Car {
    var capacity:Int;

    override init(){
        self.capacity = 10
        super.init()
        self.image = UIImage(named: "van.png")
    }

    override init(fare: Float){
        self.capacity = 10
        super.init(fare: fare)
        self.image = UIImage(named: "van.png")
    }

}
```

8. As you can see, we need two images to help the user visualize when it is a car and when it is a van. Drag the corresponding images from the `resources` folder of this book into the `Supporting Files` group.

9. It's obvious that we can't stop here. We have to change the view controller so that the new class can be represented with its specific information. Click on the `ViewController.m` file and make these changes. First, change the `cellForRowAtIndexPath` method, it will be displayed in a more complete way. The code is as follows:

```
- (UITableViewCell *)tableView:(UITableView *)tableView
  cellForRowAtIndexPath:(NSIndexPath *)indexPath{
    UITableViewCell * cell;
    cell = [self->tableView
      dequeueReusableCellWithIdentifier:@"vehiclecell"];
    if(cell == nil) {
        cell = [[UITableViewCell alloc]
          initWithStyle:UITableViewCellStyleSubtitle
          reuseIdentifier:@"vehiclecell"];
    cell.textLabel.numberOfLines = 1;
    }
```

```objectivec
Car * currentCar = self->vehicles[indexPath.row];

cell.textLabel.text = [NSString
    stringWithFormat:@"Distance %.3f meters",
    currentCar.distance];
NSString * detailText = detailText = [NSString
    stringWithFormat:@"Pax: %d Fare: %.2f",
    currentCar.pax, [currentCar getFare] ];
if ([currentCar isKindOfClass:[Van class]]) {
    detailText = [NSString stringWithFormat:@"%@,
        Volume: %ld",detailText,
        (long)[(Van*)currentCar capacity]];
}
cell.detailTextLabel.text = detailText;
cell.imageView.image = currentCar.image;
return cell;
}
```

10. Now the compiler is going to complain about the `Van` class, the reason is that you need to import it. How can we import a Swift file in Objective-C? The answer is very simple; just import a file with your project name and concatenate the `-Swift.h` suffix. If your project has whitespace in its name, replace it with underscores as follows:

```objectivec
#import "Chapter_8_Vehicles-Swift.h"
```

11. Then, you have to add one more element to the `vehicles` array, so go to `viewDidLoad` and add a `van` object after `car4`:

```objectivec
- (void)viewDidLoad {
    [super viewDidLoad];
    Car * car1 = [[Car alloc] init];
    car1.distance = 1.2;
    Car * car2 = [[Car alloc] init];
    car2.distance = 0.5;
    Car * car3 = [[Car alloc] init];
    car3.distance = 5;
    Car * car4 = [[Car alloc] initWithFare:0.25];
    car4.distance = 4;
    Van * van = [[Van alloc] initWithFare:0.32];
    van.distance = 3.8;
    vehicles = @[car1, car2, car3, car4, van];
    [self->tableView reloadData];
}
```

Now our first migration is done. Click on play, and you will see that your application is still working, but with the possibility of hiring a van:

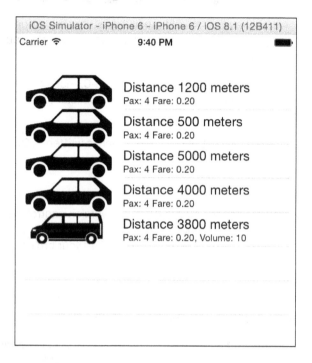

iOS Simulator - iPhone 6 - iPhone 6 / iOS 8.1 (12B411)

Carrier 📶   9:40 PM

Distance 1200 meters
Pax: 4 Fare: 0.20

Distance 500 meters
Pax: 4 Fare: 0.20

Distance 5000 meters
Pax: 4 Fare: 0.20

Distance 4000 meters
Pax: 4 Fare: 0.20

Distance 3800 meters
Pax: 4 Fare: 0.20, Volume: 10

How it works...

When you mix Swift with Objective-C and are using the Swift code into the Objective-C part, you have to create a bridge file. Usually, you are guided by a wizard that creates the bridge file and sets it into the build settings, but bear in mind that you may need to create the file if the wizard doesn't appear.

You have to import every header file that you want to use in Swift; in this case, you had to import `Car.h`.

Swift classes can inherit from Objective-C classes; however, the opposite is not allowed, which means that if you start adding the Swift code to your project, you can be sure that you are not going to continue developing classes with Objective-C.

As you've just seen, you can treat the Swift class as an Objective-C class, even if you need to use methods such as `isKindOfClass`. The Objective-C is also converted to Swift, along with its philosophy, such as creating an initializer in this manner: `init(fare:Float)` when in Objective-C, its original name was `initWithFare`.

Porting from one language to another

In the previous recipe, we learned how to add a new code into an existing Objective-C project. However, you shouldn't only add new code, but also, as far as possible, you should migrate your old code to the new Swift language.

If you would like to keep your application core on Objective-C, that's ok, but remember that the new features are going to be added to Swift, and it will be difficult to keep two languages in the same project.

In this recipe, we are going to port part of the code, which is written in Objective-C to Swift.

Getting ready

Make a copy of the previous recipe. If you are using any version control system, this is a good time to commit your changes. If you are not using a version control system, check *Chapter 1, Getting Started with Xcode and Swift*, to see how to add it to your project.

How to do it...

To port your code from one Objective-C to Swift, follow these steps:

1. Open the project and add a new file called `Setup.swift`. Here, we are going to add a new class with the same name (`Setup`), as shown here:

```
@objc class Setup {
    class func generate() -> [Car] {
        var result = [Car]()
        for distance in [1.2, 0.5, 5.0] {
            var car = Car()
            car.distance = Float(distance)
            result.append(car)
        }
        var car = Car()
        car.distance = 4
        var van = Van()
        van.distance = 3.8
        result += [car, van]
        return result
    }
}
```

2. Now that we have this `car` array generator, we can call it on the `viewDidLoad` method to replace the previous code:

```
- (void)viewDidLoad {
    [super viewDidLoad];
    vehicles = [Setup generate];
    [self->tableView reloadData];
}
```

Again, press play and check whether the application is still working.

How it works...

The reason we had to create a class instead of creating a function is that you can only export protocols, properties, and subscripts to Objective-C classes. Bear this in mind when developing a project with the two languages.

If you would like to export a class to Objective-C, you have two choices: the first one is to inherit from `NSObject` and the other one is to add the `@objc` attribute before your class, protocol, property, or subscript.

If you were paying attention you will have seen that, our method returns a Swift array, but it was converted to `NSArray`. You might as well know that there are different kinds of arrays. Firstly, because Swift arrays are mutable and `NSArray` is not, and the other reason is that their methods are different.

Can we use `NSArray` in Swift? The answer is yes, but I would recommend that you avoid it. Imagine that you have finished migrating your project to Swift, but your code still follows the old way. It would mean another migration.

There's more...

Migrating from Objective-C is something that you should do with care. Don't try to change the whole application at once. Remember that some Swift objects behave differently from Objective-C, for example, dictionaries in Swift have the key and the value types specified but in Objective-C, they can be of any type.

In the next recipe, we are going to replace the graphical components, such as the view controller.

Replacing the UI classes

At this moment, you know how to migrate the model part of an application. However, in real life, we also have to replace the graphical classes. Doing this is not complicated, but this could include a bit full of details.

Getting ready

Continuing with the previous recipe, make a copy of it or just commit the changes you have and let's continue with our migration.

How to do it...

Now, follow these steps to replace the UI classes:

1. First, create a new file called `MainViewController.swift` and start importing UIKit:

   ```
   import UIKit
   ```

2. The next step is to create a class called `MainViewController`. This class must inherit from `UIViewController` and implement the `UITableViewDataSource` and `UITableViewDelegate` protocols:

   ```
   class MainViewController:UIViewController
     ,UITableViewDataSource, UITableViewDelegate {
   ```

3. Then, add the attributes we had in the previous view controller. Keep the same name you used before:

   ```
   private var vehicles = [Car]()
   @IBOutlet var tableView:UITableView!
   ```

4. Next, we need to implement the methods. Let's start with the table view data source method:

   ```
   func tableView(tableView: UITableView,
     numberOfRowsInSection section: Int) -> Int{
       return vehicles.count
   }

   func tableView(tableView: UITableView,
     cellForRowAtIndexPath indexPath: NSIndexPath) ->
     UITableViewCell{
       var cell:UITableViewCell? =
         self.tableView.dequeueReusableCellWithIdentifier
         ("vehiclecell") as? UITableViewCell
   ```

```
if cell == nil {
    cell = UITableViewCell(style: .Subtitle,
        reuseIdentifier: "vehiclecell")
}
var currentCar = self.vehicles[indexPath.row]
cell!.textLabel?.numberOfLines = 1
cell!.textLabel?.text = "Distance
  \(currentCar.distance * 1000) meters"
var detailText = "Pax: \(currentCar.pax) Fare:
  \(currentCar.fare)"
if  currentCar is Van{
    detailText += ", Volume: \( (currentCar as
        Van).capacity)"
}
cell!.detailTextLabel?.text = detailText
cell!.imageView?.image = currentCar.image
return cell!
}
```

 Ensure that this conversion is not 100 percent equivalent; the fare, for example, isn't going to be shown with two digits of precision. There is an explanation as to why we are not going to fix this now and afterwards.

5. The next step is to add the event. In this case, we have to do the same action that is done when the user selects a car:

```
func tableView(tableView: UITableView,
  willSelectRowAtIndexPath indexPath:
  NSIndexPath) -> NSIndexPath? {
    var currentCar = self.vehicles[indexPath.row]
    var time = currentCar.distance / 50.0 * 60.0
    UIAlertView(title: "Car booked", message:
      "The car will arrive in \(time) minutes",
        delegate: nil, cancelButtonTitle: "OK").show()
    return indexPath
}
```

6. As you can see, we need only one more step to complete our code. In this case, it's about the `viewDidLoad` function. Note that another difference between Objective-C and Swift is that in Swift, you have to specify that you are overloading an existing method:

```
override func viewDidLoad() {
    super.viewDidLoad()
    vehicles = Setup.generate()
```

```
          self.tableView.reloadData()
     }
} // end of class
```

7. Our code is complete, but of course our application is still using the old code. To complete this operation, click on the storyboard. If the document outline isn't being displayed, go to **Edit | Show Document Outline**, as shown in the following screenshot:

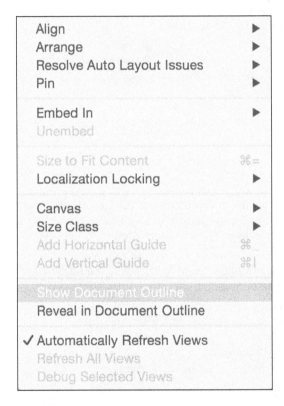

8. Now that you can see the document outline, click on the view controller, which appears as a yellow circle with a square inside, as shown here:

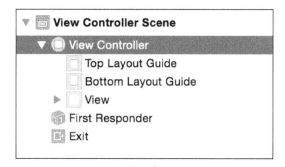

9. Then, on the right-hand side, click on the Identity inspector. Next, go to the custom class and change the value of the class from `ViewController` to `MainViewController`, as shown here:

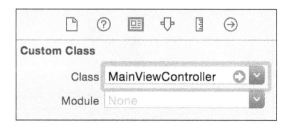

10. After this, click on play and check whether your application is running. Select a car and check whether it is working. Ensure that it is working with your new Swift class by paying attention to the fare value, which in this case isn't shown with two digits of precision. The following screenshot shows a similar fare value:

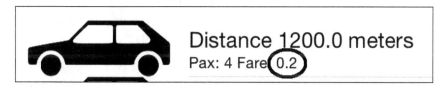

Is everything done? I would say no; it's a good time to commit your changes. Lastly, delete the original Objective-C files because you won't need them anymore.

How it works...

As you can see, it's not so hard to replace an old view controller with a Swift one. The first thing you need to do is to create a new view controller class with its protocols. Keep the same names you had on your old code for attributes and methods that are linked as `IBActions`. This will make the switch very straightforward; otherwise, you will have to link them again.

Bear in mind that you need to be sure your changes are applied and that they are working, but sometimes it's a good idea to try something different, otherwise your application would be using the old Objective-C, and you wouldn't even realize it.

> Try to modernize our code using the Swift way instead of the old Objective-C style, for example, nowadays it's preferable to use interpolation rather than using `stringWithFormat`.

We also learned that you don't need to relink any action or outlet if you keep the same name. If you want to change the name of anything, you might first keep its original name, test your app, and after that, you can refactor it following the traditional factoring steps.

> Don't delete the original Objective-C files until you are sure that the equivalent Swift file is working on the particular functionality.

There's more...

This application had only one view controller; however, applications usually have more than one view controller. In this case, the best way to update is by updating the controllers one by one, instead of all of them at the same time.

Upgrading the app delegate

As you know, there is an object that controls the events of an application called application delegate. Usually, you shouldn't have much code here, but you might have a few of them. For example, you may deactivate the camera or the GPS requests when your application goes to the background, and reactivate them when the app returns active.

Certainly, it's a good idea to update this file even if it doesn't have any new code in it. This will avoid any issues cropping up in the future.

Getting ready

If you are using the version control system, commit your changes from the last recipe or if you prefer, just copy your application.

How to do it...

To upgrade the app delegate, follow these steps:

1. Open the previous application recipe, and create a new Swift file called `ApplicationDelegate.swift`, then you can create a class with the same name.

2. As in our previous class, we didn't have any code for the application delegate, so we can differentiate it by printing on the log console. So, add this traditional application delegate to your Swift file:

```swift
class ApplicationDelegate: UIResponder,
  UIApplicationDelegate {
    var window: UIWindow?

    func application(application: UIApplication,
      didFinishLaunchingWithOptions launchOptions:
      [NSObject: AnyObject]?) -> Bool {
        println("didFinishLaunchingWithOptions")
        return true
    }

    func applicationWillResignActive(application:
      UIApplication) {
        println("applicationWillResignActive")
    }

    func applicationDidEnterBackground(application:
      UIApplication) {
        println("applicationDidEnterBackground")
    }

    func applicationWillEnterForeground(application:
      UIApplication) {
        println("applicationWillEnterForeground")
    }

    func applicationDidBecomeActive(application:
      UIApplication) {
        println("applicationDidBecomeActive")
    }

    func applicationWillTerminate(application:
      UIApplication) {
        println("applicationWillTerminate")
    }
}
```

3. Now, go to your project navigator and expand the `Supporting Files` group. After this, click on the `main.m` file, as shown here:

4. In this file, we are going to import the magic file, the Swift header file:

```
#import "Chapter_8_Vehicles-Swift.h"
```

5. We have to specify whether the application delegate is the new class we have, so replace the `AppDelegate` class in the `UIApplicationMain` call with `ApplicationDelegate`. Your main function should look like this:

```
int main(int argc, char * argv[]) {
    @autoreleasepool {
        return UIApplicationMain(argc, argv, nil,
            NSStringFromClass([ApplicationDelegate class]));
    }
}
```

6. It's time to click on play and check whether the application is working or not. Click on the *Home* button or the combination of the *shift* + *command* + *H* keys if you are using the simulator and open your application again. Ensure that you have some messages on your log console, as shown here:

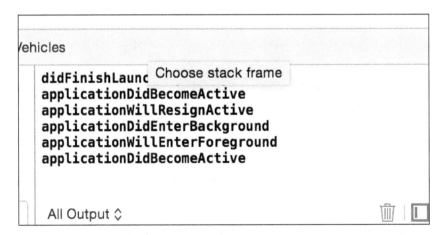

7. Now that you are sure that your Swift code is working, remove the original app delegate and its importation in `main.m`. Test your app just in case.

8. You could consider that we have finished this part, but actually, we still have another step to do: to remove the `main.m` file. Now this is very easy. Just click on the `ApplicationDelegate.swift` file and before the class declaration, add the `@ UIApplicationMain` attribute, then right-click on `main.h` and choose to delete it. Test it and your application is done.

How it works...

The application delegate is always a class that is specified at the start point of an application. In Objective-C, it follows the C start point, which is a function called `main`. In iOS, you can specify the class that you want to use as an application delegate.

 If you program for OS X, the procedure is different. You have to go to your `nib` file and change its class name to the new one.

Why did we have to change the `main` function and then eliminate it? The reason is that you should avoid massive changes; if something goes wrong, you won't know the step where you failed, so probably you will have to roll back everything again. If you do your migration step by step ensuring that it is still working, which means checking in case you find an error, it will be easier to solve it.

 Avoid making massive changes to your project, changing step by step will be easier to solve issues.

There's more...

In this recipe, we learned how to migrate an app from Objective-C to Swift code; however, we have to remember that programming is not only about applications, you can also have a framework. In the next recipe, we are going to learn how to create our own framework that is compatible with Swift and Objective-C.

Creating a framework

As you know, sometimes we have code that is meant to be shared between an application, and the best way to do this is to create a framework. In this case, we are going to create a framework which should contain a customized view. For this recipe, we are going to add only one view. This view will be painted with a gradient. This way, you can change your application's background easily.

Getting ready

Create a new project called `CustomViewsFramework`. To do this, go to **File | New | Project**, and then choose the **Framework and Library** section. Click on the **Cocoa Touch Framework** option, as shown in the following screenshot:

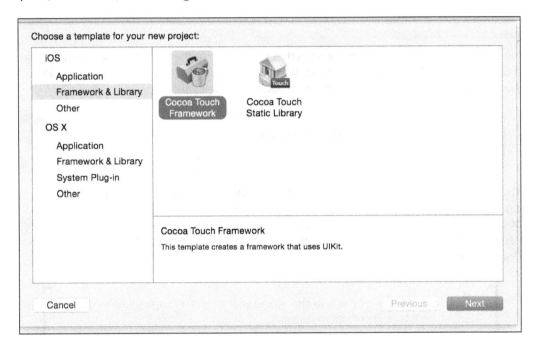

Select **Swift** as the project language.

How to do it...

Now, follow these steps to create a framework:

1. Start adding a new file to your project. In this case, you can choose the **Cocoa Touch Class** option from the **Source** section, as shown here:

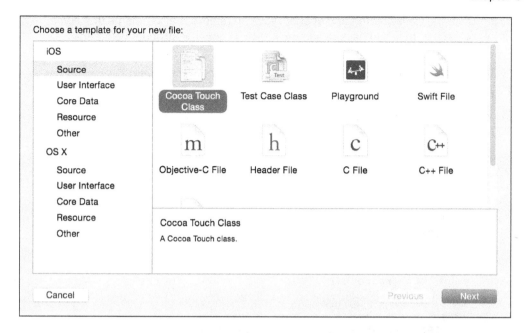

2. Now you have to write the new class name, let's call it CVGradientView. Also make sure that a subclass of UIView is selected and its language is Swift, as shown here:

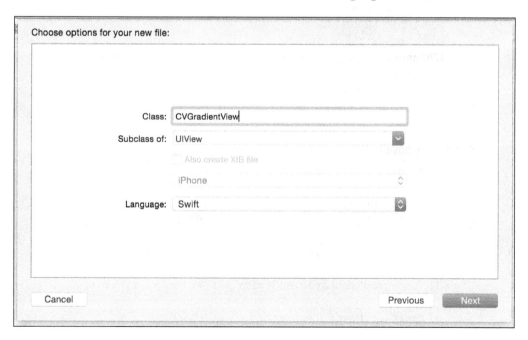

3. Once the file is created and opened, you can remove the comments that come by default, then you have to add the `@IBDesignable` attribute before the class declaration:

```
@IBDesignable public class CVGradientView: UIView {
```

4. Now we need to add some attributes. In this case, we will use properties with an observer, which will refresh the gradient view every time a property is changed:

```
@IBInspectable public var color1: UIColor =
  UIColor.redColor() {
    didSet{
        refresh()
    }
}
@IBInspectable public var color2: UIColor =
  UIColor.blackColor(){
    didSet{
        refresh()
    }
}
@IBInspectable public var roundCorners: CGFloat = 1.0
  {
    didSet{
        refresh()
    }
}
@IBInspectable public var horizontal: Bool = false {
    didSet{
        refresh()
    }
}
```

5. As you may have noticed, we may have to implement the refresh method:

```
private func refresh(){
    let colors:Array = [color1.CGColor, color2.CGColor]
    gradientLayer.colors = colors
    gradientLayer.cornerRadius = roundCorners
    if (horizontal){
        gradientLayer.endPoint = CGPoint(x: 1, y: 0)
    }else{
        gradientLayer.endPoint = CGPoint(x: 0, y: 1)
    }
    self.setNeedsDisplay()
}
```

6. Then, we need to specify some information about the gradient layer. This information is specified by following the Core Animation framework:

```
var gradientLayer: CAGradientLayer {
    return layer as CAGradientLayer
}
override public class func layerClass()->AnyClass{
    return CAGradientLayer.self
}
```

7. Now we need the last part of this method, which are the initializers:

```
override init(frame: CGRect) {
    super.init(frame: frame)
    refresh()
}

required public init(coder aDecoder: NSCoder) {
    super.init(coder: aDecoder)
    refresh()
}
}
```

8. Once it's done, we need to identify our module by going to our target build settings and searching for the word `module`. Now change the module identifier to `CustomViewsFrameWork`:

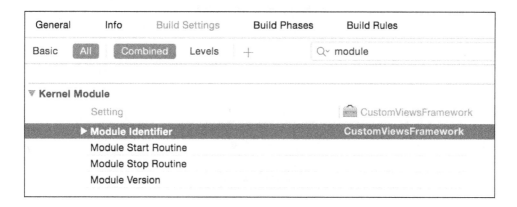

9. The class is complete, so generate the project with *command + B*. Now, we need to check whether it is working. Let's create another project called Chapter 8 Testing Views. Once it's created, click on the project in the project navigator, then click on the target **Chapter 8 Testing Views**.

10. Here, you have to click on the **Build Settings** tab, and change the **Embedded Content Contains Swift Code** field to **Yes**, as shown in the following screenshot:

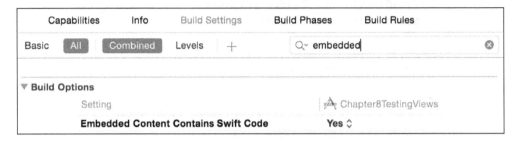

11. Next, click on the **General** tab and go to the **Embedded** Binaries section. Click on the plus button, and when a dialog appears, just click on the button with the phrase **Add other...**. Here, it is asking for your framework, so go to the built product of your framework (it should be inside a folder called `DerivedData/ CustomsViewsFramework/Build/Products/Debug-iphonesimulator/`), select it (the file called `CustomsViewsFramework.framework`) and click on **OK**. The **Linked Frameworks and Libraries** section will also show this, as is evident from the following screenshot:

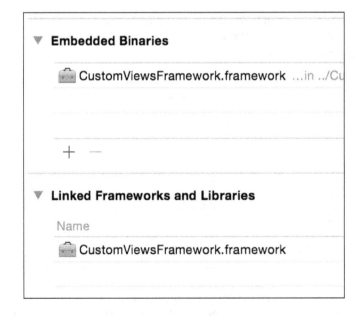

12. Good. Now that your app knows about this framework, you can click on the storyboard. Then, click on the only view you have (not on the view controller), go to the Identity inspector, and change the **Class** field to `CVGradientView` and its **Module** field to `CustomViewsFramework`, as shown here:

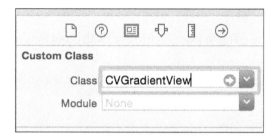

13. Click on play and check whether your background has changed. If you want you can even change your background programmatically; just click on the view controller file and start importing our framework. Here is the code statement:

```
import CustomViewsFramework
```

14. After this, change the background colors in the `viewDidLoad` method:

```
override func viewDidLoad() {
    super.viewDidLoad()
    (self.view as CVGradientView).color1 =
      UIColor.blueColor()
    (self.view as CVGradientView).color2 =
      UIColor.purpleColor()
}
```

Click on play again and see whether your background is different.

How it works...

The reason we called this project different from the others is that frameworks can't have white spaces in their names. In case of creating a project with white spaces in its name, you have to go to the **Build Settings** tab, and change the product name to something without white spaces.

The `@IBDesignable` attribute lets Interface Builder know that it should render the view directly in the canvas, but remember that this attribute can only be used if you are developing a framework; it won't work on traditional applications.

The other attribute (`@IBInspectable`) means that this property can be viewed and set by Interface Builder.

Note that we had to mark our class and some attributes and methods as public. The reason is that we want them to be accessed by external modules. If we don't do this, it means that only our framework can access this class.

There's more...

In the next chapter, we are going to learn how to deal with other languages.

9

Dealing with Other Languages

In this chapter, we will cover the following topics:

- ▶ Using your old address book
- ▶ Compressing a message
- ▶ Using assembly code with Swift
- ▶ Sharing C++ code with Swift

Introduction

Swift is a new language in a world of libraries that are already complete. Sometimes you need the help of other languages, without which you might need to spend a lot of time creating the functionalities that you want.

As you might know, since the seventies, C is the default language independently of the platform you want to develop on. There are thousands or maybe millions of libraries written in C, and you can find a lot of them that are open source, which makes it easier to port them to your iOS or Mac OS project.

In this chapter, you will learn how to use external languages on a Swift project. Here, we are going to see how to use C, C++, and even assembly code.

Using your old address book

In this recipe, we will learn how to use C code inside a Swift project. In this case, let's imagine that we want to recycle one linked list of an address book written in C, this way, we can read the contact from the device's address book and store it into a file. The advantage of storing structures on a file is that you can open the same file using other platforms that don't have Swift, such as Linux or Windows.

Getting ready

Create a new project called `Chapter 9 Address Book`, and ensure that this project is a Swift project.

We can see that the new file will be created inside an application subfolder. As you know, we can't see any device application folders without using a third-party application. In this case, we will download an application called iFunBox, which can explore our device files. This application can be downloaded for free from `http://www.i-funbox.com/`. However, if you prefer, there are other free apps and commercial apps like iBrowser and iPad Folder.

 Downloading iFunBox is only necessary if you are going to use a physical device; if you are going to use just the simulator, you can use a traditional finder window.

How to do it...

1. The first step we need to follow is to add a new file. In this case, you should select a **C file**:

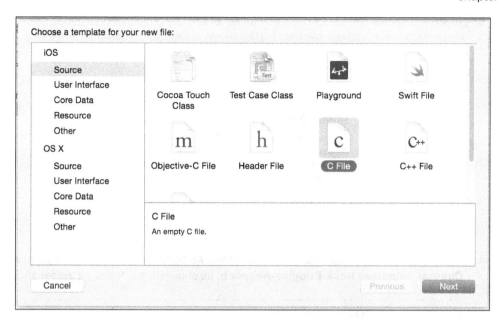

2. Then, it will ask for the filename; let's call it `AddressBook.c` and ensure that the option **Also create a header file** is checked:

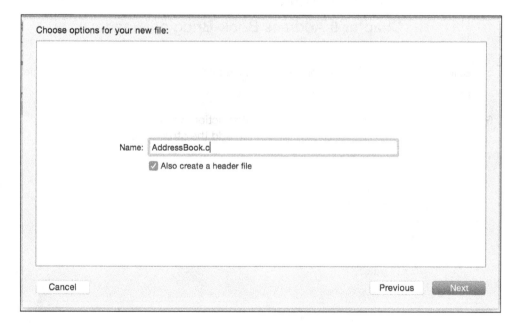

3. To store this new file, select the same folder where the project source codes are stored. After this, you will see that it asks you to create an Objective-C bridge file, click on **Yes**.

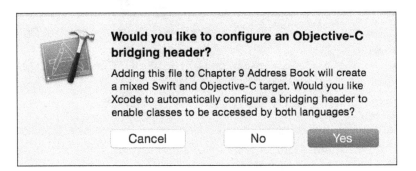

4. Now you can see that there are three new files: **AddressBook.c**, **AddressBook.h**, and **Chapter 9 Address Book-Bridging-Header.h**, as shown in the following screenshot:

5. Before coding, start clicking on the bridge file and import the `AddressBook.h` file:

```
#import "AddressBook.h"
```

6. Now go to the `AddressBook.h` file. The first action we need to take here is to remove the `stdio.h include`. After that, add the structs that are going to be used on our application:

```
struct Contact {
    char name[60];
    char phone[20];
    struct date {
        int day;
        int month;
        int year;
    } birthday;
};

struct ContactList {
```

```
    struct Contact contact;
    struct ContactList * next;
};
```

7. Once the structures and other types are defined, we will add the function headers of the operations that can be made with our contact list. For this, create a new contact, initialize the list, destroy the list, add a new contact and save the contacts list into a file as follows:

```
struct Contact createContact();
void initializeContactList(struct ContactList ** );
void insertContact(struct ContactList **, struct Contact);
void saveContactList(struct ContactList *, const char *);
void destroyContactList(struct ContactList **);
```

8. The header file is now complete. If you wish to complete it with more operations, such as finding a contact on the list or deleting a contact, feel free to do so. Now, let's go to the implementation file (AddressBook.c) and code the operations. Don't worry if you don't understand this code: usually when you are using C code into Swift, you only need to understand what the operation does by reading its header.

```
struct Contact createContact(){
    struct Contact newContact;
    strcpy(newContact.name, "");
    strcpy(newContact.phone, "");
    newContact.birthday.day = 0;
    newContact.birthday.month = 0;
    newContact.birthday.year = 0;
    return newContact;
}

void initializeContactList(struct ContactList **
  contactList ){
    *contactList = NULL;
}

void insertContact(struct ContactList ** contactList, struct
Contact contact){
    struct ContactList * newContactList =
      malloc(sizeof(struct ContactList));
    newContactList->next = *contactList;
    newContactList->contact = contact;
    *contactList = newContactList;
}

void saveContactList(struct ContactList * contactList,
  const char * filename){
```

```
        FILE * file = fopen(filename, "wb");
        if (file) {
            while (contactList) {
                fwrite(&contactList->contact, sizeof(struct
                    Contact), 1, file);
                contactList = contactList->next;
            }
            fclose(file);
        }
    }

    void destroyContactList(struct ContactList ** contactList){
        struct ContactList * aux;
        while ((aux = *contactList)) {
            *contactList = (*contactList)->next;
            free(aux);
        }
    }
```

9. The C part is done, so now you can return to the method we used to create our apps, by clicking on the storyboard and adding two buttons: one for loading the contacts and another one for saving the contacts to a file. Link the first button with a function called `fillContacts` and the other one with a function called `saveContacts`. Don't implement anything yet, we will return to these functions soon.

10. As we need to read the contacts from the device address book, we need to add them into our project. So click on the project on the project navigator, then ensure that the **General Info** tab of the target **Chapter 9 AddressBook** is selected. Here you have to scroll down to **Linked Frameworks and Libraries** and add the framework `AddressBook`:

11. Return to the view controller, scroll up to the beginning and import the address book.

    ```
    import AddressBook
    ```

12. Inside the view controller class, we will start with the attributes. In this case, we only need a list as a pointer of `ContactList`.

    ```
    var list:UnsafeMutablePointer<ContactList> = nil
    ```

13. Even if we have initialized the list assigning a nil value, we still need to initialize it using the C-specific function and we can do this using the `viewDidLoad` method:

```
override func viewDidLoad() {
    super.viewDidLoad()
    initializeContactList(&list)
}
```

14. As you might have noticed, there is also a function that destroys the list; it means that we need to call it on the deinitializer:

```
deinit{
    destroyContactList(&list)
}
```

15. Now we can implement the button events; let's start with the button that loads the contacts from the device's address book.

 Remember that on iOS and also on OS X you can't read the address book without the user's permission.

```
@IBAction func fillContacts(sender: UIButton) {
    let status = ABAddressBookGetAuthorizationStatus()

    switch status {
    case .Authorized:
        // When the user has already authorized
          previously.
        self.readContacts()
    case .NotDetermined:
        // this case happens when it is the first time
          the user opens the app, so we have to
          request his permission
        var ok = false
        ABAddressBookRequestAccessWithCompletion(nil) {
            (granted:Bool, err:CFError!) in
            if granted {
                self.readContacts()
            }
        }
    case .Restricted:
        fallthrough
    case .Denied:
```

```
            // These cases are when for any reason the app
               can't access the contacts
            UIAlertView(title: "Not authorized", message:
               "This app isn't authorized for reading your
               contacts", delegate: nil,
                  cancelButtonTitle: "OK").show()
         }
      }
```

16. As you can see, there are two calls for the `readContacts` method, so that's the method we need to implement now:

```
      private func readContacts(){
         var err : Unmanaged<CFError>? = nil
         var myAddressBook: ABAddressBook =
            ABAddressBookCreateWithOptions(nil,
            &err).takeRetainedValue()
         let myContacts =
            ABAddressBookCopyArrayOfAllPeople(
               myAddressBook).takeRetainedValue()
               as NSArray as [ABRecord]

         for aContact in myContacts {
            var newContactRecord:Contact = createContact();

            // Retrieving name
            var nameString =
              ABRecordCopyCompositeName(aContact).
                takeRetainedValue() as String
            copyIntoCString(&newContactRecord.name,
              nameString)

            // Retrieving phone
            var phones:ABMultiValue =
              ABRecordCopyValue(aContact,
              kABPersonPhoneProperty).takeRetainedValue()
              as ABMultiValue
            if(ABMultiValueGetCount(phones) > 0){
               var phoneString =
                 ABMultiValueCopyValueAtIndex(phones,
                 0).takeRetainedValue() as String
               copyIntoCString(&newContactRecord.phone,
                 phoneString)
            }
            // Retrieving birthday
```

```
        if let date = ABRecordCopyValue(aContact,
          kABPersonBirthdayProperty).
          takeRetainedValue() as? NSDate {
            var calendar =
              NSCalendar.currentCalendar().
              components(.CalendarUnitDay |
              .CalendarUnitMonth |
              .CalendarUnitYear, fromDate: date)
            newContactRecord.birthday.day =
              Int32(calendar.day)
            newContactRecord.birthday.month =
              Int32(calendar.month)
            newContactRecord.birthday.year =
              Int32(calendar.year)
        }
        insertContact(&list, newContactRecord)
    }
    UIAlertView(title: nil, message: "The contacts were
      loaded", delegate: nil, cancelButtonTitle:
      "OK").show()
}
```

17. Now let's implement the button that saves the contacts onto a file; this one is much easier because we just need to set the full path for the storing file and call the function that saves the contacts:

```
@IBAction func saveContacts(sender: UIButton) {
    var documentDir:NSString =
      NSSearchPathForDirectoriesInDomains(.
      DocumentDirectory, .UserDomainMask, true)[0]
      as NSString
    var filename:NSString =
      documentDir.stringByAppendingPathComponent(
      "contacts.dat") as NSString
    saveContactList(list, filename.UTF8String)
    UIAlertView(title: "Contacts saved", message:
      "contacts.dat was saved.", delegate: nil,
      cancelButtonTitle: "Ok").show()
}
```

18. The application looks finished but if you try compiling it, you will get an error because there is a missing implementation: the `copyIntoCString` function. This is an auxiliary function that you have to create, as you might need it in other projects. Let's implement it on a new file. Create a new file called `CstringUtils.swift` and add the following code to it:

```
func copyIntoCString<T>(inout cstring: T, swiftString:
    String) {
```

```
withUnsafeMutablePointer(&cstring, { (cstr) -> Void in
    let fullSwinftString = swiftString +
      String(UnicodeScalar(0))
    let newCString =
      fullSwinftString.dataUsingEncoding(
      NSUTF8StringEncoding,
      allowLossyConversion: true)!
    newCString.getBytes(cstr, length:
      sizeofValue(cstring))
})
}
```

19. Good. Now the application is complete, but you still need to test it. Press play, accept every permission when requested, and press the button that retrieves the contacts from the address book. When you receive a dialog that the contacts were loaded, you can press the **Save** button. On screen, the only result that you might see is just a dialog, as shown in the following screenshot:

If you think that you didn't receive much visual information, you are 100 percent right, because this app wasn't created to do something visual: rather it was created to generate a file, so let's verify it.

20. If you are using a physical device, open your iFunBox application, which was downloaded at the beginning of this recipe, expand the **User Applications** section and click on your app (**Chapter 9 Address Book**). On the right-hand side, double-click on the document folder and you might see a file called `contacts.dat`.

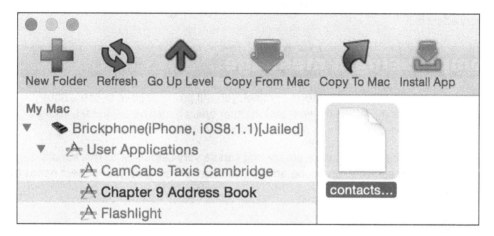

21. You can copy this file if you want, or you can also read this file on another platform; however, this task will be left as homework for you.

How it works...

Although Xcode asks you about creating an Objective-C bridge file, it actually creates a file that can also be a C bridge file. Once your C header files are imported here, you can use them on Swift.

As you might have noticed, C doesn't work with objects; the only thing you can do is create a struct (which doesn't have methods in C) and send it through some functions as arguments.

C types have their equivalent types in Swift by prefixing C to their name such as `CChar`, `CInt`, `CFloat` and so on. The structs just keep their names without the word `struct`, as you can see on the `ContactList` and `Contact`.

Another feature that you have to consider is that C works with pointers. A pointer is an information reference similar to what we had on the contact list. When you have pointers in C, they are converted to `UnsafeMutablePointer` in Swift, double pointers are converted to `UnsafeMutablePointer` of `UnsafeMutablePointer`, and so on; this is the C style of receiving function arguments by reference.

When you want to call a C function that requires an argument by reference, you have to use the & operator; it means that you are sending the memory address of that variable. However, the Swift way of declaring an argument by reference is different: you have to add the attribute `inout` before the argument name.

Using some C types on Swift sometimes requires tricks: for example, C doesn't have a type of strings, and the most similar one is the array of characters, which sometimes is converted as `[CChar]` and sometimes it is converted as a tuple of `UInt8`. If you need to use a C variable without casting it, use the `withUnsafeMutablePointer` function by retrieving its memory address.

Compressing a message

Even if you're only working on an internal project, you will probably have to use a library. Sometimes it may be a Swift framework and at other times it may be a C library. Using C libraries is very common nowadays, mainly because there are a lot of them.

For this recipe, we are going to use a library that can be very useful—BCL. This simple library can be easily compiled on Xcode and you can use it every time your project needs to compress any information.

Getting ready

Before we start with the coding for this project, let's download the BCL library, which can be found at `http://bcl.comli.eu/` and the source code can be downloaded for free. Uncompress the downloaded file and leave its finder window open.

If you are going to install this application into a physical device, you need to download the iFunBox as it was mentioned in the previous recipe.

For this recipe, instead of creating a project, start creating a workspace and call it `Chapter 9 Compressing Workspace`.

How to do it...

1. First you need to create a project, but in this case instead of creating a single view application select **Cocoa Touch Static Library** from the **Framework & Library** section and click on **Next**.

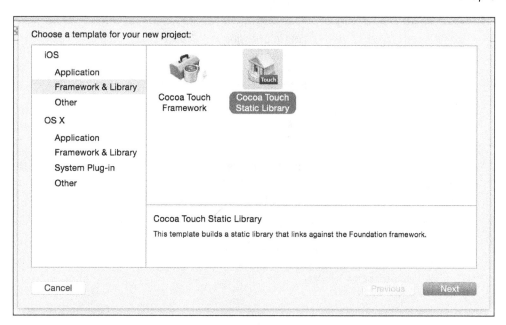

 Selecting **Cocoa Touch Static Library** implies developing it in C, C++, or Objective-C. Swift doesn't have a static library.

2. Now, call your project `Chapter 9 BCL`. Note that it is not asking whether it is a Swift project.

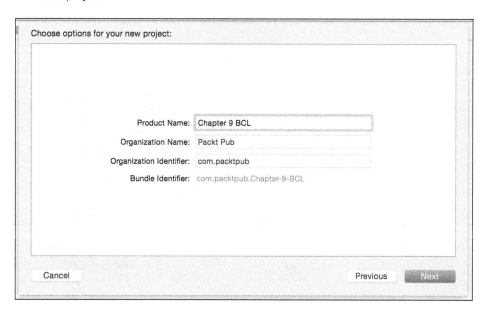

3. On the next screen, you have to select the destination folder where the project is going to be stored. However, before pressing the **Create** button, ensure that this project belongs to your workspace.

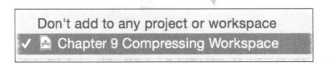

4. You can see that this project starts with two source code files: `Chapter_9_BCL.h` and `Chapter_9_BCL.m`. Delete them as they are not needed. While deleting, you can move them to trash instead of only removing the reference.

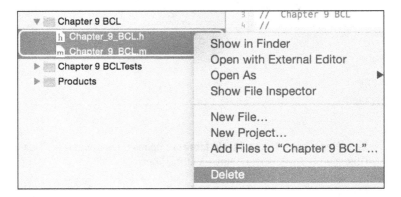

5. Now, drag the files that ends with `.c` and `.h` from the BCL library (located at the `src` folder) into you source code group.

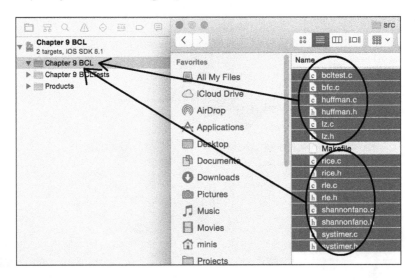

Actually, you don't need to copy the file `bcltest.c` and `bcl.c` because they belong to BCL as a program and not as a library, but copying them will make life easier.

6. Although you have the necessary files to build the library, you still need to indicate the header files that should be used externally. This is a procedure that you have to perform every time you build a library written in C, C++, or Objective-C. To do this, select the **Build Phases** tab from the target **Chapter 9 BCL**, after that expand the section **Copy Files**.

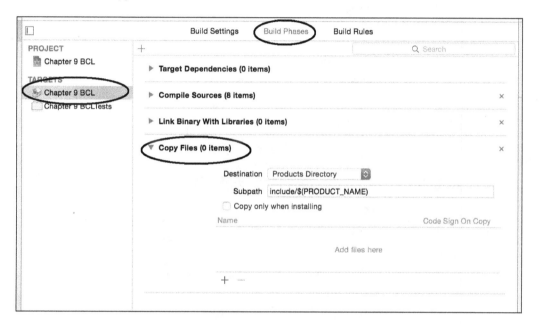

7. Now, click on the **+** icon at the bottom of this section. A new dialog will appear showing that the files can be exported; select only the header files such as `huffman.h`, `shannonfano.h`, `rle.h`, and so on.

 Remember that you can select more than one file by holding the *command* key and clicking over the files.

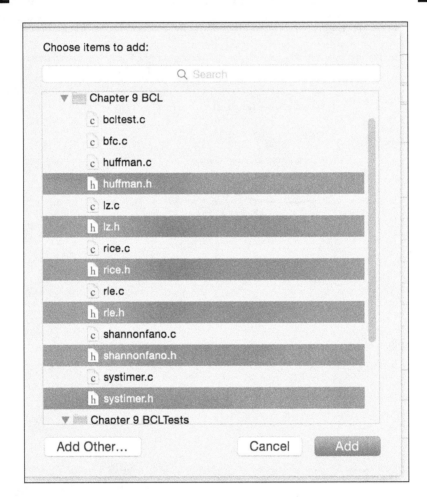

8. The library is now done. You need to check whether everything is **OK** by pressing *command+B*, this will show a message saying that the build has succeeded.

9. The next part of this recipe is creating an app that compresses a user message. To do this, don't close your project and then create a new project. This time, instead of a static library, select a single view application done with Swift and call it `Chapter 9 BCLApp`. Here, it is very important that you add this project to the workspace and group `Chapter 9 Compressing Workspace`.

10. Pay attention to the fact that we now have two projects. Ensure that the app is selected by clicking on it, then click on the target **Chapter 9 BCLApp** and select the **General Info** tab. Scroll down until you reach the **Linked Framework and Libraries** section, expand it if necessary and click on the **+** icon.

11. A dialog will appear, but this time with a new group called **Workspace**, where you have to select **libChapter 9 BCL.a**.

 The static libraries always have the prefix `lib` and the extension `.a` to their names.

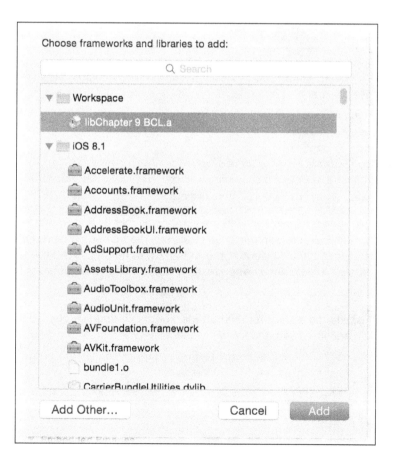

Choose frameworks and libraries to add:

Q Search

▼ Workspace
    libChapter 9 BCL.a

▼ iOS 8.1
    Accelerate.framework
    Accounts.framework
    AddressBook.framework
    AddressBookUI.framework
    AdSupport.framework
    AssetsLibrary.framework
    AudioToolbox.framework
    AudioUnit.framework
    AVFoundation.framework
    AVKit.framework
    bundle1.o
    CarrierBundleUtilities.dylib

Add Other...   Cancel   Add

12. Once you add the library, you will need to add a new header file to your project, let's call this file `BridgeHeader.h`.

13. Before we start coding this file, let's set this file as the bridge file for the app. For this, go to the **Build Settings** of your app, write `Bridging` on the search box, and once you find the **Objective-C Bridging Header** field, write `Chapter 9 BCLApp/BridgeHeader.h`.

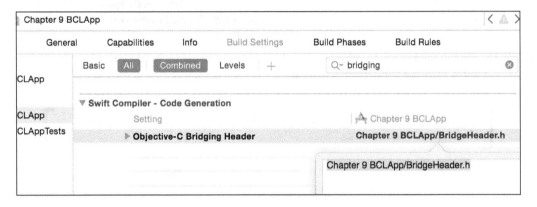

14. Let's return to `BridgeHead.h` and add a few `include` statements for using the compression library:

```
#include <Chapter 9 BCL/huffman.h>
#include <Chapter 9 BCL/lz.h>
#include <Chapter 9 BCL/rice.h>
#include <Chapter 9 BCL/rle.h>
#include <Chapter 9 BCL/shannonfano.h>
#include <Chapter 9 BCL/systimer.h>
```

15. The application is now linked with the library; this means that from now on, you can return to Swift programming. Go to the storyboard and add a text view and two buttons. Usually, the text views come with a text by default, and if you want you can leave this as it will be handy when testing. Link the text view naming it as `textView`:

```
@IBOutlet var textView: UITextView!
```

16. After this, add the actions for the buttons. For the first button, change its label to `Huffman` and link it with the following action:

```
@IBAction func huffman(sender: UIButton) {
    let text = self.textView.text
    let textIn:UnsafeMutablePointer<UInt8> =
        UnsafeMutablePointer<UInt8>((text as
        NSString).UTF8String)
```

```
     let textOut:UnsafeMutablePointer<UInt8> =
     UnsafeMutablePointer<UInt8>.
     alloc(countElements(text) * 101 / 100 + 320)
     let outsize = Huffman_Compress(textIn, textOut,
       UInt32( countElements(text)))
     save("huffman.dat", data: textOut, dataSize:
       Int(outsize))
   }
```

17. With the second button, you can do the same. Change its label to LZ and link it with a similar code:

```
@IBAction func lz(sender: UIButton) {

   let text = self.textView.text

   let textIn:UnsafeMutablePointer<UInt8> =
     UnsafeMutablePointer<UInt8>((text as
     NSString).UTF8String)

   let textOut:UnsafeMutablePointer<UInt8> =
     UnsafeMutablePointer<UInt8>.alloc(
     countElements(text) * 257 / 256 + 1)

   let outsize = LZ_Compress(textIn, textOut, UInt32(
     countElements(text)))

   save("lz.dat", data: textOut, dataSize:
     Int(outsize))

}
```

18. The last step, as you might imagine, is implementing the save function, which can be as easy as this code:

```
private func save(filename: String, data:
   UnsafePointer<UInt8>, dataSize: Int){
   let nsData = NSData(bytes: data, length: dataSize)
   let path =
     NSSearchPathForDirectoriesInDomains(.
     DocumentDirectory, .UserDomainMask, true)[0] as
     String + "/\(filename)"
   NSFileManager.defaultManager().createFileAtPath(
     path, contents: nsData, attributes: nil)
}
```

19. The application is now complete. However, it is still necessary to test it. To do this, ensure that the app is selected at the schema combo, otherwise nothing will happen when you press play.

20. Now click on play, write a message on the text field and click on the **huffman** button, and then press the **lz** button. Similar to the previous recipe, you won't see anything visually attractive but if you open your iFunBox, expand the app and open the document folder. If you would like to see the files' size without copying them, just click on the list view.

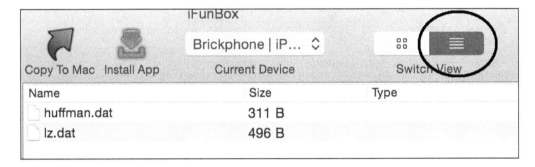

How it works...

When you have a big project you can divide it into small components, and you can divide your project into small projects. A good way of doing this is by creating workspaces.

Workspace is like a connection between projects, making it easy to use one project (in this case, the BCL static library) in the other project (in this case, the application).

 Avoid creating a huge project. Try to divide it into small projects; this will make it easy to maintain your project, to find issues and solutions, and even to create unit tests.

A static library is something that is copied into your project as is, meaning that your project will grow in size but you won't be worried about a library update that can break your app. Every time you create a static library, you must export the header files, which contain the functions that can be used publicly.

 Remember that even if you have a static library on the same workspace, you still need to link it on your project and create a bridge file.

You can also see that we used a new method, `alloc`. The method `alloc` was used to create the C array with a specific size; remember that arrays in C are not resizable and if you want to store anything on them, you must allocate enough memory to it.

There is also a new type: `UnsafePointer`. The reason is that C functions can receive constants or variables as arguments, for example, receiving `const char *` is different from `char *`; the first one is considered an `UnsafePointer` and the second one is `UnsafeMutablePointer`. Unsafe mutable pointers can be casted to unsafe pointers implicitly, but it is not true the other way round.

There's more...

As you can see, there are more compression types in this library. You can try using a few of them to see which one is the best.

In the next recipe, you will learn how to use assembly code with Swift. This feature is very useful if you really need performance.

Using assembly code with Swift

In this recipe, you will learn how to use assembly code with Swift. Of course, nobody develops using only assembly code nowadays, but using it in parts of an app is very common when you need performance. Image manipulation programs, for example, use assembly code as it is much faster when you have to process something using hardware rather than using software.

Obviously, programming with assembly language has its drawbacks. The first drawback is that you might have to rewrite your source code for different processors. For example, if you have an assembly code ready for old iPhones (32 bits ARM processor), you might have to rewrite it for the new devices (64 bits ARM processor), and even after writing both codes, you might have to write your code for the third time if you wish to see your app working on the iPhone simulator (Intel processor).

This time, we will use a very simple code as it is beyond the scope of this book to teach the ARM architecture. In this case, we will create a simple variable swap function.

Getting ready

For this recipe, it is recommended to have a physical device but it is not mandatory, because you can compile the code from the command line specifying the architecture that you want to compile for.

Create a new Swift single view application called Chapter 9 Assembly, add a new file called AssemblyCode.c, and click on **Yes** when Xcode asks for the bridging file.

How to do it...

1. Firstly, click on the bridging header file (Chapter 9 Assembly-Bridging-Header.h) and include the AssemblyCode.h file:

   ```
   #include "AssemblyCode.h"
   ```

2. Then, go to AssemblyCode.h and add the following header:

   ```
   void swap(int * firstnumber, int * secondnumber);
   ```

3. Once the definition is done, code the implementation on AssemblyCode.c. Here, we will use a very simple code that can be used on 32 bits and 64 bits, but bear in mind that you might need to separate them in case of more complex codes:

   ```
   void swap(int * firstnumber, int * secondnumber){
   #if defined __arm64__ || defined __arm__
       asm volatile (
                   "EOR %[first],%[first], %[second] \n\t"
                   "EOR %[second],%[second], %[first] \n\t"
                   "EOR %[first],%[first], %[second] \n\t"
                   : /* outputs */
                     [first] "=r" (*firstnumber),
                     [second] "=r" (*secondnumber)
                   : /* inputs */ [first] "r" (*firstnumber),
                         [second] "r" (*secondnumber)
                   );
   #else
   #error "Architecture not allowed"
   #endif
   }
   ```

4. The assembly part is done; click on the storyboard and create a layout with two labels, two text fields, and a button. Change the labels' text to First Number and Second Number. On the text fields, replace the place holders with some sample numbers and change the button's text to Swap numbers. The final result should be something similar to this:.

5. Click on each text field on the storyboard and change the keyboard type on the attribute inspector to `Number and Punctuations`.

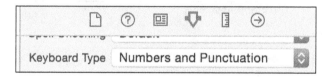

6. After placing the user views into the storyboard, link the text fields with the view controller and call them `firstNumberTextField` and `secondNumberTextField`:

```
@IBOutlet var firstNumberTextField: UITextField!
@IBOutlet var secondNumberTextField: UITextField!
```

7. Then, link the button with the following action:

```
@IBAction func swapNumbers(sender: UIButton) {
    var number1 =
        Int32(self.firstNumberTextField.text.toInt()!)
    var number2 =
        Int32(self.secondNumberTextField.text.toInt()!)
    swap(&number1, &number2)
    self.firstNumberTextField.text = "\(number1)"
    self.secondNumberTextField.text = "\(number2)"
}
```

8. The application is ready, let's test it. First, change the device to iPhone 6 simulator and click on play.

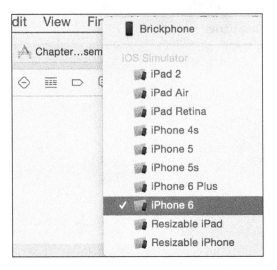

9. If you receive an error message, it's alright. You will see that the message is the same as the one you wrote on the `AssemblyCode.c` file.

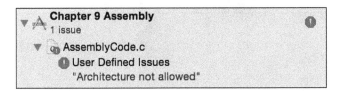

10. Now plug your Apple device into the computer, select it on the active schema, and press play again. You will see the app, so type two different numbers (one on each text field) and press the swap button. The result is that they exchange their text fields.

How it works...

Writing assembly code is something that you need to do in the C or Objective-C layer, meaning that you still need to know how these languages are converted to Swift. Using the `asm volatile` statement allows you to write assembly code. Inside this statement, you have upto four parts delimited by colon, which are as follows:

▸ The first part is a string (only one) that is your assembly template: we haven't written more than one string. In C and Objective-C, if you write two constant strings, they are treated as one. Here, you can specify the variables using `%[assembly variable name]` or `%0`, `%1` and so on.

- ▸ The second part is the output variables. You can name them for your assembly template using square brackets and by specifying the equivalent C variable between parentheses.

- ▸ The third part is the input variables, which work similar to the output variables.

- ▸ The last part (which we haven't used) is called **clobbers**. Clobber registers are registers that have their value modified in the assembly chunk. Compiler will know not to expect that the old register value is preserved.

Take care while writing huge assembly code, debugging it can be very hard.

As discussed earlier, assembly code is platform dependent, meaning that it can be different when you use it on the simulator, on an old Apple device, or when using the new 64 bits device. To differentiate them, you can use the macro __arm__ for 32 bits devices and __arm64__ for new arm devices.

Usually, you will see functions that contain assembly code with the keyword `inline`. This is done because assembly code is used when performance is really necessary, and the programmer is trying to tell the compiler to copy the function code by calling it instead of jumping to the function implementation. Unfortunately, to do this, you have to implement the function on the header file and Swift doesn't accept it.

There's more...

Assembly code is also very interesting when you need to debug an application that was compiled on release configuration. The website at `http://www.peter-cockerell.net/aalp/html/frames.html` is a good source from which to learn about the arm assembly code.

You can also investigate NEON to find out how to work with vectors, double word registers, and so on. If you would like to know even more, you can investigate intrinsics, which are C functions that call arm instructions.

If you are asking yourself how games that require big performance are developed if assembly code is very complicated, the answer is using C++. In the next recipe, we are will use it with Swift.

Sharing C++ code with Swift

If you have some code or an external library written in C++ or Objective-C++, you'll probably be surprised when you receive Apple's note that you can't use C++ on Swift directly, as we did with C or Objective C.

The solution is creating your own wrapper. There are some attempts such as SwiftPP (`https://github.com/sandym/swiftpp`) but they are still very immature. In this recipe, we will see how you can wrap your C++ class to use it on Swift.

In this recipe, we will wrap a C++ XML creator for using it on Swift. Don't worry if you don't know C++, the idea of this recipe is just letting you know how to create this kind of proxy class.

Getting ready

For this recipe, we will need to download a pure C++ library for creating XML files. In this case, the library chosen is PugiXml. So before you start, open your web browser, go to `http://pugixml.org/` (or just google `pugixml`) and uncompress it. After this, create a new Swift single view project called `Chapter 9 Xml Wrapper`.

How to do it...

1. First of all, we will create two project groups; so right-click on the source code group, select **New Group** and call it `Pugi`. Repeat this operation calling the second group `PugiWrapper`.

2. Now return to the pugi source code finder window. Here, open the folder `src`, select all files with the the shortcut *command+A*, and drag them to the group Pugi. Accept the creation of the bridging file when it is requested.

3. Now, go to the `PugiWrapper` group and create a new file. This time, choose **Cocoa Touch Class** from the **iOS source** section. This file should be named `PugiBase` and it must be a subclass of `NSObject`. Ensure that Objective-C is selected as the language.

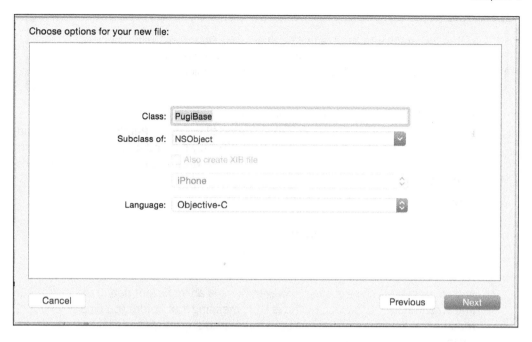

Choose options for your new file:

Class: PugiBase

Subclass of: NSObject

Also create XIB file

iPhone

Language: Objective-C

Cancel   Previous   Next

4. Click on the `PugiBase.h` file, which was just created. Start including the `pugixml.hpp` file if it is being imported from a C++ file.

```
#ifdef __cplusplus
#include "pugixml.hpp"
#endif
Now we can define this class with the following code:
@interface PugiBase : NSObject
@property (nonatomic, assign) void * element;
-(instancetype) init;
@end
```

5. Once this class interface is defined, we can implement it. In this case, only the initializer is necessary by setting the property to NULL:

```
@implementation PugiBase
-(instancetype) init{
    self = [super init];
    if(self){
        self.element = NULL;
    }
    return self;
}
@end
```

Be careful with `NULL` and `nil` when using Objective-C with C or C++. These values are equivalent but not the same. For C and C++, always use `NULL` and check this value before using the object.

6. This class is done, so the next step is to create the first class that will inherit from `PugiBase`. To do this, add a new **Cocoa Touch Class** to the **PugiWrapper** group and call it `PugiNodeAttribute`. For this class, the only method that we will create is the `setValue`. With this knowledge, go to the `PugiNodeAttribute.h` file and add the following code:

```
#import "PugiBase.h"

@interface PugiNodeAttribute : PugiBase
-(void) setValue:(NSString *) value;
@end
```

7. Implementing this class is easy; however, there is an important detail, the implementation of this class will have C++, meaning that before you type anything, rename this file from `PugiNoteAttribute.m` to `PugiNodeAttribute.mm` (Objective-C++ extension).

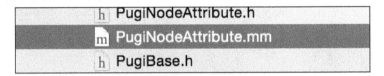

8. Click on the renamed file and complete the class implementation with the following code:

```
@implementation PugiNodeAttribute

-(void) setValue:(NSString *) value{
    if(self.element){
        reinterpret_cast<pugi::xml_attribute
        *>(self.element)->set_value([value
        UTF8String]);
    }
}

@end
```

9. Now that the attribute is done, we can repeat the operation for the node (XML tag). To do this, create a **Cocoa Touch Class** file called `PugiNode`, rename `.m` to `.mm`, go to the header file, and add the following code:

```
#import "PugiBase.h"
#import "PugiNodeAttribute.h"

@interface PugiNode : PugiBase
-(PugiNode*) appendChild:(NSString *) name;
-(PugiNodeAttribute *) appendAttribute:(NSString *) name;
@end
```

10. For the implementation, just add the following code:

```
#import "PugiNode.h"
#import "PugiNodeAttribute.h"

@implementation PugiNode

-(PugiNode*) appendChild:(NSString *) name{
    if (self.element) {
        PugiNode * newNode = [PugiNode new];
        newNode.element = new
          pugi::xml_node(reinterpret_cast<
          pugi::xml_node*>(self.element)-
          >append_child([name UTF8String]));
        return  newNode;
    }
    return nil;
}
-(PugiNodeAttribute *) appendAttribute:(NSString *) name{
    if (self.element){
        PugiNodeAttribute * newAttribute =
          [PugiNodeAttribute new];
        newAttribute.element = new
          pugi::xml_attribute(reinterpret_cast<
          pugi::xml_node*>(self.element)-
          >append_attribute(name.UTF8String));
        return newAttribute;
    }
    return nil;
}

@end
```

11. To finish the wrapper classes, we only need to create another class that represents an XML document. Again, create a new **Cocoa Touch Class** and this time call it `PugiDocument`. Rename the implementation file from `.m` to `.mm` and add the following code into the `.h` file:

```
#import "PugiBase.h"
#import "PugiNode.h"

@interface PugiDocument : PugiBase

-(instancetype) init;
-(PugiNode *) appendChild:(NSString *) name;
-(void) saveFile:(NSString *) path;


@end
```

12. On the implementation file (`PugiDocument.mm`), add the following code:

```
@implementation PugiDocument

-(instancetype) init{
    self = [super init];
    if(self){
        self.element = new pugi::xml_document;
    }
    return self;
}


-(PugiNode *) appendChild:(NSString *) name{
    if(self.element){
        PugiNode * newNode = [PugiNode new];
        newNode.element = new
          pugi::xml_node(reinterpret_cast<
          pugi::xml_document *>(self.element)-
          >append_child([name UTF8String]));
        return newNode;
    }
    return nil;
}

-(void) saveFile:(NSString *) path{
    if (self.element) {
```

```
    reinterpret_cast<pugi::xml_document
      *>(self.element)->save_file(path.UTF8String);
  }
}
```

`@end`

13. Now the wrapping step is finished, we can use these classes in our app. However, we still need to create another class that is going to be used by our app and will store the user information before creating the XML file. This class will be a pure Swift class, so add a new Swift file called `Task.swift` into the project and add the following code:

```swift
class Task {
    var description:String
    var important :Bool

    init(description:String, important: Bool){
        self.description = description
        self.important = important
    }
}
```

14. Before you start coding the view controller, don't forget to import the header files of the wrapper classes into the bridging file. So, click on the bridging file (`Chapter 9 Xml Wrapper-Bridging-Header.h`) and add the following lines:

```
#import "PugiDocument.h"
#import "PugiNode.h"
#import "PugiNodeAttribute.h"
```

15. Now let's mock up our view by clicking on the storyboard file and adding three labels, two buttons, one text field, and one `UISwitch`. This looks something like the image below:

16. Now, connect the text field with the view controller and call it `taskTextField`; the `UISwitch` should be called `importantSwitch`. So the generated code should be as follows:

```
@IBOutlet var taskTextField: UITextField!
@IBOutlet var importantSwitch: UISwitch!
```

17. Now we can add a new attribute for storing the user tasks:

```
var tasks = [Task]()
```

18. The last thing we need to do is create the events for the buttons. Connect the **Add** button with the following code:

```
@IBAction func addTask(sender: AnyObject) {
    tasks.append(Task(description: taskTextField.text,
        important: importantSwitch.on))
    taskTextField.text = ""
    importantSwitch.on = false
}
```

19. Good. Now we can finalize the code by linking the **Save** button with the following action:

```
@IBAction func saveXml(sender: AnyObject) {
    var document = PugiDocument()!
```

```
var mainNode = document.appendChild("tasks")
var path =
    (NSSearchPathForDirectoriesInDomains(
    .DocumentDirectory, .UserDomainMask, true)[0]
    as NSString).stringByAppendingPathComponent(
    "tasks.xml") as String;
for task in tasks {
    let node = mainNode.appendChild("task")
    let attributeDescription =
        node.appendAttribute("description")
    attributeDescription.setValue(task.description)
    let attributeImporant =
        node.appendAttribute("important")
    attributeImporant.setValue(task.important ?
        "yes" : "no")
}
document.saveFile(path)
}
```

20. Congratulations, the app is ready! Press play and add some tasks, such as "Clean the room" or "Study Swift very hard". Once you finish, you can press the **Save** button. What happened? Open your iFunBox or equivalent application and check the `Documents` folder of your app.

How it works...

PugiXML is a minimalist XML library that can easily be used. In this case, we wrapped only the minimal necessary code that was the `tag` attribute, the `xml` tag (called node), and the complete XML called document. Of course, there are more classes in this library and you can complete the code if you want.

As was mentioned earlier, C++ can't be used directly on Swift, but you can create an Objective-C class that calls C++. Here, note that you can create Objective-C classes but not Objective-C++ classes; it means that the class interface can't contain any C++ object.

How can we solve this issue? Every C++ object (like attributes or properties) must be declared as `void*` (an unsafe pointer to anything) and the arguments or retuning values must be another wrapper class.

 For better compatibility between Swift and Objective-C, try to use types that are common to both languages instead of the C or C++ types, such as `NSString` instead of `char*`.

10

Data Access

In this chapter, we will cover the following topics:

- ▶ Creating an SQLite database
- ▶ Checking where your IP is from
- ▶ Tracking your phone activity
- ▶ Controlling your stock
- ▶ Voting devices

Introduction

As you may know, nowadays it is very difficult to imagine an app that doesn't store anything on the hard disk. Simple apps, such as a calculator or a compass might not need to store any information, but you will usually need to create apps with more complex features to keep the information even if the device reboots.

When you have to store a minimum amount of information, such as a simple date or just the current app version, you can use a file as we have done in the previous chapters of this book, but when you have to store a few records with different data structures, you need the help of a database.

In this chapter, we are going to learn how to use databases on Swift, and you will see the advantages of each method.

Creating an SQLite database

Usually, storing information on a mobile app is done with a local database. To do this, it is very common to use SQLite because even if it is a bit limited, this database has some advantages. For example, it is a serverless and a zero configuration database, and is built on iOS and Mac OS X.

Getting ready

For this recipe, we are going to download a SQLite file; therefore, you will need a SQLite client to read this file. So, apart from iFunBox downloaded in the previous chapter, you will also need to download a program, such as SQLiteBrowser (`http://sqlitebrowser.org/`).

Create a new project called `Chapter 10 SQLite`, and keep in mind where you have saved this recipe because we are going to complete this in the next recipe.

How to do it...

Perform the following steps:

1. When the project is created, click on the **General** tab, and scroll down until you get to the section **Linked Frameworks and Libraries**. Click on the plus sign to add a new library, and select **libsqlite3.dylib**:

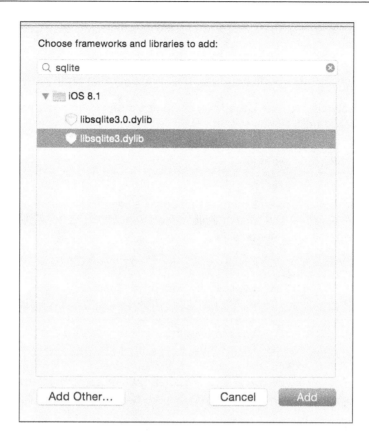

Choose frameworks and libraries to add:

> sqlite

▼ iOS 8.1

　　libsqlite3.0.dylib

　　libsqlite3.dylib

Add Other...　　　　　　　Cancel　　　Add

2. After this, let's create a new bridging file by adding a new header file called `BridgingHeader.h`, and check whether it is set as a bridging header in **Build Settings**. In this file, include `sqlite3.h`:

```
#include <sqlite3.h>
```

3. Now add a new file called `SQLite.swift`. Here, we are going to start coding a class called `SQLite`, and inside this class, we will start coding an enumeration called `status`:

```
public class SQLite {
    public enum Status {
        case CONNECTED,
        DISCONNECTED
    }
```

4. Now let's create two attributes, one for the connection with the database and another one for the current connection status:

```
private var _connection:COpaquePointer = nil
private var _status = SQLite.Status.DISCONNECTED
```

5. The next step is to create a read-only computed attribute that returns the current connection status:

```
public var status:SQLite.Status {
    return _status
}
```

6. After this, you can create a method that opens a connection with the database. For this method, we will only need the file name as an argument; however, we are going to store it in the documents folder:

```
public func connect(filename:String) -> Bool{
    let documentsPath =
        (NSSearchPathForDirectoriesInDomains
        (.DocumentDirectory, .UserDomainMask, true)[0] as
        NSString).stringByAppendingPathComponent(filename)
    let error = sqlite3_open(documentsPath,&self._connection)
    if error == SQLITE_OK {
        // Adding a table just in case
        let statement = "CREATE TABLE IF NOT EXISTS ips
            " + "(ipstart text, ipend text, " +
            "iipstart integer, iipend integer, " +
            "country text);" as NSString
        var errmessage:UnsafeMutablePointer<CChar> =
            nil
        if sqlite3_exec(self._connection,
            statement.UTF8String, nil, nil,
            &errmessage) == SQLITE_OK {
            self._status = .CONNECTED
            return true
        }
        return false
    return false
}
```

7. The last step for this class is the deinitializer that should close the database connection:

```
deinit {
    switch self._status {
        case .CONNECTED:
            sqlite3_close(self._connection)
        default:
```

```
            break;
        }
    }
}
```

8. The model part is done. Now, let's create the view part by clicking on the storyboard and adding a label, a text field, and a button, which looks something similar to this layout:

9. Now, connect the text field to the view controller and call it `databaseNameTextField`:

```
@IBOutlet var databaseNameTextField: UITextField!
```

10. Once it is done, you can create an action for the only button. In this case, we are going to open the database connection, create a table, and check whether everything was done successfully:

```
@IBAction func createDatabase(sender: AnyObject) {
    var database = SQLite()
    if self.databaseNameTextField.text == "" {
        UIAlertView(title:"No database name", message:
            "You must introduce a database name",
            delegate: nil, cancelButtonTitle:
            "Ok").show()
        return
```

```
    }
    let dbname = self.databaseNameTextField.text +
        ".sqlite"
    if database.connect(dbname) {
        UIAlertView(title: nil, message: "Database was
            created", delegate: nil, cancelButtonTitle:
            "OK").show()
    }else {
        UIAlertView(title: nil, message: "Failed
            creating the database", delegate: nil,
            cancelButtonTitle: "OK")
    }

}
```

11. This app is now done, or in other words, this first version is now done. Now click on play and write a filename for your database, for example, `mydatabase`, and then click on the button to create a database.

12. Now let's check the real application. So open your iFunBox and search for the app `Chapter 10 SQLite`, Open its document folder, select the only file that is in this folder, then click on the **Copy to Mac** button, and save it in your local documents folder:

13. Once you have the empty database, let's check whether we are able to open it. Open your SQLite browser and click on the **Open Database** button:

14. Choose the database file you downloaded and open it. In the main panel, you should see a table called **ips** in the database schema. This means that your database was created successfully, and can create a table without any errors:

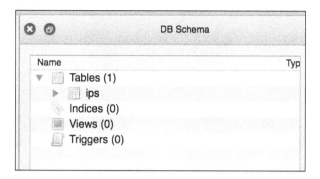

How it works...

SQLite is not a framework, rather it is a library that uses the traditional C functions instead of objective-C or Swift objects.

As you might know, using a C function implies using C types, and that's the reason we had to use UnsafeMutablePointer<CChar> for the error message and COpaquePointer for the database handle.

 COpaquePointer represents a C pointer, such as UnsafeMutablePointer, but it is used when you can't represent the pointer type in Swift, such as with some structs for example.

In this recipe, we used three SQLite functions:

▶ sqlite3_open: This opens a database. It creates a new database file if it doesn't exist. This function receives the filename and a handle pointer by reference as arguments.

 If you don't want to create a database file, you can use in-memory databases. You can check this information at https://www.sqlite.org/inmemorydb.html.

▶ sqlite3_close: This closes the connection with the database and frees the resources that are being used for this connection. Bear in mind that C has no objects, garbage collectors, and automatic reference counters; therefore, if you don't free the resources, they are going to be there until your application finishes or crashes.

> ▸ `sqlite3_exec`: This executes a SQL statement; in this case, it wasn't really necessary because we just wanted to check whether the file was created or not. However, sometimes, SQLite creates only an empty file if you don't use the database.

There's more...

SQLite has a lot of options and functions. You can find out more about them at the official website `https://www.sqlite.org/cintro.html`. Now that you know how to create a database, let's work with it by creating registers and querying results.

Checking where your IP is from

Sometimes, you need to query from a remote database, but as you know SQLite works with a local database, which means that you have to populate it before querying. In this recipe, we are going to convert a CSV file to a SQLite database, and after this, we are going to query some results.

Getting ready

For this recipe, we will need a CSV file with the range of IPs of each country. There are some websites that will give or sell it to you and you can download it for free from `https://db-ip.com/db/download/country`, uncompress it, and add it to your SQLite application.

 Right now, this file is called `dbip-country-2014-12.csv`, but it changes its name every month so we need to replace the filename where it is mentioned with the one you have.

How to do it...

Perform the following steps:

1. Let's start completing the SQLite class by adding two additional methods: one for executing statements that don't return any result, such as the insert, delete, and update queries. To do this, click on the `SQLite.swift` file, and inside the SQLite class, add the following code:

    ```
    func exec(statement: String) -> Bool {
        var errmessage:UnsafeMutablePointer<CChar> = nil
        return sqlite3_exec(self._connection, (statement as
            NSString).UTF8String, nil, nil, &errmessage) ==
            SQLITE_OK
    ```

```
        }

        func query(statement:String) -> [[String]]? {
            var sqliteStatement:COpaquePointer = nil
            if sqlite3_prepare_v2(self._connection, (statement
                as NSString).UTF8String , -1, &sqliteStatement,
                nil) != SQLITE_OK {
                return nil
            }
            var result = [[String]]()
            while sqlite3_step(sqliteStatement) == SQLITE_ROW {
                var row = [String]()
                for i in
                    0..<sqlite3_column_count(sqliteStatement) {
                        row.append(String.fromCString
                            (UnsafePointer<CChar>
                            (sqlite3_column_text
                            (sqliteStatement, i)))!)
                }
                result.append(row)
            }
            return result
        }
    }
```

2. Now, let's add a new file called `Functions.swift` to your project. This file will contain some auxiliary functions. The first function that we are going to create is the one that reads a CSV file and returns its contents inside a double array of string:

```
func csv2array(filename: String) -> [[String]]? {
    var error: NSErrorPointer = nil
    var url = NSBundle.mainBundle().URLForResource
        (filename, withExtension: "csv")
    if let  fileContent = String(contentsOfURL: url!,
        encoding: NSUTF8StringEncoding, error: error){
        var records = [[String]] ()
        fileContent.enumerateLines({ (line, _) -> () in
            var fields:[String] =
                line.componentsSeparatedByString(",")
                .map({ (field:String) -> String in
                return
                    field.stringByTrimmingCharactersInSet
                    (NSCharacterSet(charactersInString:
                    "\""))
            })
            if isIPv4(fields[0]) {
                records.append(fields)
```

```
            }
        })

        return records
    }else {
        return nil
    }
}
```

3. Now, we need two additional functions related to the IP string. The first one will check whether the input string has an IPv4 format:

```
func isIPv4(ip:String) -> Bool {
    var error: NSErrorPointer = nil
    return NSRegularExpression(pattern: "^\\d{1,3}\\.\\
d{1,3}\\.\\d{1,3}\\.\\d{1,3}$", options: .CaseInsensitive, error:
error)!.matchesInString(ip, options: nil, range:NSMakeRange(0,
countElements(ip))).count > 0
}
```

4. The second function will convert the IP from a string to an unsigned integer, and it will allow us to check whether an IP falls within a range:

```
    func ip2int(ip:String) -> UInt32 {
        return CFSwapInt32(inet_addr((ip as
            NSString).UTF8String))
    }
```

5. We are now done with the auxiliaries functions, and need to update the storyboard. Go to your storyboard and add two more buttons: one with the word **Populate** and another one with the word **Search**, so that it shows something similar to the following screenshot:

6. Now, we need to set these buttons as hidden by default, because we are not going to insert any registers before we create the database. To do this, click on one of these new buttons, go to the attribute inspector, check the **Hidden** option, and then repeat the operation with the other button:

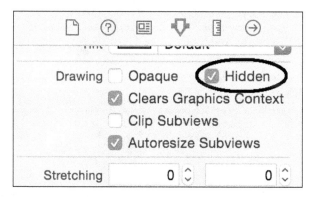

7. Once the storyboard is done, we have to update the view controller. Let's start by connecting the label and the three buttons to the view controller:

```
@IBOutlet var inputLabel: UILabel!
@IBOutlet var createButton: UIButton!
@IBOutlet var populateButton: UIButton!
@IBOutlet var searchButton: UIButton!
```

8. We still need another attribute, that is, the database connection, which is inside the action of creating a database. So what we are going to do is move the declaration with the initialization from inside the `createDatabase` method to outside of it:

```
var database = SQLite()
@IBAction func createDatabase(sender: AnyObject) {

    if self.databaseNameTextField.text == "" {
```

9. As we are working with the `createDatabase` method, we can take advantage of it, and update it by hiding the some unneeded views and displaying only the **Populate** button:

```
@IBAction func createDatabase(sender: AnyObject) {

    if self.databaseNameTextField.text == "" {
        UIAlertView(title:"No database name", message:
            "You must introduce a database name",
            delegate: nil, cancelButtonTitle:
            "Ok").show()
        return
    }
    let dbname = self.databaseNameTextField.text +
        ".sqlite"
    if database.connect(dbname) {
        UIAlertView(title: nil, message: "Database was
            created", delegate: nil, cancelButtonTitle:
            "OK").show()
        self.createButton.hidden = true
        self.populateButton.hidden = false
        self.inputLabel.text = ""
        self.databaseNameTextField.text = ""
        self.databaseNameTextField.hidden = true
    }else {
        UIAlertView(title: nil, message: "Failed
            creating the database", delegate: nil,
            cancelButtonTitle: "OK")
    }
}
```

10. After this, we can connect the populate button to a new action. This action will be called `populate`, and it will call the insert statement in our database, then it will display the search button:

```
@IBAction func populate(sender: AnyObject) {
    if let data = csv2array("dbip-country-2014-12"){
        println("total \(data.count)")
```

```
        var statements = data.map{ record -> String in
            return "INSERT INTO ips (ipstart, ipend,
                iipstart, iipend, country) VALUES " +
            "('\(record[0])', '\(record[1])',
                \(ip2int(record[0])),
                \(ip2int(record[1]))," +
            "'\(record[2])' )"
        }

        database.exec("delete from ips;")

        for statement in statements {
            database.exec(statement)
        }
        self.searchButton.hidden = false
        self.populateButton.hidden = true
        self.inputLabel.text = "Enter an IP"
        self.databaseNameTextField.text = ""
        self.databaseNameTextField.hidden = false
    }
    else {
        UIAlertView(title: nil, message: "Unable to
            parse the file", delegate: nil,
            cancelButtonTitle: "OK").show()
    }
}
```

11. As you can see, we need to develop the search action. Firstly, it needs to check whether the input is correct, and then it will look for an IP range where it belongs. If it is able to find it, this will show you the country where the IP belongs, otherwise it will show you that the country wasn't found:

```
@IBAction func search(sender: AnyObject) {
    let iptext = self.databaseNameTextField.text
    if !isIPv4(iptext) {
        UIAlertView(title: "Error", message: "Wrong
            format", delegate: nil, cancelButtonTitle:
            "OK").show()
        return
    }
    let ipnumber = ip2int(iptext)
    let sql = "SELECT country FROM ips where
        \(ipnumber) between iipstart and iipend"
    if let result = database.query(sql){
```

```
            if result.count > 0 && result[0].count > 0 {
                UIAlertView(title: "Found", message: "This
                ip belongs to \(result[0][0])", delegate:
                nil, cancelButtonTitle: "OK").show()
            }else {
                UIAlertView(title: "Not Found", message:
                    "No result was found", delegate: nil,
                    cancelButtonTitle: "OK").show()
            }
        }else {
            UIAlertView(title: "Error", message: "Failed to
                execute your query", delegate: nil,
                cancelButtonTitle: "OK").show()
        }
    }
```

12. Once again, we have completed another app, and we need to test it. Click on play, write `mydatabase` in the test field and click on `Create database`. You should see only the populate button on the screen, tap on it, and it will take a while until it finishes.

If you would like to know when the app starts writing on the disk when you are developing, you can click on the debugger navigator, and then on the disk report, and you should see some bars with the disk-writing activity, as shown in the following screenshot:

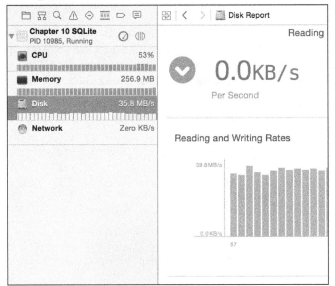

13. The last step is to look for the country of a specific IP. So, we need to type an IP in the text field when it appears, for example, `74.125.230.52` and click on search. You should receive an alert, displaying where this IP belongs to.

How it works...

SQL has two kinds of queries:

▸ There are queries that modify the data structure, such as CREATE TABLE, ALTER TABLE, or modify the data content, such as INSERT, DELETE, or UPDATE, which will be discussed in the next section. These queries usually don't return any data. For these kind of queries, you can use the `sqlite3_exec` function.

▸ There are queries that retrieve information, such as SELECT. Here, you have to work in a different way; you need to use the `sqlite3_prepare_v2` function to execute the query and `sqlite3_step` to retrieve each record.

If you check the SQLite API documentation, you will see that `sqlite3_exec` can also return a result from a SELECT statement; however, it needs a pointer to a function for each record received (what is called a callback).

If you have developed your function in C, you can have a pointer to it using a variable of type `CFunctionPointer`, but bear in mind that this data type can't be used for pointing Swift functions. Make sure that SQLite has its own constants, such as SQLITE_OK to indicate that the operation has finished successfully. SQLITE_ROW tells us that it can receive a record from the statement result, or SQLITE_DONE tells us that there are no more records in this statement result.

In this case, we covered a common case of converting a text file to database records. Let's take a look at a few details you will need for completing a similar task. First, we added every record in an array; it took approximately 80 megabytes of RAM until we finished inserting the records. This isn't a problem here because even low-end devices, such as the iPhone 4S has 512 megabytes of RAM, but if you decide to load the cities IP database, it can consume a lot of memory, so probably you would need to split the file or store each record directly in the database without using an intermediate array.

Another detail is that we didn't use the transactions, which means that if for any reason we had to stop inserting the records halfway through, we will need to remove every record previously inserted; otherwise, we will have duplicated records or errors when trying to reinsert everything again.

One good question is: Why did we use IP ranges instead of one record for each IP? The reason is very simple: space. If we were going to use one record for each IP, we would need 4,294,967,296 records; if each record occupies 1 kilobyte of disk space, it would need 4,398,046,511,104 bytes (approximately 4 terabytes), which we don't have on any Apple mobile device except for Apple computers, but it wouldn't be worth wasting such space for only an IP table.

Another good question is: why did we have to convert IP strings to an unsigned integer? Even if you see an IP as a sequence of four numbers, actually it is a 32-bit unsigned integer, which allows us to check whether an IP is within a range, otherwise we would do a string comparison, which is not valid.

There's more...

SQLite has a lot of functions, some of them are used more often than others, and some of them are more specialized than others. For these reasons, it's a good idea to check out the C functions that are available at `https://www.sqlite.org/c3ref/intro.html` and the SQL statements at `https://www.sqlite.org/lang.html`.

Here, you learned how to use the SQLite in an application; however, it gives a lot of work to do because SQLite is not a framework, it is a C library. In the next recipe, we are going to learn how to use a SQLite "precooked" class to save time when developing.

Tracking your phone activity

Imagine that you would like to track where your phone received (or made) a call by recording when a human head was close to the phone; you would want to create an app that will register some data, such as the current time and the phone coordinates, every time the proximity sensor detects something near the front face of the phone.

Although we are going to use SQLite again, we are not going to write any SQL statements. This time, we are going to use a framework that uses only Swift types and objects so that we don't have to worry about converting types from Swift to C and from C to Swift.

Getting ready

For this recipe, we will need to download an external framework called `SQLite.swift`. To do this, open your favorite web browser and go to `https://github.com/stephencelis/SQLite.swift`. Once the website is open, click on the "Download ZIP" icon. If you have used Safari, the downloaded file would probably be already unzipped. In case of using another web browser, unzip it yourself by double-clicking on the file icon on your finder window. Using this framework requires Xcode 6.1 or greater, so make sure that you are using an updated version of Xcode.

As this recipe will use the proximity sensor, it is necessary to use it with a physical phone, otherwise you won't be able create any records.

You are now ready to create a new project called Chapter 10 Activity Recording.

How to do it...

Peform the following steps:

1. First of all we need to add the SQLite.swift to our project. To do this, just drag the SQLite.swift Xcode project file (**SQLite.xcodeproj**) into your project, and you will now see two projects in the project navigator:

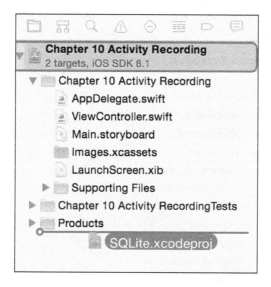

2. Now click on your project to add this framework. So, click on the **General** tab of your target, scroll down to the **Linked Frameworks and Libraries** section and click on the plus sign. When the dialog appears, you can check whether there is a section called **Workspace** with two frameworks with the same name, and select the one that is for iOS:

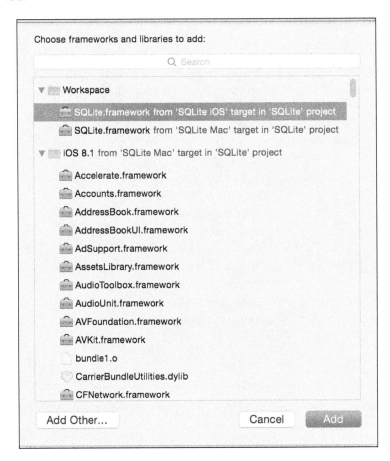

3. Click on the plus sign again and select another framework, the CoreLocation framework.

4. In this recipe, we are going to develop only the view controller, and we are not going to add any new file. So, click on the storyboard and add a text field and a button to your view. Remove the text in your text field, and change the button label to **Print records**. Now, connect the text field to the view controller and call it **textView**:

```
@IBOutlet var textView: UITextView!
```

5. Connect the button to a new action called `printRecords`. We are not going to develop it right now, so just leave it empty for future use:

```
@IBAction func printRecords(sender: AnyObject) {
}
```

6. Now click on the view controller file, and place the prompt at the beginning of this file. Here, we have to import two frameworks besides UIKit: SQLite and `CoreLocation`:

```
import SQLite
import CoreLocation
```

7. Before we start developing the view controller code, we are going to create an auxiliary type for our common variables:

```
typealias activityTuple = (activity: Query,
    id:Expression<Int>,
    latitude: Expression<Double?>,
    longitude:Expression<Double?>,
    time:Expression<String>, away:Expression<Bool>)
```

8. We will need to use the core location to receive the current location. We will need to implement the view controller as a core location delegate:

```
class ViewController: UIViewController,
    CLLocationManagerDelegate {
```

9. Now, we can add the attributes. We will need one attribute for database connection, one for the location manager, and another one for keeping a record of the last location received:

```
var database:Database?
var locationManager = CLLocationManager()
var lastLocation: CLLocation?
```

10. It is time to develop the methods. We will start with the `viewDidLoad` method, and we need to set up everything:

```
override func viewDidLoad() {
    super.viewDidLoad()
    if !openDatabase(){
        UIAlertView(title: "Error", message: "Can't
            open the database", delegate: nil,
            cancelButtonTitle: "OK").show()
        return
    }
    if !createStructure() {
        UIAlertView(title: "Error", message: "Can't
            create database structure", delegate: nil,
            cancelButtonTitle: "OK").show()
```

```
            return
        }
        setLocationManager()
        setProximitySensor()
    }
```

11. As you can see, we have a few methods to be implemented. Let's start with the
    `openDatabase` method, which creates the database and handles the connection:

```
        private func openDatabase() -> Bool{
            let documentsPath =
                (NSSearchPathForDirectoriesInDomains
                (.DocumentDirectory, .UserDomainMask, true)
                [0] as NSString).stringByAppendingPathComponent
                ("database.sqlite")
            database = Database(documentsPath)
            return database != nil
        }
```

12. The next step is to create the database structure. This will create a table called
    activity with its columns:

```
        private func createStructure() -> Bool {
            var actVars = self.activityVars()
            var result = database!.create(table:
                actVars.activity, ifNotExists: true) { t in
                // Autoincrement means that we don't have to set this
    value because it will be automatic.
                t.column(actVars.id, primaryKey:
                    .Autoincrement)
                t.column(actVars.latitude)
                t.column(actVars.longitude)
                t.column(actVars.time, unique: true)
                t.column(actVars.away)
            }
            return !result.failed
        }
```

13. The database initialization is done; we need to start receiving information about the
    device's position by setting up the core location:

```
        private func setLocationManager(){
            locationManager.delegate = self
            locationManager.distanceFilter =
                kCLDistanceFilterNone
            locationManager.desiredAccuracy =
                kCLLocationAccuracyBest
```

```
        if (UIDevice.currentDevice().systemVersion as
            NSString).floatValue >= 8 &&
            CLLocationManager.authorizationStatus() !=
            CLAuthorizationStatus.AuthorizedAlways {
                locationManager.requestAlways
                    Authorization()
        }
        locationManager.startUpdatingLocation()
    }
```

14. As you know, we need to implement the method that updates the current location:

```
    func locationManager(manager: CLLocationManager!,
        didUpdateLocations locations: [AnyObject]!){
            if locations.count > 0 {
                lastLocation = locations[0] as? CLLocation
            }
    }
```

15. Now, we need to get notifications from the proximity sensor. To do this, we need to use the notification center:

```
    private func setProximitySensor(){
        var device = UIDevice.currentDevice()
        device.proximityMonitoringEnabled = true
        if device.proximityMonitoringEnabled {
            NSNotificationCenter.defaultCenter()
                .addObserver(self, selector:
                Selector("proximity:"),
                name: "UIDeviceProximityState
                DidChangeNotification", object: device)
        }
    }
```

16. As you can see, when we receive a proximity sensor, change the `proximity` method needs to be called. That's the moment we have to store in the database recording that an activity has started or ended:

```
    func proximity(notification:NSNotification){
        var device: AnyObject? = notification.object
        var latitude:Double?
        var longitude:Double?
        if lastLocation != nil {
            latitude = lastLocation!.coordinate.latitude
            longitude = lastLocation!.coordinate.longitude
        }
        let dateFormatter = NSDateFormatter()
```

```
dateFormatter.dateFormat = "yyyy-MM-dd HH:mm:ss" //
    superset of OP's format
let dateString:String =
    dateFormatter.stringFromDate(NSDate())


let actVars = self.activityVars()


if let id = actVars.activity.insert(actVars.away <-
    !device!.proximityState!,
    actVars.time <- dateString, actVars.latitude <-
        latitude, actVars.longitude <- longitude ) {
    println("Register inserted with id \(id)")

    }

}
```

17. Now we need to create the method that returns the variables that are related to the activity table:

```
private func activityVars() -> activityTuple{
    return (activity:database!["activity"],
        id:Expression<Int>("id"),
        latitude: Expression<Double?>("latitude"),
        longitude:Expression<Double?>("longitude"),
        time:Expression<String>("time"),
        away:Expression<Bool>("away") )

    }
```

18. The last part of the development is the button event, which was empty until now. We just need to retrieve the data from the activity table and add it to the text view:

```
@IBAction func printRecords(sender: AnyObject) {
    self.textView.text = ""
    let actVars = activityVars()
    for record in actVars.activity {

        textView.text = textView.text +  "id:
            \(record[actVars.id]), time:
            \(record[actVars.time]), away:
            \(record[actVars.away])"
        if record[actVars.latitude] != nil {
            textView.text = textView.text + ",
            latitude: \(record[actVars.latitude]!),
            longitude: \(record[actVars.longitude]!)"
        }
        textView.text = textView.text +  "\n"

    }

}
```

19. There is one more step that you might need to do; click on the `Info.plist` of your project and add a new row. In this row, set `NSLocationAlwaysUsageDescription` as the key and `This app needs GPS` as the value. The reason for this is that on iOS 8, when you request permission to use the GPS (core location), it is ignored if there is no message. Some people say that it is a bug and it should be fixed soon.

20. Once again, the app is done and we need to test it. So click on play and put your phone next to your head, as if you were talking on the phone. Repeat it a few times, and then check the table content by pressing the button. Your result should look similar to this screenshot:

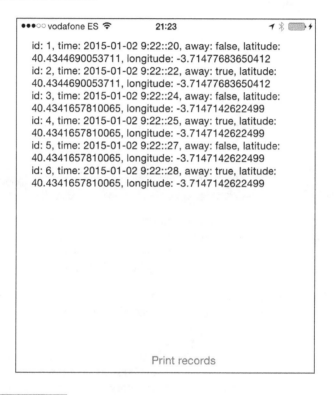

How it works...

`SQLite.swift` is a good layer in the SQLite library. You can create a database by creating an object of a Database type. You can define the table fields with a generic class called Expression. This class works with integers (Int), double precision (Double), strings, and Boolean types (Bool). All of them can be declared as optionals, which means that the database can store null values in them.

You can use methods, such as insert or update, to add or change a record. Both of them receive a type called setter, which is similar to the relationship between a field and its value. To create an object of the setter type, you have to use the `<-` operator.

To retrieve the results, you can iterate over a Query object like we did for loop and access its fields with the subscript using the expression fields as index.

 You can use the filter method to retrieve only the records that complain with a criteria, such as the where clause in the SQL language.

There's more...

As you can check with this framework, we didn't have the need to write SQL statements; however, `SQLite.swift` allows you to work with the SQL statements if you want. To do this, you can use the methods, such as `run` or `prepare`.

Another excellent feature of `SQLite.swift` is that it is transaction ready. The `transaction` method and how it works for using transactions.

Apple has another solution for using a database in its own laye, which called core data. In the next recipe, we are going to learn how to use it.

Controlling your stock

The idea of an application connected with a database came with the need of keeping some data even if the application finishes. However, SQL is another language, and you have to repeat the development twice, similar to how a new field in a class is also a new field in the database.

When Xerox developed the first window system based on Smalltalk, they didn't use any kind of database. The argument for this was that if an application doesn't finish, the data will always be stored in the RAM memory.

The idea itself is very intelligent, but we know that the real world doesn't work like that. Applications crash and finish and devices need to reboot sometimes. Besides this, you also need to consider that up to the present the RAM memory is still more expensive than hard disks. The new iPhone 6, for example, has only 1 gigabyte of RAM and at least 32 gigabytes of permanent storage.

Based on the problems mentioned earlier, Apple recommends that you use its own ORM called Core Data. An ORM is a framework that allows your objects to be stored in a permanent storage system without wasting time writing SQL statements. Actually, what Core Data does is that it writes the SQL for us.

In this recipe, we are going to develop a small app using Core Data by simulating a product control of a warehouse.

Getting ready

We can start by creating a new app called Chapter 10 Stock Control; however, make sure that the Use Core Data option is checked, as shown in the following screenshot:

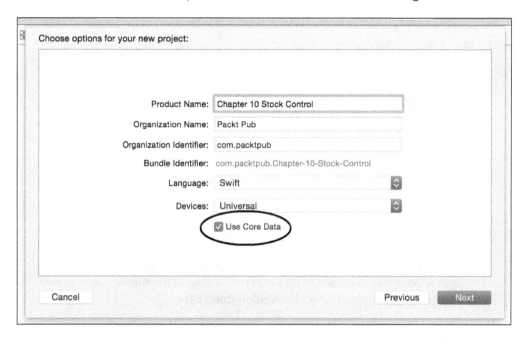

How to do it...

Perform the following steps:

1. Firstly, we will need to create a database model, so don't think in SQLite when creating this model because there will be some different types. So, click on the Chapter_10_Stock_Control.xcdatamodeld file. Here, you should see a different layout with some empty fields. Let's start by clicking on the plus sign, which is located on the text **Add Entity**:

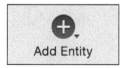

2. Rename the new entity **Product**:

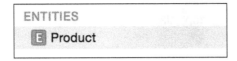

3. After this, add three attributes to this entity: one called **name**, which should be of type string, **price**, which is of type double, and **units**, which is an integer of 32 bits:

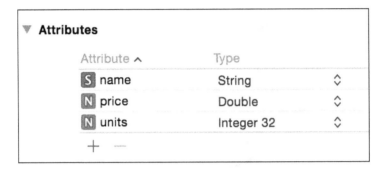

4. That's all for the data part. Now we need to click on the storyboard file. Select the only view controller you have by clicking on it, and go to the **Editor** menu, expand the **Embedded In** option and select **Navigation Controller**:

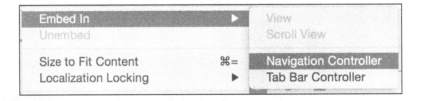

5. If don't want the navigation bar for this app, you can click on the navigation controller you just created, and uncheck the **Show navigation bar** option that is on the attribute inspector:

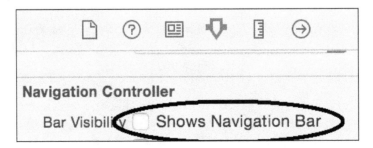

6. Now add a button to the only view controller we have with the text **New product**, and under this option, add a table view. You should have a layout similar to the following screenshot:

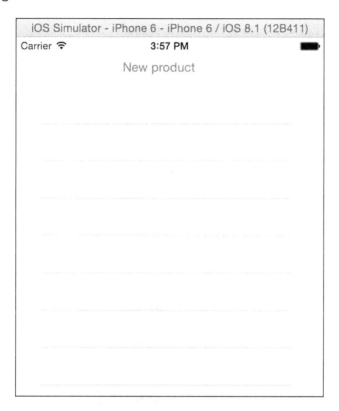

7. Now go to the view controller and import Core Data:

```
import CoreData
```

8. You have to add the `UITableViewDataSource` protocol to the view controller, and in this way, we can display the results on the table view:

```
class ViewController: UIViewController,
    UITableViewDataSource {
```

9. Now, connect the table view to the view controller as the data source and as an attribute of it. As we are adding an attribute, we can also add a new attribute that will contain our records:

```
@IBOutlet var tableView: UITableView!
var products = [NSManagedObject] ()
```

10. Once this is done we have to implement the methods that update the table view information. In this case, the number of records is the size of the array, but their contents are the values of some keys of NSManagedObject:

```
func tableView(tableView: UITableView,
    numberOfRowsInSection section: Int) -> Int{
        return products.count
}

func tableView(tableView: UITableView,
    cellForRowAtIndexPath indexPath: NSIndexPath) ->
    UITableViewCell {
    var cell: UITableViewCell? =
        tableView.dequeueReusableCellWithIdentifier
        ("cell") as UITableViewCell?
    if (cell == nil) {
        cell = UITableViewCell(style:
            UITableViewCellStyle.Value1,
            reuseIdentifier: "cell")
    }
    cell!.textLabel?.text =
        products[indexPath.row].valueForKey("name") as?
        String
    var units = products[indexPath.row].valueForKey
        ("units") as? Int
    cell!.detailTextLabel?.text = "\(units!) units"
    return cell!
}
```

11. If we create a new record, it's necessary to reload the table view data. We can create a button to refresh it, but it wouldn't be as intuitive, so the best way in which we can do is to refresh the data as well as update the product array when the view appears again:

```
override func viewWillAppear(animated: Bool) {
    var appDelegate:AppDelegate =
        UIApplication.sharedApplication().delegate as
        AppDelegate
    var moc: NSManagedObjectContext =
        appDelegate.managedObjectContext!
    var request = NSFetchRequest(entityName: "Product")
    request.returnsObjectsAsFaults = false
    var err : NSError?
    products  = moc.executeFetchRequest(request, error:
        &err) as [NSManagedObject]
    self.tableView.reloadData()
}
```

12. Good. Click on play and check what happens. Nothing? The reason is that we are able to list the records but not able to insert them, so it is time to add a functionality to the **New product** button. Return to the storyboard and add a new view controller. Place it on the right-hand side of the previous one, and click on the **New product** button with the ⌘ key pressed and drag it until the new view controller.

13. Click on play; of course, you are not going to see any records, but if you tap on the button, you can see that a new view is called. At this moment, we need to develop this view. However, before we can continue, this view needs a view controller file; in this case, you have to add a new file of type **Cocoa Touch Class** and name it `NewProductViewController`. Make sure that it inherits from **UIViewController**:

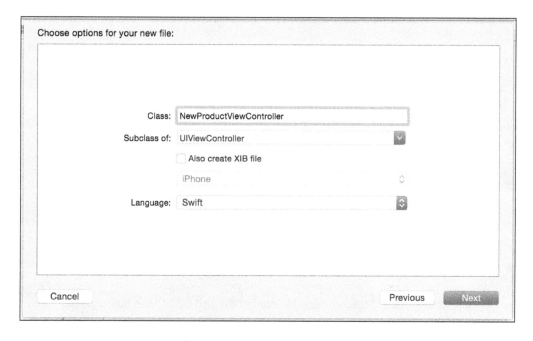

14. Return to your storyboard, and change the class of this view controller on the identity inspector to a new file that we created:

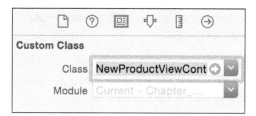

15. Now let's create a layout for this view. We have to add three text fields (one for each entity field), three labels to explain these fields, one button to save the records, and lastly, one label just to display the view title (as we don't have the navigation bar):

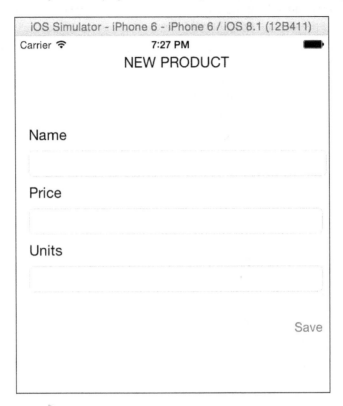

16. Once the layout is done, we have to connect the text field to the new product view controller:

```
@IBOutlet var nameTextField: UITextField!
@IBOutlet var priceTextField: UITextField!
@IBOutlet var unitsTextField: UITextField!
```

17. Finally, we need to develop the save. As it is going to use a few Core Data classes, you have to start by importing it:

```
import CoreData
```

18. Now connect your save button to an action called save, and develop it by retrieving the text fields data and saving it in Core Data:

```
@IBAction func save(sender: UIButton) {
    var appDelegate:AppDelegate =
        UIApplication.sharedApplication().delegate as
        AppDelegate
```

```
        var moc: NSManagedObjectContext =
            appDelegate.managedObjectContext!

        var newProduct =
            NSEntityDescription.insertNewObject
            ForEntityForName("Product",
            inManagedObjectContext: moc) as NSManagedObject
        newProduct.setValue(self.nameTextField.text,
            forKey: "name")
        newProduct.setValue( (priceTextField.text as
            NSString).floatValue, forKey: "price")
        newProduct.setValue(unitsTextField.text.toInt()!,
            forKey: "units")
        var err:NSError?
        moc.save(&err)
        if let error = err {
            println(error.localizedDescription)
        }else{
            println(newProduct)
        }
        self.navigationController?.
            popViewControllerAnimated(true)
    }
```

19. The last step is to test your app, so click on play, and add a few products, such as computers, potatoes, and cars, and check whether they appear on your table view.

How it works...

We should be very thankful to Apple because the old versions of Xcode didn't have the option of creating a Core Data application, which means that the code for the initialization done on the AppDelegate class had do be done manually. What it does is that it creates some attributes, such as managedObjectModel that reads the entity model and interprets it, while persistentStoreCoordinator converts from Core Data to a persistent system (SQLite by default, but it can be configured to be a XML file for example) and managedObjectContext controls the objects/records that belong to Core Data.

For this reason, every time that we had to use something from Core Data, we had to access the AppDelegate class a few times. If you prefer, you can create your own singleton class and transfer the Core Data code to this class.

When we need a new record, we need an object of type NSManagedObject. If it is a new record, we can ask for the help of the insertNewObjectForEntityForName method from the NSEntityDescription class. Accessing its fields is very easy; we just need to use valueForKey for retrieving its value or setValue for modifying it.

If you need to access the objects, you have to use `NSFetchRequest`, which is like a SQL statement. The `managedObjectContext` is the one that can execute this request and return its data.

There's more...

If you want to filter some data, you can use `NSPredicate`, which is similar to the where clause of SQL.

We've seen some ways of storing data in your local device, but how about a network database? In the next recipe, we are going to use a centralized database for storing our data.

Voting devices

As we learned before, usually on mobile apps we can access a local database, but sometimes we need to use only one database with a lot of devices connected to it. For example, when you do a Google query, you don't download the whole Google Index to your mobile phone, you just send a request to Google for some information and retrieve the result.

In this recipe, we are going to learn how to use a centralized database; here, we are going to use a database called CouchDB.

Getting ready

For this recipe, you need to download a CouchDB server. I assume that you are developing on a Mac computer, so we will demonstrate how to use it with Mac OS X. In case you want to use another platform, such as Linux or Windows, feel free to use it.

Download CouchDB from `http://couchdb.apache.org`. Once it is downloaded and unzipped, right-click on its icon, and choose the **Show Package Contents** option from the menu:

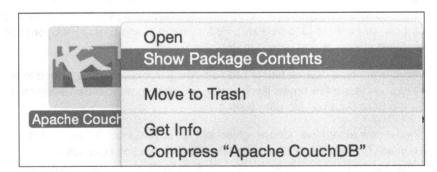

Now follow the `Contents/Resources/couchdbx-core/etc/couchdb` path. Here, you should see a file called `default.ini`: open it and search for the `bind_address` variable. Here, you have to change 127.0.0.1 to 0.0.0.0. Now return to the folder, where CouchDB app is located, and open the app by double-clicking on it. Your web browser should open displaying the CouchDB frontend (called Futon), and keep it open for checking the results later.

One important detail that you need to bear in mind is that if you are going to use a physical device, it must use the same Wi-Fi network as your computer; otherwise, your device won't be able to find your database server.

Return to your Xcode and create a new project called `Chapter 10 Voting`. Here you won't need Core Data.

How to do it...

Perform the following steps:

1. The first step is to set up the database. To do this, go to your web browser and click on the **Create** button. If for any reason you closed your browser, just type the URL `http://127.0.0.1:5984/_utils/`. When the website asks for a database name, write `voting`, as shown in the following screenshot:

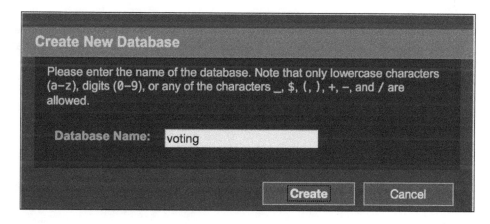

2. Inside this database, we need to add a few documents. So, click on the button that says **New document**.

 Documents in CouchDB are JSON dictionaries.

3. For the first document, click on **Source** and complete it, as shown in the following code. Do not modify the `_id` value, leave the one that CouchDB gave to you:

```
{
    "_id": "608d7c9174f7caba4ab618d6810004cf",
    "question": "What is your favorite computer programming
language?",
    "answers": [
        {
            "answer": "Swift",
            "votes": []
        },
        {
            "answer": "Objective-C",
            "votes": []
        },
        {
            "answer": "C",
            "votes": []
        }
    ]
}
```

4. Now click on save document, and let's repeat the operation with another document; in this way, we can be sure that the questions are being received from the database:

```
{
    "_id": "608d7c9174f7caba4ab618d681001467",
    "_rev": "3-41c057820d6cbd595e7db2bdf05610fe",
    "question": "What is your favorite book?",
    "answers": [
        {
            "answer": "Swift cookbook",
            "votes": []
        },
        {
            "answer": "Divine Comedy",
            "votes": []
        },
        {
            "answer": "Oxford dictionary",
            "votes": []
        }
    ]
}
```

5. Now we need to create an update handler, which is similar to a function that receives data and completes a document for us. Click on the new document, and this time, we need to change the document ID because it will be called _design/voting:

```
{
    "_id": "_design/voting",
    "updates": {
        "addvote": "function(doc, req) { var json =
            JSON.parse(req.body); doc.answers[parseInt(json.
answer)].votes.push(json.uid); return [doc, toJSON(doc)]}"
    }
}
```

6. The database part is done; therefore, you now need to go back to your Xcode project.

 Explaining how CouchDB works is beyond the scope of this book. If you would like to learn how to use this database, there are good books and tutorials on this.

7. Once you've returned to your Xcode project, click on the storyboard, and add two labels and three buttons to your view. Write TODAY'S QUESTION in the first label, which should be located at the top of the view. Below it, place the other label that will contain the received question, and under it, the three buttons. Don't worry about the text of these components as they will be changed programmatically.

8. We have to link some components to the view controller; in this case, we have to connect the question label and the three buttons:

```
@IBOutlet var questionLabel: UILabel!
@IBOutlet var answer1button: UIButton!
@IBOutlet var answer2button: UIButton!
@IBOutlet var answer3button: UIButton!
```

9. Besides this, we will also add two attributes: one for the document ID and another one for the common part of the request's URL. Remember that if you are using a device, you have to change the IP from 127.0.0.1 to the one of your computer:

```
var documentId:String?

let baseurl = "http://127.0.0.1:5984/voting/"
```

10. Connect the three buttons to the same action called vote. Leave this action empty for now:

```
@IBAction func vote(sender: UIButton) {
}
```

11. When the application starts, we need to receive the current questions that our database has, so let's just start calling a function that will do this for us in the `viewDidLoad` method:

```
override func viewDidLoad() {
    super.viewDidLoad()
    self.chooseQuestion()
}
```

12. As you can see, we have to implement the `chooseQuestion` method. This method will call the `_all_docs` "action", which returns the ID of every document in the database, including the special document "_design/voting". Once we have received the document, we can choose one of them and request its data:

```
private func chooseQuestion(){
    var url = NSURL(string: baseurl + "_all_docs")!
    var task = NSURLSession.sharedSession().
        dataTaskWithURL(url, completionHandler: {
        data, response, error -> Void in
        if error != nil {
            println(error.localizedDescription)
        }
        var err: NSError?
        var jsonResult = NSJSONSerialization.
            JSONObjectWithData(data, options:
            NSJSONReadingOptions.MutableContainers,
            error: &err) as NSDictionary
        var invalid = true
        var docid:String = ""
        while invalid {
        let rows   = jsonResult.valueForKey("rows") as
            NSArray
        srandom(UInt32(time(nil)))
        var choosenRow:Int = random() % rows.count
        docid = (rows[choosenRow] as
            NSDictionary).valueForKey("id") as String
            invalid = startsWith(docid, "_")
        }
        self.getQuestion( docid )
    })
    task.resume()
}
```

13. Once the application has decided which document it wants, we can request its data. This mechanism is similar to the previous one, but with the difference that when we receive the data, we have to update the UI, and as you know this must be done on the main thread:

```
private func getQuestion(id:String){
    self.documentId = id
    var url = NSURL(string: baseurl + id)!
    var task = NSURLSession.sharedSession()
        .dataTaskWithURL(url, completionHandler: {
        data, response, error -> Void in
        if error != nil {
            println(error.localizedDescription)
        }
        var err: NSError?
        var jsonResult = NSJSONSerialization.
            JSONObjectWithData(data, options:
            NSJSONReadingOptions.MutableContainers,
            error: &err) as NSDictionary

        dispatch_async(dispatch_get_main_queue(), {
            self.questionLabel.text =
                jsonResult.valueForKey("question") as?
                String
            var answers = jsonResult.valueForKey
                ("answers") as [NSDictionary]
            self.answer1button.setTitle
                (answers[0].valueForKey("answer") as?
                String, forState: .Normal)
            self.answer2button.setTitle
                (answers[1].valueForKey("answer") as?
                String, forState: .Normal)
            self.answer3button.setTitle(answers[2].
                valueForKey("answer") as? String,
                forState: .Normal)

        })
    })
    task.resume()
}
```

14. If you click on play now, you will see a screen similar to the following screenshot. This means that you have received a question with its possible answers from the database. However, if you choose any answer, nothing happens:

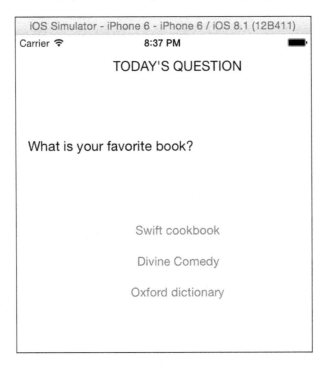

15. Now it's time to implement the vote action. The idea is to check which button was pressed and then send this information with the device ID to the database. In this way, our vote will be registered:

```
@IBAction func vote(sender: UIButton) {
    var answer:Int
    switch sender {
    case answer1button:
        answer = 0
    case answer2button:
        answer = 1
    case answer3button:
        answer = 2
    default:
        return
    }
    // input
```

```
        var params = ["answer":"\(answer)",
            "uid":UIDevice.currentDevice().
            identifierForVendor.UUIDString] as
            Dictionary<String, String>
        var request = NSMutableURLRequest(URL:
            NSURL(string: baseurl +
            "_design/voting/_update/addvote/\
            (documentId!)")!)
        request.HTTPMethod = "POST"
        var err: NSError?
        request.HTTPBody =
            NSJSONSerialization.dataWithJSONObject(params,
            options: nil, error: &err)
        request.addValue("application/json",
            forHTTPHeaderField: "Content-Type")
        request.addValue("application/json",
            forHTTPHeaderField: "Accept")
        var task = NSURLSession.sharedSession().
            dataTaskWithRequest(request, completionHandler:
            {data, response, error -> Void in
            UIAlertView(title: nil, message: "Thanks for
                voting", delegate: nil, cancelButtonTitle:
                    "OK").show()
        })
        task.resume()
    }
```

16. The application is done. Now, we have to check whether it communicates with the database correctly, so click on play again and choose an answer. You should receive an alert view thanking you, which is a good sign. After this, go the web browser again and open the chosen document, check whether your device ID is there in the answer that you had selected:

```
"question": "What is your favorite book?",
"answers": [
    {

        "answer": "Swift cookbook",
        "votes": [
            "A4655357-34DD-42E2-9484-CF2E35CC52EE"
        ]
    },
```

How it works...

If you have worked with remote SQL databases, you may know that you usually need a driver/connector that should be compatible with your platform and can also be blocked by some firewalls.

CouchDB is a NoSQL database that works by exchanging JSON messages via the HTTP protocol, which makes our life easier because we don't have to add any controller we just receive and send JSON messages. Due to the way this database works, we had to develop a function to update/insert a new vote on the client size. Remember that Swift is not JavaScript adding a new element to a JSON array can be more work than just developing a simple function.

Why did we have to cast to NSArray and NSDictionary a few times? The reason is that the NSJSONSerialization was created in the objective C era, which means that it is still not 100 percent prepared for Swift.

It is true that the way in which we worked could be better organized. The ideal way is to create a layer for CouchDB, such as a framework or a library; however, this task will be left as homework.

There's more...

In this chapter, we learned the different ways of using database in Swift; some of them are very straightforward and others require a better analysis. In the next chapter, we are going to learn some new tricks: mainly those that are related to the new Xcode 6 and the iOS 8.

11
Miscellaneous

In this chapter, we will cover the following topics:

- ▶ The geekest keyboard
- ▶ Time to take your pill
- ▶ Adding effects to your photos
- ▶ Being a film critic
- ▶ Leaving breadcrumbs
- ▶ Exchanging money

Introduction

This is the last chapter of this book. Here, we will learn different topics that weren't mentioned in the previous chapters, mainly new features of Xcode 6.

The geekest keyboard

App extensions are a new feature where an application can come with some kind of plugins, which can even interact inside other apps.

In this case, we will develop a keyboard for the geeks. This keyboard will contain only two keys: `key 0` and `key 1`. When you type a combination of eight keys, you will get a new character.

Getting ready

For this recipe, make sure that you have iOS 8; it doesn't matter whether you are using the simulator or a physical device. The custom keyboard feature is only available on iOS 8.

Create a new single view application called `Chapter 11 Geekboard` and let's start coding.

How to do it...

To create the geekest keyboard, follow these steps:

1. The main development of this recipe is based on the app extension of the custom keyboard; however, as we will need a view for testing our keyboard, let's start by clicking on the storyboard and adding a text field on our view. Link this text field with the view controller, calling it "inputTextField":

    ```
    @IBOutlet var inputTextField: UITextField!
    ```

2. Now, let's make this text field the first responder; just as the application is about to launch, you won't need to tap on the field for displaying the keyboard. Here is the code to do this:

    ```
    override func viewDidLoad() {
        super.viewDidLoad()
        self.inputTextField.becomeFirstResponder()
    }
    ```

3. This is everything we have to code with this view controller; everything else will be done on the application extension. The next step is to open the menu and add a new target to our project. In this case, select **Custom Keyboard** from the **Application Extension** section:

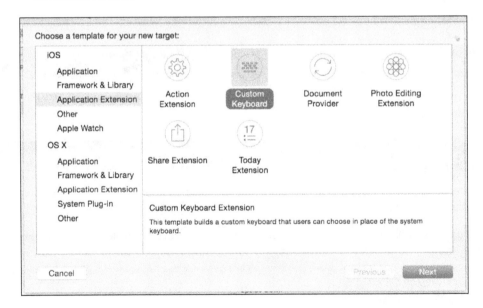

4. Call this target `Geekboard` and click on **Yes** when a dialog asks for activating the Geekboard scheme.

5. Before coding, let's start by adding a new view to this target. Therefore, click on the new file from the menu and choose **View** from the **User Interface** section.

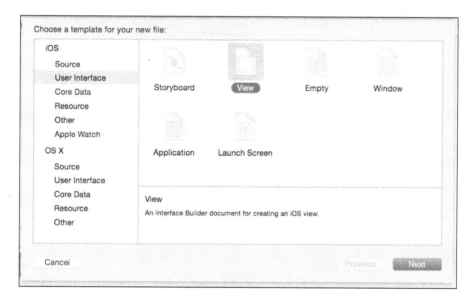

6. Call this view Geekboard (again), but before clicking on the **Create** button, ensure that this file belongs to the extension target, as shown in the following screenshot:

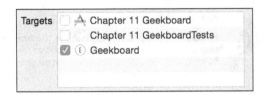

7. Once it is created, click on the new file (Geekboard.xib); select the only view it has. Let's change some properties of it by clicking on the Attribute Inspector. Here, you have to change the size to **Freeform**, the status bar to **None**, and the background color to **Silver**:

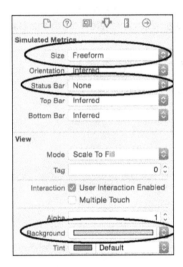

8. After this, click on the **Size Inspector** and change the view size to 320 by 160:

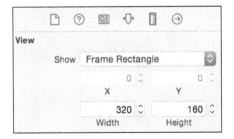

9. The view properties are done. Now, we need to set the file's owner class. To do this, click on the file's owner icon (the yellow cube), select the Identity inspector, and change the class name to `KeyboardViewController`:

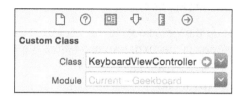

10. There is one more thing we need to in this XIB file—we need to add a few components for this layout. Add a label to let the user know about the binary combination that was done, and two buttons: one that represents digit *0* and another one that represents digit *1*. This would look something similar to the following screenshot:

11. Of course, the label will be changed and the buttons don't need a different action due to the only difference—the digit value. Therefore, we will create the same action for both buttons and differentiate them by checking the sender. To summarize, link the label and the buttons with `KeyboardViewController`, as shown in the following code:

```
@IBOutlet var button0: UIButton!
@IBOutlet var button1: UIButton!
@IBOutlet var label:UILabel!
```

 Don't remove any code created by Xcode on `KeyboardViewController` yet. It will be explicitly written to remove any code if it's necessary to remove it.

12. Link both buttons with an empty action called `addBit`. Don't worry about its contents, we will develop it later:

```
@IBAction func addBit(sender: UIButton){
}
```

13. On `KeyboardViewController`, we will also add two attributes to control the current keyboard state:

```
var currentBinaryText:String = ""
var currentBinaryNumber:Int = 0
```

14. Now, we need to set up the view, so go to the `viewDidLoad` method and add some lines of code after `super.viewDidLoad` and before the Apple precooked code:

```
override func viewDidLoad() {
    super.viewDidLoad()
    // Perform custom UI setup here
    var geekNib = UINib(nibName: "Geekboard",
      bundle: nil)
    self.view = geekNib.instantiateWithOwner(self,
      options: nil)[0] as UIView
    self.label.text = currentBinaryText
    self.nextKeyboardButton =
      UIButton.buttonWithType(.System) as UIButton
...
```

15. Once we have typed this, we can complete our app by developing the buttons event:

```
@IBAction func addBit(sender: UIButton){
    var number: Int
    switch sender{
    case button0:
        number = 0
    case button1:
        number = 1
    default:
        return
    }
    currentBinaryText += "\(number)"
    currentBinaryNumber = currentBinaryNumber * 2 +
      number
    if countElements(currentBinaryText) == 8 {
        var proxy = textDocumentProxy as
          UITextDocumentProxy
        proxy.insertText(String(UnicodeScalar(
          currentBinaryNumber)))

        currentBinaryNumber = 0
        currentBinaryText = ""
    }
    self.label.text = currentBinaryText
}
```

16. The application is done; let's test it. Click on play and when the application launches, the keyboard is shown, but this is not our keyboard! What happened? The reason is that you have to add this keyboard the same way you add another language keyboard on your device.

17. Bearing this in mind, press the home button, go to **Settings**, choose **General**, then **Keyboard**, then another option of keyboards, and at last, the option **Add New Keyboard**.

18. You should see some suggested keyboards and another section with third-party keyboards. Select Geekboard from this section.

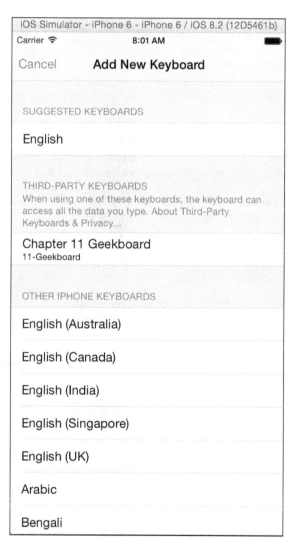

19. Return to your app (Chapter 11 Geekboard), and you will see that the keyboard is not there yet. So, you have to tap the globe icon until you get your keyboard and voila! It's working. Type this binary message: 01001000 01000101 01001100 01001100 01001111 for example, but if you are really a geek, you can go to the Mail application and write an e-mail using only this keyboard. Do you accept the challenge?

How it works...

The custom keyboard has a feature called **App Extension**. This has some limitations, for example, it can't be used for passwords and other text field types, such as contact phones. It also can't display anything on top of itself.

Creating a custom keyboard implies creating a controller of the type `UIInputViewController`, which is a class that inherits from `UIViewController`, meaning that you can use the `UIViewController` methods if it is necessary.

To make the keyboard development simpler, we added a new XIB file, which allowed us to visually create the layout. Some developers think that the XIB files were removed from Xcode since the storyboard was incorporated; however, you can see that this is not true. You can still use the XIB files for customizing some view, such as a keyboard or a table cell.

Submitting a text to the text field is very easy; you only need to create a `UITextDocumentProxy` object and use the `insertText` method. It will know the active text field magically.

There's more...

The custom keyboards communication is a bit limited because it can't use the network or share any file with the containing app by default. If you desire to use these features, you have to go to its `Info.plist` file and set the option `RequestsOpenAccess` to **Yes**.

On the next recipe, we will learn something different; we will develop an app for the Apple Watch.

Time to take your pill

Who in this world has never fallen sick? Let's face it, sooner or later, we fall sick and we have to follow the doctor's prescription. If you are like me and look at the watch frequently when it's time to take the pill, maybe what we need is just an app that can remind us about it, and this time, it will be an Apple Watch application.

Getting ready

For this recipe, you will need Xcode 6.2 or higher, because we will use the WatchKit, which is not available on the previous versions.

Start as usual by just creating a single view iOS application and call it `Chapter 11 Red Pill`.

How to do it...

To create the Apple Watch app, follow these steps:

1. The first thing we need to do is just create a new target, but this time you have to click on **WatchKit App** to add it from the **WatchKit** section.

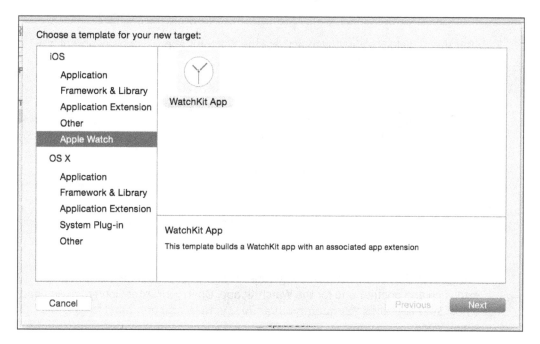

2. On the next dialog, uncheck the notifications and glance its options; this will make the project cleaner:

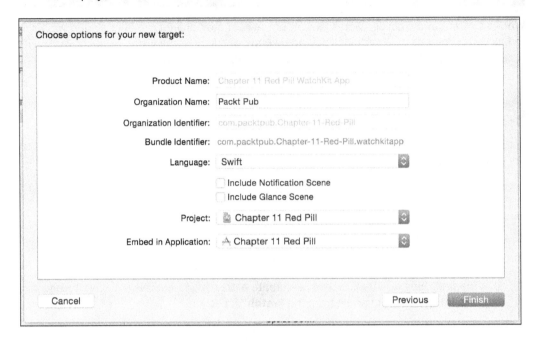

3. After this, a dialog requesting to activate the WatchKit App will appear, accept it by clicking on the **Activate** button.

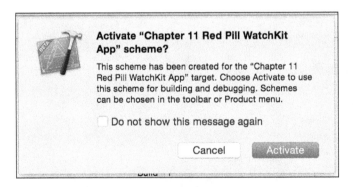

4. You can see that there are two new groups on your project: one for the WatchKit extension and another one for the WatchKit app. Open your extension group and add a new Swift file called FrequencyData.swift. Here, you only need to type this simple code:

```
class FrequencyData: Printable {
    var description: String {
```

```
switch self.time {
case 0 ..< 60:
    return "Every \(self.time) minutes"
case 60 ..< (24 * 60):
    return "Every \(self.time/60) hours"
default:
    return "Every \(self.time/60/24) days"
}
}

var time:Int // minutes

init(time:Int){
    self.time = time
}
}
```

5. Now, go to your WatchKit app group, expand it and click on the storyboard. Here, you have something like the view controller, but here, it's called interface. On your interface, add a label and try to make it fit on the entire screen. Connect it with the interface controller as an `IBOutlet` object:

```
@IBOutlet var label:WKInterfaceLabel!
```

6. Create a new interface and place another label. Here, you don't have to connect it, just change its text to `It's time to take your pill`. If it doesn't fit, change the label number of lines to two.

7. Now, click on the first interface, hold the control key, and drag it to the second interface. You should now have your storyboard like this:

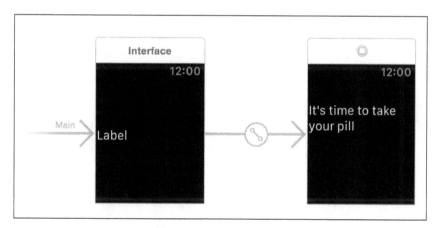

8. Select the second interface and go to its attribute inspector. Set the identifier to `its_time`:

9. Return to the extension group and open the `InterfaceController` file. As usual, we will start by adding the necessary attributes:

```
var timer:NSTimer?
var remainingTime:Int?
var context:AnyObject?
var options = [FrequencyData(time: 2),
  FrequencyData(time:4 * 60), FrequencyData(time: 8
  * 60), FrequencyData(time: 24 * 60)]
```

10. Now, initialize the context on the `awakeWithContext` method:

```
override func awakeWithContext(context: AnyObject?) {
    super.awakeWithContext(context)
    self.context = context
}
```

11. After this, we have to request the user to select the time he needs for taking his pill. Do it on the "willActivate" method:

```
override func willActivate() {
    super.willActivate()
    let texts = options.map({ (freq) -> String in
        return freq.description
    })
    self.presentTextInputControllerWithSuggestions
      (texts, allowedInputMode: WKTextInputMode.Plain,
      completion: {
    selections in
        var index = find(texts, selections[0]
          as String)!
        var frequency = self.options[index]
        self.timer?.invalidate()
        self.remainingTime = frequency.time * 60
```

```
            self.timer = NSTimer.
                scheduledTimerWithTimeInterval(1, target:
                self, selector: Selector("tick"),
                userInfo: nil, repeats: true)
        })
    }
```

12. As you can see, we need a method called `tick`, which will be called every second. Code it this way:

```
func tick(){
    var rt = remainingTime!
    let formatter = NSDateComponentsFormatter()
    formatter.unitsStyle = .Short
    let components = NSDateComponents()
    components.second = rt % 60
    rt = rt / 60
    components.minute = rt % 60
    rt = rt / 60
    components.hour = rt % 24
    rt = rt / 24
    components.day = rt
    if components.hour > 6 {
        label.setText("Still have time")
    }else if components.hour == 0 &&
      components.minute == 0{
        label.setText("A few secs:
            \(components.second)")
    }else {
        label.setText( formatter.
            stringFromDateComponents(components))
    }
    remainingTime!--
    if(remainingTime == 0){

        presentControllerWithName("its_time",
            context: self.context)
        timer?.invalidate()
    }
}
```

13. The app is done. Let's test it by changing the current scheme to `Chapter 11 Red Pill WatchKit App` and click on play. You should see a dialog like the one shown here:

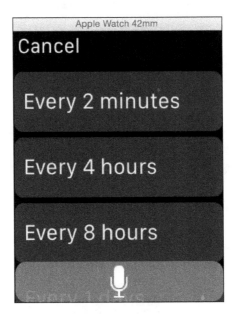

14. Choose 2 minutes, which was done just for testing and wait until you get your alert.

How it works...

If you have ever worked with or studied remote objects such as Corba or Java RMI, the idea of Apple Watch may sound familiar to you. The Apple Watch app by itself doesn't execute your code, it is done on your iPhone through the WatchKit extension, and just a few data is stored on the Apple Watch, such as the storyboard and application resources.

As you can see, the component classes are different, for example, instead of `UIViewController`, we have `WKInterfaceController`, and instead of `UILabel`, we have `WKInterfaceLabel`. Some methods are different; for example, the interface controller initializes its attributes on the `awakeWithContext` method rather than `viewDidLoad`.

There's more...

There is one component called `WKInterfaceTimer`, which works as a label with `NSTimer` like we did. In this recipe, we used `WKInterfaceLabel` with `NSTimer` because it is more flexible, and you can customize the text that is on your component.

WatchKit has more features such as notifications and glance. Try to have a look at the official documentation at `https://developer.apple.com/library/ios/documentation/` `General/Conceptual/WatchKitProgrammingGuide/index.html#//apple_ref/` `doc/uid/TP40014969`.

In the next recipe, we will return to iOS and learn how to use the camera to take pictures.

Adding effects to your photos

It is unbelievable how mobile phones have replaced traditional photo cameras. I remember when we used to take a camera only to special events and nowadays, our cameras follows us everywhere. We can say that the mobile phone has gone even further; you can take a picture of yourself on the phone, edit it, and share it with your friends and family.

In this recipe, we will learn how to take a picture with your phone and edit it in a very easy way.

Getting ready

As we will use the device camera for this recipe, you will need a physical device for testing this app. You can change it for using photos from the gallery, but you will also need to upload some pictures to the simulator.

Create a project called `Chapter 11 Photo Effects` and let's move on.

How to do it...

To add effects to your photos, follow these steps:

1. Open your project, click on the **General Settings** option of your target and add a framework called CoreImage. After this, go to the storyboard, add an image view, and four buttons under it. Change the button's labels to `Take photo`, `Sepia`, `Blur`, and `Dots`.

2. Connect the image with the view controller as an attribute and call it `imageView`. Now, create one action for each button and call them `takePhoto`, `sepia`, `blur`, and `dots`. Don't worry about their contents now; we will fill them later:

   ```
   @IBOutlet var imageView: UIImageView!
   @IBAction func takePhoto(sender: UIButton) {
   }
   @IBAction func sepia(sender: AnyObject) {
   }
   @IBAction func blur(sender: AnyObject) {
   }
   @IBAction func dots(sender: AnyObject) {
   }
   ```

3. Click on the view controller source code and let's start completing it by adding a new attribute called `image` of the optional type `UIImage`:

```
var image:UIImage?
```

4. The `UIImagePickerController` requires a delegate and only accepts objects that are also navigation controller delegates; therefore, append to the view controller definition these protocols:

```
class ViewController: UIViewController,
  UIImagePickerControllerDelegate,
  UINavigationControllerDelegate {
```

5. It's almost time to start coding functions; however, we still need to add a detail—we have to import the core image on the top of the file:

```
import CoreImage
```

6. Now, at this time, we can start coding the view controller methods, start by checking whether your device has a camera or not on the `viewDidLoad` method:

```
override func viewDidLoad() {
    super.viewDidLoad()
    if !UIImagePickerController.isSourceTypeAvailable
      (.Camera){
        UIAlertView(title: "Error", message: "There
          is no camera", delegate: nil ,
          cancelButtonTitle: "OK").show()
    }
}
```

7. The next step is to complete the `takePhoto` method. This method initializes the image picker and calls the camera view:

```
@IBAction func takePhoto(sender: UIButton) {
    let imagePicker = UIImagePickerController()
    imagePicker.delegate = self
    imagePicker.allowsEditing = true
    imagePicker.sourceType = .Camera
    self.presentViewController(imagePicker,
      animated: true, completion: nil)
}
```

8. As you might imagine, the delegate needs to have at least a method; in this case, we need one method to receive the picture from the user and another in case of canceling it:

```
func imagePickerController(picker:
  UIImagePickerController,
  didFinishPickingMediaWithInfo info: [NSObject
  : AnyObject]){
```

```
        image = info[UIImagePickerControllerEditedImage]
          as? UIImage
        self.imageView.image = image;
        picker.dismissViewControllerAnimated(true,
          completion: nil)
    }
    func imagePickerControllerDidCancel(picker:
      UIImagePickerController){
        picker.dismissViewControllerAnimated(true,
          completion: nil)
    }
```

9. Once we have done this, we only need to complete the effects code. They are very similar, but not the same, so here you have them:

```
    @IBAction func sepia(sender: AnyObject) {
        if image != nil {
            var ciImage = CIImage(image: image)
            let filter = CIFilter(name: "CISepiaTone")
            filter.setValue(ciImage, forKey:
              kCIInputImageKey)
            filter.setValue(0.8, forKey: "inputIntensity")
            ciImage = filter.outputImage
            self.imageView.image = UIImage(CIImage:
              ciImage)
        }
    }
    @IBAction func dots(sender: AnyObject) {
        if image != nil {
            var ciImage = CIImage(image: image)
            let filter = CIFilter(name: "CIDotScreen")
            filter.setValue(ciImage, forKey:
              kCIInputImageKey)
            ciImage = filter.outputImage
            self.imageView.image = UIImage(CIImage:
              ciImage)
        }
    }
    @IBAction func blur(sender: AnyObject) {
        if image != nil {
            var ciImage = CIImage(image: image)
            let filter = CIFilter(name: "CIGaussianBlur")
            filter.setValue(ciImage, forKey:
              kCIInputImageKey)
            ciImage = filter.outputImage
```

```
                        self.imageView.image = UIImage(CIImage:
                           ciImage)
                  }
            }
```

10. The app is done, now click on play, take a photo, and choose the effect you like the most.

How it works...

`UIImagePickerController` was created for using the camera easily. This way we don't have to use complicated camera settings and worry about different states of it. To use `UIImagePickerController`, you need a delegate and on its method, you can retrieve the taken picture as `UIImage`.

After receiving the picture, you can use the CoreImage to add some effects; however, you need to convert `UIImage` to `CIImage`. If you loaded `UIImage` from a local file, you can convert it easily by calling a property `ciImage`; however, this is not the case. As this picture was loaded from the camera, you need to create a new object and send your `UIImage` as an argument.

Now, you can use the filter that you want with the corresponding values. When you use `CIFilter`, you have to check the attributes that are accepted by it; sometimes, you can use the default values, and sometimes, you can change them.

After using the filter, you can retrieve your picture by using the `outputImage` attribute, and after this, you can construct a new `UIImage` object with the `CIImage` object generated.

There's more...

CoreImage has a lot of filters, so nowadays, it's not necessary looking for libraries or algorithms that modifies our pictures. Check the filters that are available at `https://developer.apple.com/library/ios/documentation/GraphicsImaging/Reference/CoreImageFilterReference/index.html#//apple_ref/doc/uid/TP40004346` and test them with different attributes.

In the next recipe, we will learn how we can send information from the iPhone to our Mac.

Being a film critic

There are times that an app needs to transfer information from your device to the computer and vice versa, for example, you might be watching a movie on your iPad on your way home (assuming that you are not the driver), and then you will continue watching it on your computer.

For scenarios like this one, Apple has created a new technology called **Handoff**. The idea is simple: continue the task you are doing on another.

In this recipe, we will create an app where the user can start writing his opinion about a film on one device and check it on a Mac application.

Getting ready

The Handoff framework has software and hardware requirements. The software requirements are Xcode 6, iOS 8, and Mac OS X Yosemite (10.10). Therefore, make sure that your hardware is able to use all of these software versions (or higher). Unfortunately, Handoff can't be used with the simulator. Another software requirement is that both devices (the computer and your Apple mobile device) must be logged into the same iCloud account and they must be paired.

The requirements for the hardware are having Bluetooth LE 4.0. The easiest way to check whether your iPhone or iPad can use this feature is by opening your settings, going to **General**, and checking whether there is an option called **Handoff & Suggested Apps**.

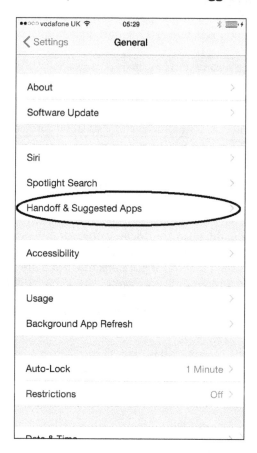

Make sure that the **Handoff** option is on.

Once you have checked the device requirement, it's time to check whether the computer meets the requirements. On your Mac computer, open the system preferences, then open the **General** option and ascertain that there is a **Handoff** option and it is checked.

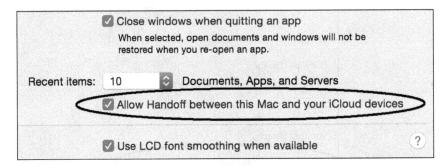

However, of all requirements, the most complicated one is that this technology needs the application signed by a team (or a developer), which implies being enrolled on the Apple Development program for each platform. This means that if you are going to use this technology between mobile devices and Mac computers, you need both subscriptions.

In this recipe, we will use both platforms, but if you only have an iOS subscription, it is very straightforward changing the Mac app to an iOS app.

Now, we can start coding the project; in this case, start creating a workspace called `Chapter 11 Films`.

How to do it...

To create an app making use Handoff, follow these steps:

1. Create on the workspace a group called `Common Code`. Here, you need to add new Swift file called `FilmData.swift`. Now, we will add this simple class:

```swift
class FilmData {
    var name:String
    var year:Int?
    var director:String?
    var score:Int?
    var opinion = ""

    init(name:String){
        self.name = name
    }
}
```

2. Let's create a new iOS project called `Chapter 11 Films iOS` and ensure that it will be added to your workspace on the combo box:

3. Repeat the procedure with a Mac OS X Cocoa application called `Chapter 11 Films MacOSX`, but note that you have to add it to the workspace and the group must be added to the workspace too.

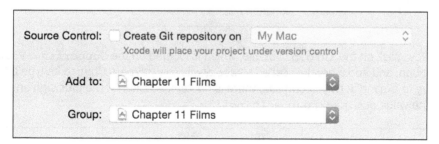

4. Once we have both projects, let's add to both of them the first file we created at the beginning of this recipe (`FilmData.swift`). This way we don't have to repeat the code for each project.

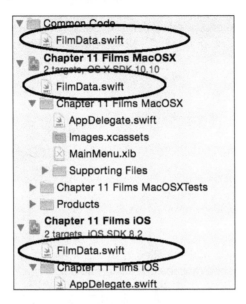

5. Once we have these common parts, we will continue with the Mac application. So, click on the Mac project, go to the **General** settings, change the **Signing** section to `Developer ID`, and select your team account.

6. Now, click on the `info.plist` file, which is located on the `Supporting Files` group, and add a new key called `NSUserActivityTypes`. Change its type to array, try to expand it; as you can see, there is no item, so click on the plus sign and write the value `com.packtpub.editingfilm`.

Key	Type	Value
▼ Information Property List	Dictionary	(15 items)
▼ NSUserActivityTypes	Array	(1 item)
Item 0	String	com.packtpub.editingfilm
Localization native development r...	String	en

7. The next step is to click on the XIB file and add five labels into the only window we have. Put one under the other, and after this, start from the first, connecting to `AppDelegate.swift`:

```
@IBOutlet var titleLabel: NSTextField!
@IBOutlet var directorLabel: NSTextField!
@IBOutlet var yearLabel: NSTextField!
@IBOutlet var scoreLabel: NSTextField!
@IBOutlet var opinionLabel: NSTextField!
```

8. After that, we only need to add the following code to `AppDelegate`:

```
func application(application: NSApplication,
  willContinueUserActivityWithType userActivityType:
  String) -> Bool {
      return userActivityType ==
        "com.packtpub.editingfilm"
  }


  func application(application: NSApplication,
    continueUserActivity userActivity: NSUserActivity,
    restorationHandler: ([AnyObject]!) -> Void) -> Bool
    {
      func setField (fieldName:String,
        uiField:NSTextField) {
          if let value =
            userActivity.userInfo![fieldName]
            as? String {
              uiField.stringValue = value
          }else if let value =
            userActivity.userInfo![fieldName] as? Int {
              uiField.stringValue = String(value)
          }
          else{
              uiField.stringValue = "-"
          }
      }
      setField("title", titleLabel)
      setField("director", directorLabel)
      setField("year", yearLabel)
      setField("score", scoreLabel)
      setField("opinion", opinionLabel)

      return true
  }
```

9. The Mac application is done. Before you click on play, remember that you have to log in on the iCloud. To do this, you have to open **System Preferences**, then go to **iCloud**, and log in to it. Remember that this account must be the same one that you will use on the mobile device. Once it is done, return to your app, and click on play. You should see just a window with some labels; don't worry about them now, we will check them later.

10. At this time, we are ready for developing the iOS part. Firstly, you have to set your team on the main project target, and also add the key `NSUserActivityTypes` on `info.plist`. As we did on the Mac application, change its type to `Array` and add the value `com.packtpub.editingfilm`, as we also did on the Mac application.

11. Click on the storyboard, and as usual, you might see only a view controller. Click on it to select it, go to **Editor Menu**, move down to the option **Embed In**, and select **Navigation controller**. As you might expect, we will add a second view controller later. Now, just remove the navigation bar by clicking on the navigation controller, select the attribute inspector, and uncheck the option **Show Navigation Bar**.

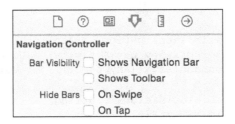

12. Now, return to the original view controller and simply add a table view on this. In this case, we need to display some cell with contents and also do something when they are selected. This means that we will need to set the view controller to `UITableViewDelegate` and `UITableViewDatasource`:

```
class ViewController: UIViewController,
   UITableViewDataSource, UITableViewDelegate {
```

13. After this, bind the table view with the view controller as data source and delegate. As a data source, we need an array of `FilmData`, which will be an attribute initialized with a private function:

```
let movies = createBasicMovieArray()
```

14. Of course, we will receive an error here because we need to implement this function, so do this outside of the class:

```
private func createBasicMovieArray() -> [FilmData] {
    var movieArray = [FilmData]()

    var filmData = FilmData(name: "A Clockwork Orange")
    filmData.year = 1971
    filmData.director = "Stanley Kubrick"
    movieArray.append(filmData)

    filmData = FilmData(name: "Monty Python and
      the Holy Grail")
    filmData.year = 1975
    filmData.director = "Terry Gilliam"
    movieArray.append(filmData)

    filmData = FilmData(name: "Kill Bill")
    filmData.year = 2003
    filmData.director = "Quentin Tarantino"
    movieArray.append(filmData)

    filmData = FilmData(name: "Ghost Busters")
    filmData.year = 1984
    movieArray.append(filmData)

    return movieArray
}
```

15. After that, we need to complete the data source methods on the view controller class:

```
func tableView(tableView: UITableView,
  numberOfRowsInSection section: Int) -> Int{
        return movies.count
    }


    func tableView(tableView: UITableView,
      cellForRowAtIndexPath indexPath: NSIndexPath) ->
UITableViewCell{
```

```
var cell  = tableView.
  dequeueReusableCellWithIdentifier("filmcell")
  as? UITableViewCell

if (cell == nil) {
    cell = UITableViewCell(style:
      UITableViewCellStyle.Subtitle,
      reuseIdentifier: "filmcell")
}

let currentFilm = movies[indexPath.row]
cell!.textLabel?.text = currentFilm.name
let unknown = "????"
cell!.detailTextLabel?.text = "\(currentFilm.year
  != nil ? String(currentFilm.year!) : unknown) -
  \(currentFilm.director != nil ?
  currentFilm.director! : unknown)"

return cell!
}
```

16. Even though the app is not finished, yet you should click on play and test it, and you must see a view similar to the one shown here. Don't forget to make sure that you have chosen the right schema, otherwise it will restart the app application.

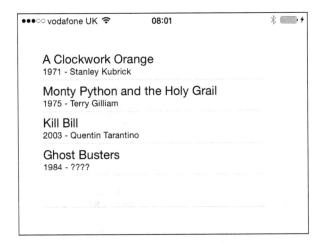

17. Once this phase is done, we can return to our view controller and implement the last method. Don't worry when you get some compile errors, they will be fixed soon:

```
func tableView(tableView: UITableView,
    didSelectRowAtIndexPath indexPath: NSIndexPath) {
    var filmDetailViewController =
        self.storyboard?.
        instantiateViewControllerWithIdentifier(
        "film_detail") as FilmDetailViewController
    filmDetailViewController.film =
        movies[indexPath.row]
    self.navigationController?.
        pushViewController(filmDetailViewController,
        animated: true)
}
```

18. This view controller is done; the next step is to create a new Cocoa Touch class that inherits from `UIViewController` called `FilmDetailViewController`. Uncheck the XIB option.

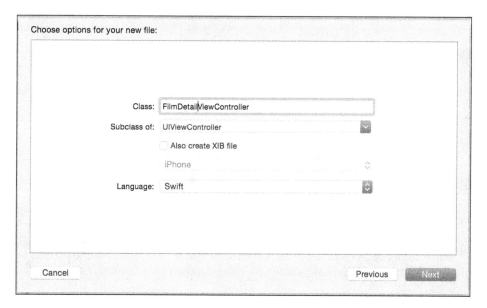

19. Once you have your new Swift file, you can return to the storyboard and add a new view controller. In this storyboard, add five labels, one stepper, a text view, and a button. Change the text view background to gray. You should have a layout similar to this one.

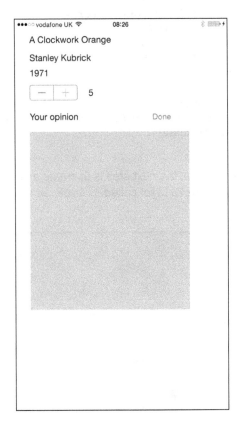

20. The new view controller needs to know that its class is not the default view controller; therefore, select the view controller, go to its Identity inspector and change its class to `FilmDetailViewController`. Leveraging that we are here, we should also set the storyboard ID to `film_detail`:

21. Now, link the labels, the stepper, and the text view with the view controller:

```
@IBOutlet var movieTitle: UILabel!
@IBOutlet var director: UILabel!
@IBOutlet var year: UILabel!
@IBOutlet var score: UILabel!
@IBOutlet var opinion: UITextView!
@IBOutlet var stepper: UIStepper!
```

22. Once we have these attributes, we can set the actions. The only one that will need a protocol is the text view; then, start adding `UITextViewDelegate` to the class header:

```
class FilmDetailViewController: UIViewController,
    UITextViewDelegate {
```

23. After this, we can connect the view controller as the text view delegate, create an action called `done` for the button, and another one called `changeScore` as the stepper value changed event:

```
@IBAction func done(sender: AnyObject) {
}
@IBAction func changeScore(sender: UIStepper) {
}
```

24. Great! Now, we can code this class without worrying about the storyboard. Let's start with the attribute `film`, which will contain the information of the movie that is on screen:

```
var film:FilmData?
```

25. Then, we can initialize the views we have on screen and an inherited attribute called `userActivity`. Remember that here, we suppose that the attribute film was already set:

```
override func viewDidLoad() {
    super.viewDidLoad()
    movieTitle.text = film?.name
    director.text = film?.director
    year.text = film?.year != nil ? "\(film!.year!)"
        : "???"
    if let score = film?.score {
        self.score.text = String(score)
        self.stepper.value = Double(score)
    }else {
        self.score.text = ""
        self.stepper.value = 1
    }
    self.opinion.text = film?.opinion
    self.userActivity = NSUserActivity(activityType:
      "com.packtpub.editingfilm")
    self.userActivity!.userInfo = [NSObject:
      AnyObject]()
}
```

26. After this, we can complete the views events. Here, we will add a new one called `textViewDidChange`, which belongs to `UITextViewDelegate`:

```
@IBAction func done(sender: AnyObject) {
    self.userActivity!.invalidate()
    self.navigationController?.
      popViewControllerAnimated(true)
}
@IBAction func changeScore(sender: UIStepper) {
    self.film?.score = Int(sender.value)
```

```
        self.score.text = String(self.film!.score!)
        self.updateUserActivityState(self.userActivity!)
    }
    func textViewDidChange(textView: UITextView) {
        film?.opinion = self.opinion.text
        self.updateUserActivityState(self.userActivity!)
    }
```

27. The last part of this code is about getting the whole information we want to transmit and updating the `userActivity` state:

```
    override func updateUserActivityState(activity:
        NSUserActivity) {
        self.userActivity!.userInfo!["title"] = film?.name
        self.userActivity!.userInfo!["year"] = film?.year
        self.userActivity!.userInfo!["director"] =
            film?.director
        self.userActivity!.userInfo!["score"] = film?.score
        self.userActivity!.userInfo!["opinion"] =
            film?.opinion
        super.updateUserActivityState(activity)
    }
```

28. The app is done, and as you know, we have to test it. Before clicking on play, make sure that the right schema is selected and the app will be installed on your mobile device, not on the simulator.

29. Click on play, select a movie you like the most (or hate the most), set a score for it, and write your comment. Return to your Mac (remember that you haven't stopped the Mac application) and check that your dock has a new icon. This means that it has detected a user activity that can be read. Click on this icon.

30. You will see that your Mac app is going to the foreground, and it will show the information received from your device.

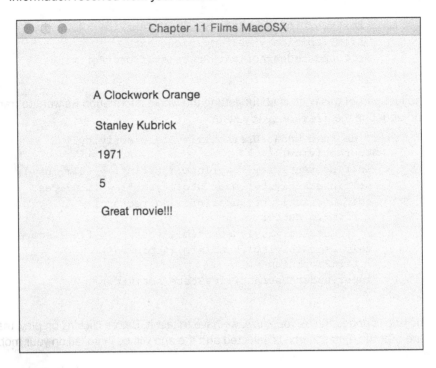

How it works...

Handoff works with a feature called **Activity**. Activities are some kind of information about what the user is doing right now, such as composing an e-mail, editing a video, and so on.

When using Handoff, you have to plan three phases for your activities: creating the activity, updating it, and destroying it. We created it on the `viewDidLoad` method, updated it every time the user changed the score or the opinion text, and destroyed it when the user clicked on the `done` button.

If you want to use Handoff in your own classes, you have to add an NSUserActivity object. A good feature about this class is that it is the same as using the AppKit (Mac OS X) and the UIKit (iOS). Some classes already have this object as a property, such as NSDocument, UIDocuments, NSResponder, and UIResponder.

As UIViewController inherits from UIResponder, we can use the existing attribute userActivity. Every time we or the app think that the activity needs to be updated, the updateUserActivityState method is called. Here, it should set the whole information that should be transmitted even when the information hasn't changed such as the movie title, the director, or the production year, because after updating the state, the userInfo dictionary is going to be empty.

 Don't overload the user info dictionary. Apple recommends storing up to 3 KBs of information; more than that can affect the application performance.

To receive the information, we need two steps: the first one is to check whether the app accepts the activity at that moment by implementing the willContinueUserActivityWithType method on the app delegate; the other one is to implement the app delegate method continueUserActivity for retrieving the information and sending it to the corresponding view or object.

An important detail is that Handoff is used between apps of the same company or developer and only with the same user. This is the reason that you have to use the same team signature, and that the user must be logged in.

There's more...

In this case, we created an app that edits your movie opinion and another one that can receive it. However, you can modify the Mac application in a way that it can also edit and retransmit it to the device application. Try to do it as homework.

Apple has a good sample about how to use handoff with photos. Visit https://developer.apple.com/library/ios/samplecode/PhotoHandoff/Listings/README_md.html to download it.

Leaving breadcrumbs

Have you ever gone somewhere and started thinking whether your path was the best one? At times, we would like to review our journey once we've reached the destination. Usually, we do this when the journey has been a very long one. In this recipe, we will create an app for recording our steps and then we can check the path we took.

Getting ready

Create a new single view application called `Chapter 11 Breadcrumbs`, add the Core Location Framework and the MapKit Framework. You can use the simulator or a physical device to test this app; however, if you are as lazy as me, it will be better using the simulator; this way, you don't have to stand up and walk to test it.

How to do it...

Once you have added the frameworks, you just need to follow these steps to create the app.

1. Open the storyboard; add a label on the top, a button under it, and a map view under it, something for which the result can be similar to the following screenshot:

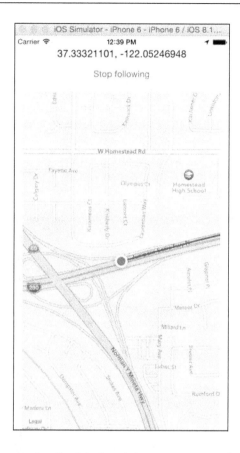

2. As usual, start connecting the label and the map view with the view controller:

```
@IBOutlet var mapView: MKMapView!
@IBOutlet var positionLabel: UILabel!
```

3. Now, you can click on the view controller and start by importing the core location and the MapKit frameworks, and of course, don't remove `UIKit`:

```
import UIKit
import MapKit
import CoreLocation
```

4. After this, complete the `ViewController` class by adding the `CLLocationManagerDelegate` and `MKMapViewDelegate` protocols:

    ```
    class ViewController: UIViewController,
      CLLocationManagerDelegate, MKMapViewDelegate {
    ```

5. The next step is to add the view controller attributes; in this case, we will need the location manager to receive the current position, an array of positions that we have passed through, and a Boolean attribute to follow the user on the map:

    ```
    var manager = CLLocationManager()
    var locationsStack = [CLLocation]()
    var follow = true
    ```

6. Now, we need to initialize the manager attribute and the map view. To do this, we will use the method `viewDidLoad`:

    ```
    override func viewDidLoad() {
        super.viewDidLoad()

        manager.delegate = self
        manager.desiredAccuracy = kCLLocationAccuracyBest
        manager.requestAlwaysAuthorization()
        manager.startUpdatingLocation()

        mapView.delegate = self
        mapView.mapType = .Standard
        mapView.showsUserLocation = true
    }
    ```

7. Then, we need to update the map view and `locationStack` every time we receive a new location:

    ```
    func locationManager(manager:CLLocationManager,
    didUpdateLocations locations:[AnyObject]) {

        var currentLocation = locations[0] as CLLocation
        positionLabel.text =
          "\(currentLocation.coordinate.latitude),
           \(currentLocation.coordinate.longitude)"
        locationsStack.append(currentLocation)

        if follow {
            var currentRegion = MKCoordinateRegion(center:
              mapView.userLocation.coordinate, span:
              MKCoordinateSpanMake(0.01, 0.01))
    ```

```
mapView.setRegion(currentRegion, animated:
    true)
}

if locationsStack.count > 1{
    var destination = locationsStack.count - 2
    let sourceCoord =
        locationsStack.last!.coordinate
    let destinationCoord =
        locationsStack[destination].coordinate
    var coords = [sourceCoord, destinationCoord]
    let polyline = MKPolyline(coordinates:
        &coords, count: coords.count)
    mapView.addOverlay(polyline)
}

}
```

8. The app is still not displaying the path; the reason is that we need to draw it by writing the map view method `renderForOverlay`:

```
func mapView(mapView: MKMapView!, rendererForOverlay
    overlay: MKOverlay!) -> MKOverlayRenderer! {
    if overlay is MKPolyline {
        var polylineRenderer =
            MKPolylineRenderer(overlay: overlay)
        polylineRenderer.strokeColor =
            UIColor.blueColor()
        polylineRenderer.lineWidth = 3
        return polylineRenderer
    }
    return nil
}
```

9. Now, the app is working; however, it can be quite difficult to check our journey because it is always being updated, so it is time to add the button event:

```
@IBAction func followAction(sender: UIButton) {
    follow = !follow
    if follow {
        sender.setTitle("Stop following", forState:
            .Normal)
    }else {
        sender.setTitle("Resume following", forState:
            .Normal)
    }
}
```

10. The app is almost done. There is one detail that you still need to set up—the permission on iOS 8. So, go to your `info.plist`, then add a new record with the key `NSLocationAlwaysUsageDescription`, and write a string value, for example, `Please allow the GPS usage`.

Key	Type	Value
▼ Information Property List	Dictionary	(16 items)
NSLocationAlwaysUsageDescription ⬍ ⊕ ⊖	String ⬍	Please allow the GPS usage
Localization native development region ⬍	String	en

11. Now, the app is done, click on play, and walk around if you are using a physical device or click on **Debug**, then scroll down to location and select a freeway drive if you are using the simulator.

How it works...

The core location framework allows us to retrieve the current device position, but of course it needs a delegate. This is the reason we had to implement the `CLLocationManagerDelegate` protocol. This protocol receives positions from the method `didUpdateLocations`.

Once we receive it, we can store the locations into the `locationStack` array. Actually, if you don't want to keep information of the whole journey, you can just store the last location.

After storing a new location, we can create a polyline, which is like a segment of our journey. This information is submitted to the map view.

The map view needs to render it with the `rendererForOverlay` method of the `MKMapViewDelegate`. The reason for this is that you are free to draw what you want on the map; you can create shapes such as circles, squares, and so on for highlighting an area.

There's more...

Drawing a route on a map view is something very common, mainly if you would like to use directions. Have a look at `MKDirections`, which can be very useful.

Exchanging money

Nowadays, our apps must be prepared to be executed everywhere; therefore, your app should have as many languages as possible. Consider that internationalization is very important for using different languages to a different number of formats.

In this recipe, we will create an app that will show us the currency exchange rate, but more important than that is it will be adapted to the current location.

Getting ready

Create a single view application called `Chapter 11 Currency Converter` and place the two flag pictures on `images.xcassets`. These pictures can be downloaded from the book resources.

How to do it...

Follow these steps to create the Currency Converter app:

1. Firstly, click on the supporting files group and add a new file. In this case, go to the **Resource** section and select **Strings File**:

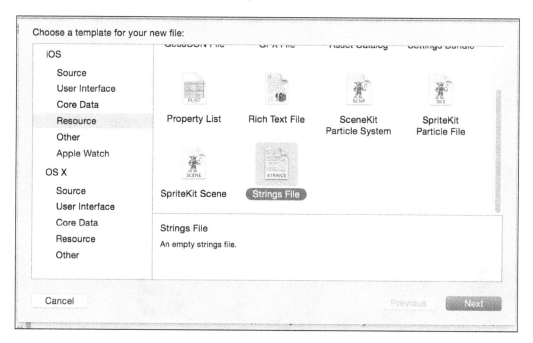

2. Inside this file, add some of these keys with their corresponding values:

```
"Rate" = "Rate: %@";
"Total" = "Total: %@";
"Choose Currency" = "Choose a currency";
"flagicon" = "english";
"Cancel" = "Cancel";
```

3. Now, go to the storyboard and add four labels, two buttons, a text field, and an image view on the bottom, something similar to the following screenshot:

4. Once you have your layout done, connect the `ui` components (except the title label) with the view controller with the following names:

```
@IBOutlet var fromButton: UIButton!
@IBOutlet var toButton: UIButton!
@IBOutlet var amountTextField: UITextField!
```

```
@IBOutlet var dateLabel: UILabel!
@IBOutlet var rateLabel: UILabel!
@IBOutlet var totalLabel: UILabel!
@IBOutlet var flagImage: UIImageView!
```

5. Change the text field keyboard type to `Numbers and Punctuation` at the attribute inspector:

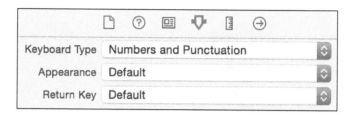

6. Add the `UITextFieldDelegate` protocol to the view controller:

```
class ViewController: UIViewController,
    UITextFieldDelegate {
```

7. Now, set the view controller as the text field delegate and write `Amount of money` as the text field placeholder.

8. Another important action is to change the view class from `UIView` to `UIControl` so that we can hide the keyboard easily.

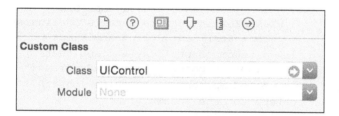

9. Go to the view controller and add the following attributes:

```
let currencies = ["AUD", "BGN", "BRL", "CAD", "CHF",
    "CNY", "CZK", "DKK", "EUR", "GBP", "HKD",
    "HRK", "HUF", "IDR", "ILS", "INR", "JPY", "KRW",
    "MXN", "MYR", "NOK", "NZD", "PHP", "PLN", "RON",
    "RUB", "SEK", "SGD", "THB", "TRY", "USD", "ZAR"]
let baseurl = "http://api.fixer.io/latest"
var fromCurrency = "USD"
var toCurrency = "EUR"
```

10. At this time, we can start coding the view controller methods; starting from the beginning, we will implement the `viewDidLoad` method:

```
override func viewDidLoad() {
    super.viewDidLoad()
    flagImage.image = UIImage(named:
      NSLocalizedString("flagicon", comment: ""))
    setup()
}
```

11. As you can see, there is a private method called `setup`, which we will implement right now. This method is responsible for retrieving the currency rate from the Internet and calculating the value of the amount of money that the user has entered:

```
private func setup(){
    fromButton.setTitle(fromCurrency,
      forState: .Normal)
    toButton.setTitle(toCurrency, forState: .Normal)
    var session = NSURLSession.sharedSession()
    var url = NSURL(string: "\(baseurl)?base=
      \(fromCurrency)&symbols=\(toCurrency)")!
    var err:NSError? = nil

    session.dataTaskWithURL(url, completionHandler:
      { (data, response, error) -> Void in
        var json = NSJSONSerialization.
          JSONObjectWithData(data, options:
          NSJSONReadingOptions.MutableContainers,
          error: &err) as [String:AnyObject]
        let dateComponentsArray = (json["date"] as
          String).componentsSeparatedByString("-")
        let dateComponents = NSDateComponents()
        dateComponents.year    =
          dateComponentsArray[0].toInt()!
        dateComponents.month   =
          dateComponentsArray[1].toInt()!
        dateComponents.day     =
          dateComponentsArray[2].toInt()!

        let rates = json["rates"] as [String:Double]
        let date = NSCalendar.currentCalendar().
          dateFromComponents(dateComponents)
        let ratio = rates[self.toCurrency]
```

```
        let amount = self.amountTextField.text ==
          "" ? 1.0 : (self.amountTextField.text as
        NSString).doubleValue

        NSOperationQueue.mainQueue().
          addOperationWithBlock({ () -> Void in
            let dateFormatter = NSDateFormatter()
            dateFormatter.dateStyle = .LongStyle
            self.dateLabel.text =
              dateFormatter.stringFromDate(date!)

            let currencyFormatter = NSNumberFormatter()
            currencyFormatter.currencyCode =
              self.toCurrency
            currencyFormatter.numberStyle =
              .CurrencyStyle
            self.rateLabel.text = String(format:
              NSLocalizedString("Rate", comment: ""),
              arguments: [currencyFormatter.
              stringFromNumber(ratio!)!])
            let total = amount * ratio!

            self.totalLabel.text = String(format:
              NSLocalizedString("Total", comment: ""),
              arguments: [currencyFormatter.
              stringFromNumber(total)!])

        })
      }).resume()

    }
```

12. We are going to implement the button event. The event is the same for both of them, so connect the touch up event with this method.

```
@IBAction func chooseCurrency(sender: UIButton) {
    let alertController = UIAlertController(title:
      NSLocalizedString("Choose Currency", comment:
      ""), message: nil, preferredStyle: .ActionSheet)

    let cancelAction = UIAlertAction(title:
      NSLocalizedString("Cancel", comment: ""), style:
      .Cancel) { (action) in
    }
```

```
alertController.addAction(cancelAction)

for currency in currencies {
    let currAction = UIAlertAction(title: currency,
        style: .Default) { (action) in
        if sender == self.fromButton {
            self.fromCurrency = action.title
        }else {
            self.toCurrency = action.title
        }
        self.setup()
    }
    alertController.addAction(currAction)
}

self.presentViewController(alertController,
    animated: true, completion: nil)
}
```

13. Connect the main view (the one that we changed to UIControl), and touch up the event with the view controller by creating a method called touchup:

```
@IBAction func touchup(sender: UIControl) {
    self.amountTextField.resignFirstResponder()
    self.setup()
}
```

14. Now, we can complete the view controller with the last method that allows us to hide the keyboard when the return key is pressed:

```
func textFieldShouldReturn(textField: UITextField) ->
  Bool {
    self.touchup(self.view as UIControl)
    return true
}
```

15. The app is basically done; however, we can only say that it is ready for localization, but except for the currency format, we can say that there is nothing that can demonstrate it. So, click on your project on the project navigator, and go to the **Info** tab of the project. Make sure that you have selected the project and not the target. Scroll down to the **Locations** section and click on the plus sign. Select **Spanish**, a new language.

16. Now, expand your storyboard and select `Main.strings`.

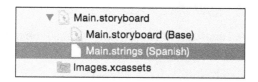

17. Change the title from `Currency Converter` to `Conversor de monedas` and the text field place holder from `Amount of money` to `Cantidad de dinero`. The modified lines should be similar to the ones shown here:

```
/* Class = "UILabel"; text = "Currency Converter";
   ObjectID = "hFW-19-dID"; */
"hFW-19-dID.text" = "Conversor de Monedas";


/* Class = "UITextField"; placeholder =
   "Amount of money"; ObjectID = "vzh-tY-rr3"; */
"vzh-tY-rr3.placeholder" = "Cantidad de dinero";
```

 Try to design the whole layout before translating it to other languages; adding components to your view sometimes makes you translate everything again.

18. Return to `Localizable.strings`, and on the file inspector, click on the **Localize...** button, which is located on the **Localization** section.

19. A dialog requesting to move this file to the `lproj` folder will appear. Choose the base language.

20. As you can see, the **Localization** section has replaced the old button with some languages options. Check the **Spanish** option.

21. Expand `Localizable.strings` and click on the **Spanish** one.

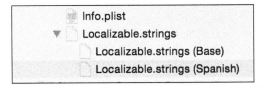

22. Now, update the values translating them to the Spanish language, like the lines shown here:

```
"Rate" = "Tasa de conversión: %@";
"Total" = "Total: %@";
"Choose Currency" = "Elija la moneda";
"flagicon" = "spanish";
"Cancel" = "Cancelar";
```

23. It's time to test our app. Click on play and check that the app works perfectly fine; then, press the home button, go to settings, enter into the general section, tap (or click) on **Language & Region**, change the region to **Spain** and the language to **Spanish**. Now, return to your app and you should see it with Spanish text, and the numbers should be represented with the Spanish format.

How it works...

When you want to translate your app to other languages, you first have to create it with the base language (default language), but bear in mind that every text can be translated; therefore, instead of using hardcoded text, you have to retrieve them from the `Localizable.strings` file.

Use `NSLocalizedString` for retrieving strings from the Localizable file; you can also get format strings and use the String format initializer.

You can also use date and number formatters using `NSDateFormatter` and `NSNumberFormatter`; this way you don't have to worry about local dates and numbers.

It's also possible to translate your storyboard, so it is not necessary to set the labels and placeholders on `viewdidload`.

There's more...

You can also translate other files, such as the Launch Screen and `Info.plist`; for example you can change the application name according to the language using the Bundle display name key (`CFBundleDisplayName`).

`NSLocalizedString` has other options that allow you to use translation in complex applications.

Index

Thank you for buying
Swift Cookbook

About Packt Publishing

Packt, pronounced 'packed', published its first book, *Mastering phpMyAdmin for Effective MySQL Management*, in April 2004, and subsequently continued to specialize in publishing highly focused books on specific technologies and solutions.

Our books and publications share the experiences of your fellow IT professionals in adapting and customizing today's systems, applications, and frameworks. Our solution-based books give you the knowledge and power to customize the software and technologies you're using to get the job done. Packt books are more specific and less general than the IT books you have seen in the past. Our unique business model allows us to bring you more focused information, giving you more of what you need to know, and less of what you don't.

Packt is a modern yet unique publishing company that focuses on producing quality, cutting-edge books for communities of developers, administrators, and newbies alike. For more information, please visit our website at www.packtpub.com.

Writing for Packt

We welcome all inquiries from people who are interested in authoring. Book proposals should be sent to author@packtpub.com. If your book idea is still at an early stage and you would like to discuss it first before writing a formal book proposal, then please contact us; one of our commissioning editors will get in touch with you.

We're not just looking for published authors; if you have strong technical skills but no writing experience, our experienced editors can help you develop a writing career, or simply get some additional reward for your expertise.

Swift Essentials

ISBN: 978-1-78439-670-1   Paperback: 228 pages

Get up and running lightning fast with this practical guide to building applications with Swift

1. Rapidly learn how to program Apple's newest programming language, Swift, from the basics through to working applications.

2. Create graphical iOS applications using Xcode and storyboard.

3. Build a network client for GitHub repositories, with full source code on GitHub.

Android Studio Essentials

ISBN: 978-1-78439-720-3   Paperback: 126 pages

A fast-paced guide to get you up and running with Android application development using Android Studio

1. Learn to install and configure Android Studio on your machine to create your own projects.

2. Test your apps using the Android emulator and learn how to manage virtual devices.

3. Familiarize yourself with the fundamentals of Android development through an exemplary coverage of practical examples, functional code, and relevant screenshots.

Please check **www.PacktPub.com** for information on our titles

Go Programming Blueprints

ISBN: 978-1-78398-802-0   Paperback: 274 pages

Build real-world, production-ready solutions in Go using cutting-edge technology and techniques

1. Learn to apply the nuances of the Go language, and get to know the open source community that surrounds it to implement a wide range of start-up quality projects.

2. Write interesting, and clever but simple code, and learn skills and techniques that are directly transferrable to your own projects.

3. Discover how to write code capable of delivering massive world-class scale performance and availability.

Raspberry Pi Cookbook for Python Programmers

ISBN: 978-1-84969-662-3   Paperback: 402 pages

Over 50 easy-to-comprehend tailor-made recipes to get the most out of the Raspberry Pi and unleash its huge potential using Python

1. Install your first operating system, share files over the network, and run programs remotely.

2. Unleash the hidden potential of the Raspberry Pi's powerful Video Core IV graphics processor with your own hardware accelerated 3D graphics.

3. Discover how to create your own electronic circuits to interact with the Raspberry Pi.

Please check **www.PacktPub.com** for information on our titles